⊕ REST IN PEACE ⊕

⊕ REST IN PEACE ⊕

A CULTURAL HISTORY OF DEATH
AND THE FUNERAL HOME IN
TWENTIETH-CENTURY AMERICA

GARY LADERMAN

OXFORD
UNIVERSITY PRESS

2003

OXFORD
UNIVERSITY PRESS

Oxford New York
Auckland Bangkok Buenos Aires Cape Town Chennai
Dar es Salaam Delhi Hong Kong Istanbul Karachi Kolkata
Kuala Lumpur Madrid Melbourne Mexico City Mumbai Nairobi
São Paulo.Shanghai Taipei Tokyo Toronto

Published by Oxford University Press, Inc.
198 Madison Avenue, New York, New York, 10016
www.oup.com

Oxford is a registered trademark of Oxford University Press

Library of Congress Cataloging-in-Publication Data

Laderman, Gary, 1962-
Rest in peace : a cultural history of death and the funeral home in twentieth-century America /
Gary Laderman.
p. cm.
Includes bibliographical references and index.
ISBN 0-19-513608-X
1.   Undertakers and undertaking—United States. 2. Funeral supplies industry—United States. I. Title.
HD9999.U53 U543 2003
363.7'5'0973—dc21   2002006682

Design and composition by Rae Grant Design

9 8 7 6 5 4 3 2 1
Printed in the United States of America
on acid-free paper

To my beautiful boys, Miles and Graham
In the midst of death, you keep me alive!

⊕ CONTENTS ⊕

⊕ ACKNOWLEDGEMENTS ⊕

WHEN I FINISHED *THE SACRED REMAINS: AMERICAN ATTITUDES TOWARD Death, 1799–1883* in 1996, I vowed never to write on the subject again. But after considering sex, violence, film, and other research topics, I kept returning to death and finally realized that the story I had told in the first book was not complete. *The Sacred Remains* ends with "the birth of the funeral industry," and the continuation of that story in twentieth-century America was too compelling to ignore. Within a short period of time, and after consulting with trusted friends, the research road ahead quickly became clear, and it led straight to the funeral home.

From that moment to the completion of this book, Emory University has been a tremendously supportive and intellectually stimulating place to work. I enjoy my interactions with everyone from the president to the grounds crew, and consider myself lucky to be there. Paul Courtright hired me in 1994 and has since become my closest friend and advisor. Indeed, he has been involved with this project from the beginning and at every step along the way—listening to my early ramblings about Disney and death, reading carefully through the final manuscript—and has encouraged me with his insights, questions, and sense of humor. Whether we were in a seminar together, walking in the woods, sipping coffee, or simply listening to the Grateful Dead, Paul helped me read the data and identify its significance in the larger scheme.

My colleagues in the Department of Religion and the Graduate Division of Religion were especially helpful during the researching and writing of the manuscript. I presented material to them in various settings and received a great deal in return. Surprisingly, they never seemed to mind talking about funerals, embalming, and the return of the dead. In particular, I want to thank E. Brooks Holifield, Steve Tipton, Laurie Patton, Mark Jordan, Joyce Flueckiger, Richard C. Martin, Bobbi Patterson, Michael Berger, Deborah Lipstadt, Eric Reinders, Vernon Robbins, Nancy Eiesland, and Thomas G. Long. Also, thanks go to office staff in the Department of Religion and the Graduate Division of Religion, and to graduate students from the departments of English and History, the Institute of Liberal Arts, the Candler School of Theology, and the Graduate Division of Religion who enrolled in two seminars I gave that were critical to the book: "Death, Ritual, Power" and "Cultures of Death in America." Jennifer Saunders, a graduate student in West and South Asian Religions, was an exceptional research assistant, transcriber, and conversation partner. Graduate students Justin Holcomb, in Theological Studies, Christian Noble, in West and South Asian Religions, and Graham Reside, in Ethics and Society, also helped at various points during the production of the book.

Former Provost Rebecca S. Chopp, former Emory College Dean Steve Sanderson, and current Dean Robert A. Paul have given me personal as well as institutional support, for which I am very grateful. I received a University Research Committee Grant near the end of this project and that assistance proved crucial to completing the manuscript in a timely manner. Portions of this book were presented in various Emory settings, including the Myth and Ritual in American Life Center and the History of Medicine Group. These discussions were particularly helpful. Individual conversations with the following Emory faculty also proved to be highly valuable: Arri Eisen (Biology), Howard Kushner (Public Health), Rebecca Stone-Miller (Art History), Matthew Bernstein, (Film Studies), Jonathan Prude (History), P. V. Rao (Physics), Walt Reed (English), and Allen Tullos (Institute of Liberal Arts). Thanks to all the dinner guests at the Emory Boys Night Out, too—it was truly inspiring to be sitting around the table with all of you. Library staff and reference librarians at the Woodruff Library, including the Interlibrary Loan Division and the Marian K. Heilbrun Music and Media Library, were always friendly and cooperative. A special thanks to Nowell Briscoe, Coordinator of Special Gifts to the Woodruff Library and a former funeral director, who read the manuscript and let me look through some of the old funeral trade magazines in his collection. I cannot leave Emory without also giving a heartfelt thanks to Amy Benson Brown, associate editor of Emory's *Academic Exchange*. Amy read the entire manuscript and her editorial and substantive guidance in the final stages made an incredible difference in the life of this book.

In addition to financial support from Emory, I also received fellowships from the American Council of Learned Societies, which allowed me to take a year leave in the early stages of research, and from the Louisville Institute, which provided crucial funding for travel to interview funeral directors and engage in other research. The first award I received for this project was from the National Endowment of the Humanities, which supported a summer institute at Columbia University on the history of death. Many people involved in this institute contributed to the conceptualization of the book at a very formative stage. In particular, I would like to thank Thomas W. Laqueur (History, University of California, Berkeley), Suzanne E. Smith (History, George Mason University), Erik R. Seeman (History, State University of New York Buffalo), and James Green (Anthropology, University of Washington). I would not have received any of these awards without the recommendations of good friends Brooks Holifield, Richard D. Hecht (Religious Studies, University of California, Santa Barbara), and Colleen McDannell (History, University of Utah). Colleen also read through the manuscript and gave me her usual no-nonsense, straightforward, and penetrating comments, for which I am extremely appreciative. My former advisor at UCSB and lifelong friend, Richard, read the manuscript as well and gave me thoughtful suggestions.

I presented material from the book at numerous professional conferences, public lectures, and guest lectures. Whether I found myself in a church, a hospital, a college auditorium, or a convention center, at every event questions and comments enriched and expanded my own thinking about the book. The level of engagement from audience members and their willingness to bring up their own personal experiences with death always surprised me. But these responses—as difficult as they could be at times—also encouraged me to believe that many people are more than willing to enter into a conversation about the dead. One of the more memorable events took place at the Doreen B. Townsend Center for the Humanities at the University of California, Berkeley. Associate Director Christina Gillis organized "Seeing the Difference/Seeing Differently: Viewing Death and Dying in Interdisciplinary Perspective," a fascinating array of doctors, artists, scholars, therapists, and others brought together for a weekend to consider matters of death and life. Also, thanks to Stephen Prothero (Religion, Boston University), Robert Orsi (Religion, Harvard University), Luis León (Religious Studies, Arizona State University), and Louis Ruprecht Jr. (Religion, Mercer University) for their contributions and conversations along the way.

I knew early on that my book would include interviews with individuals in the funeral industry. My research took me all over the country, including Milwaukee, Wisconsin (National Funeral Directors Association); Houston, Texas (National Funeral Director's Museum); Nashville, Tennessee (Gupton Mortuary School); Los Angeles, California (Museum of Radio and Television); New York, New York (Columbia Library and the New York Public Library); Reno, Nevada (University of Reno, Nevada Library); and New Brunswick, New Jersey (Rutgers University Library). In most of these places I arranged to interview an undertaker, usually someone whose family had been in the business for generations. I am appreciative to all of the funeral directors who let me into their homes and took the time to sit down and talk frankly with me about their past experiences, personal memories, and current observations. All of the people I spoke with in funeral homes, mortuary schools, funeral museums, and especially at the national headquarters of the National Funeral Directors Association were exceptionally helpful and gracious with their time.

Family and friends deserve a very special thanks as well. My dear wife, Elizabeth, took care of our two boys—born when I was in the middle of researching the book—and read the final copy of the manuscript. I always feel better when she tells me she likes it. The encouragement, support, and love from all the Ladermans and Hardcastles proved quite invaluable during this long, often grueling process. Thanks especially to David, Carol, Pete, and Gladys, for their comments and suggestions. My close friends Dave Orleans, Jeff Morgen, and Larry Schapiro, convinced me to do additional research in Las Vegas and Los Angeles and, as usual, they steered me in the right directions.

I am very glad I made the decision early on to publish this book with Oxford University Press. Cynthia Read is a fabulous editor, an insightful reader, and a delightful dinner partner. Thanks to all the editors at Oxford who had a hand in the production of the book. Many thanks to Stanley Burns and staff at the Burns Archive for help with the photographs.

Finally, I would like to acknowledge not an individual nor an institution, but a space, and a state of mind. As a young graduate student, I had the luxury of having an office in the two-bedroom apartment I shared with Liz in Santa Barbara. My dissertation, which later became *The Sacred Remains*, was written in this spacious, familiar setting. Although we have our own house now, the two boys would prefer I play with them rather than work—a sentiment I wholeheartedly agree with. Since I could not write undisturbed in my regular departmental office, I secured a small cubicle in the Woodruff Library. This intimate space on the seventh floor, with its off-white and dark yellow walls, brown vinyl chair, and small window, had barely enough room for pacing, a necessary consideration when finding a good place to write. Early on I made the best of it, and drew on an earlier experience living for a year in a maid's quarters—slightly bigger than a walk-in closet with a sink and a toilet—at the top of a seven-story apartment building in Paris.

Writing in this tiny library space soon acquired a strange significance for me when I found myself leaving my departmental office early in the morning and excitedly heading for the library smiling and singing "Heigh-Ho, Heigh-Ho, it's off to work we go" under my breath. Indeed, part of the charm of this room, and an integral component of the writing process for me, relates to music. My solitary days in the study, often regrettably too short for my own desires, began after I turned on the laptop and donned the headphones. I organized my data and wrote the manuscript listening to music that put me in the right frame of mind, a soundtrack that consisted of Radiohead's "Lucky," U2's "Dirty Day," Dave Mathews' "Say Goodnight," Led Zeppelin's "Down by the Seaside," Moby's "Porcelain," Madonna's "Ray of Light," Smashing Pumpkins' "Soma," Tom Petty's "Mary Jane's Last Dance," Neil Young's "Out on the Weekend," REM's "Night Swimming," and Pink Floyd's "Time," to name only a few. Sometimes the right combination of mood, music, and material would put me in a writing groove that was downright inspiring. I am sorry it all has to end. And so quickly, too.

⊕PROLOGUE⊕

THE CHAOS OF DEATH DISTURBS THE PEACE OF THE LIVING. NOTHING represents this chaos more forcefully to human senses and the imagination than the biological process of bodily disintegration. This unsettling fact of life has proven to be a rich source of inspiration for human efforts to find order in disorder, meaning in suffering, eternity in finitude. Religion, culture, social structures, the vitality of these rudimentary elements of communal life depends upon ritually putting the dead body in its place, managing the relations between the living and the dead, and providing explanations for the existence of death. Throughout human history the problem of bodily decay has had to be solved in a meaningful way—the social body cannot function without agreed upon principles to respond to the universal presence of dead bodies.

After death, the body once so critical to identity is fated to decompose, raising difficult questions about the very nature of individual and social identity. A body without life is immediately recognizable, usually because the face, the primary marker of identity, begins to change. Sherwin Nuland, noted surgeon and historian of medicine, writes: "The appearance of a newly lifeless face cannot be mistaken for unconsciousness. Within a minute after the heart stops beating, the face begins to take on the unmistakable gray-white pallor of death; in an uncanny way, the features very soon appear corpse-like, even to those who have never before seen a dead body."[1] Critical to the appearance of the lifeless face is the eyes, which become dull, vacant, empty. The body follows the face, emitting transparent visual and olfactory cues that, indeed, life is no more and that identity no longer completely resides here in this transformed and transforming flesh and blood.

Gravity then does its work, with liquid and mass moving to those areas of the body closest to the ground, and skin growing more and more discolored, starting to slip away, altering the shape and form of the corpse in decay. After the muscles relax, rigor mortis sets in and makes the body rigid. The corpse soon starts to putrefy, and the odor it emits—largely a consequence of intestinal bacteria producing a noxious gas that enters the blood vessels and tissues—contributes to the rapid distancing of the body from any type of postmortem identity. This gas leads to bloating, ultimately turns the skin black, makes the eyes and tongue protrude, forces the intestines out of the body, and produces a blood-stained fluid that seeps from body orifices.

After about one week, the skin begins to slip from the blistering, foul-smelling mass. Distinctions between inside and outside, form and substance, even life and death, no longer make much sense in the face of decomposition; internal organs make their way outside, solid matter becomes liquid, microbes thrive and spread throughout the cadaver, and body parts swell until they finally explode. Exposure to sun, moisture in the air, and dangers from the animal and insect world are only a few of the additional factors that determine the exact details of a body in decay. In the end, the body, so beloved and indulged when alive, breaks down rather violently in death, dissolving as a result of the work of various chemicals released by dead tissues, and losing any vital connection between post-mortem identity, either as spirit or memory, and the natural materials disintegrating into their final skeletal form.

From the Paleolithic era to the present, human societies have felt compelled to take specific actions to dispose of the dead body. Some eat it, others burn it, many bury it; some leave it exposed to the elements, still others regard its decay and meditate with that in mind, and a few in California freeze it with a view to future reanimation. In most cases, the choice both reflects and authorizes constitutive cultural sentiments about the true nature of personal and cosmic identity. The final ceremonies that accompany a corpse's disposal, as well as its preparation for these ceremonies and the manner in which it vanishes from living society, reveal a great deal about the animating cultural values and integrating social principles at work in any particular community. But they are often also about a more immediate concern: Ritual actions by the living can make a dif-

ference in the postmortem journey and final destiny of the deceased, and therefore affect relations between the living and the dead.

Given this association between ritual enactments with the body and the future status of the disembodied identity, control of the dead carries significant social weight. This is made more powerful, and more complicated, because the decaying body generally evokes revulsion and fears of contamination along with lingering reminders of an identity that is here but not here. While some cultures will erase these liminal, ambiguous, confusing signs by attempting to preserve the body, others work to annihilate the human form as quickly as possible by expeditious disposition in the ground or on the pyre. Religious leaders are generally identified as the authorities who are closest to the dead, and who will determine and remind group members about the ultimate meaning of death. But many cultures have other classes of authorities singled out to prepare the corpse or manage the presence of the dead.

Anthropologists and ethnographers provide numerous accounts of corpse-handlers who are social outcasts and occupy a marginal place in the social order. James L. Watson describes an array of ritual funeral specialists in two Cantonese villages in China whose social position and status are determined by communal notions of death pollution. He notes that what distinguishes "professional" from "non-professional" ritual death specialists is a single factor: do they get paid or not? If they do, villagers think of them as professionals, though that does not necessarily improve their social standing in the community. Indeed, Watson characterizes those hired to handle the dead and prepare them for burial as "the lowest of the low," an abhorred class of men who work with religious priests and have the undignified and dangerous task of removing the polluting body from living society. They are identified with rotting flesh, awful odors, and social corruption, and avoided at all costs—except when payment is made. Still, along with other specialists involved in funeral rituals, they are essential to Chinese society and identity: "Paid professionals always play a key role in the performance of Chinese funerary ritual . . . I would contend that it is not possible for people who conceive of themselves as 'Chinese' to hold what amounts to a do-it-yourself funeral, with untrained and unpaid personnel performing the rites."[2]

Anthropologist Jonathan P. Parry identifies the complex cultural, social, and religious meanings and practices associated with handling the dead in Banaras, India. Parry describes the world of sacred specialists who

interact with people who bring their dead to the holy city for final disposal in the Ganges. Parry states explicitly and clearly a simple truth revealed by his study: "Death in Banaras is very big business."[3] He describes the division of mortuary labor that drives much of the local economy and a variety of death specialists who manage the relations between the living and the dead. Some specialists take care of the corpse, some manage the ghosts of the recent dead who are believed to threaten living society, and others are primarily concerned with more friendly ancestors. The specialists responsible for immediate matters of corpses consumed by fire and malevolent ghosts on the prowl are generally considered to be impure, inauspicious, and rapacious characters who, despite their often ruthless tactics and fierce competition, carry out essential ritual work that keeps order in the cosmos and assists the dead after they lose their physical body.

Pascal Boyer reiterates a fairly accepted point of view: "The pollution of the dead is also the reason why, in so many places in the world, grave-digging and the handling of the corpse are carried out by a specialized, ritually avoided and generally despised class."[4] But there are exceptions to this general cultural model such as the hevra kadisha, or holy burial society in traditional Jewish communities. Members of this society are highly regarded for the volunteer work they do, which requires them to stay close to the body during its short stay above ground. They watch over it, wash it, dress it, and arrange its final interment with simple but deeply meaningful ceremonies. In this case, intimacy with the polluting and potentially dangerous corpse confers respect and admiration on those singled out to perform difficult mortuary duties.

Regardless of cultural setting, the dead body poses a significant and complex problem that requires careful ritual actions by the survivors, who simply cannot live with bodies hanging around. While twentieth-century anthropologists have considered the place of the dead and the role of funeral ritual specialists in a variety of global settings, very little attention has been given to these issues in America. Reviled by some, caricatured in the media and popular culture, and greatly appreciated by many who desire their mediation, funeral directors came of age in the twentieth century. During this period, these professionals embalmed and brought the dead into the presence of the living one last time, often in their own homes; and they continue to manage the critical body before disturbing and dangerous signs of decomposition threaten the association between identity and physical appearance. According to the homepage for the

Wyoming Funeral Directors Association, modern Americans embalm for three reasons: disinfection of the potentially dangerous corpse; preservation to facilitate proper ceremonial steps in the final disposition and to ward off "odors and other unpleasantness" that accompanies a corpse in decay; and restoration of the body to a semblance of life for the sake of therapeutic healing among survivors.

The same website explains the standard procedure of embalming as consisting of several steps that include washing and disinfecting the body, shaving the face if necessary, closing the eyes, wiring the mouth shut, and tending to the lips. With the use of an embalming machine, an electric pump forces chemical fluids through a tube into either the cartoid artery or the femoral artery. Another tube is inserted into the accompanying vein to drain the blood out of the body and into the sewer system. It generally takes three gallons of embalming fluid to get the body in the right shape. After removing the tubes and suturing the incision, suctioning out the abdominal cavity with a trocar or hollow tube and injecting additional chemicals, the body is then washed a final time. Cream is used to prevent dehydration on the hands and face, hair is shampooed, finger nails cleaned, and after the bloodless body is dressed and placed in the casket, cosmetics are employed to restore the natural color of the face.[5]

The twentieth century was indeed the "embalming century." This form of corpse preservation and presentation gave funeral directors the necessary authority, purpose, and values to promote their services to the living in a credible, profitable, and meaningful way. However, embalming could not have taken root in American society without implicit and explicit forms of support from across the larger cultural landscape throughout the century. This new, deeply complicated cultural convergence transformed the presence of the dead in both the social and imaginative worlds of modern Americans.

⊕ INTRODUCTION:1963 ⊕

Death, I come to take the soul, leave the body and leave it cold, to drop the flesh off of the frame, the earth and worms both have a claim. O Death, O Death, won't you spare me over 'til another year.

**"O! Death," traditional American folk song,
Doc Boggs, recorded June 26, 1963, North Carolina**

Funeral Service Under the Gun

O Death, where is thy sting? O grave, where is thy victory?
Where, indeed. Many a badly stung survivor, faced with the
aftermath of some relative's funeral,
has ruefully concluded that the victory has been won hands
down by a funeral establishment—in disastrously unequal battle.[1]

**Opening paragraph of Jessica Mitford's
The American Way of Death, published August, 1963.**

FROM THE BEGINNING OF THE TWENTIETH CENTURY, JOURNALISTS, RELIGIOUS leaders, academics, community activists, and other vocal critics publicly decried the stupendous rise of American funeral homes generally, and the undeniable cultural influence of the ritual specialists who lived and worked in these homes, specifically. Public indictments of the American funeral, and disturbing questions about profiting from the death of others, haunted men and women involved in this enterprise throughout the century. For sixty years nothing had really changed the basic ingredients of their day-to-day lives: removing bodies from homes and hospitals, embalming them, dressing and displaying them, recording information, and performing other tasks that assisted the living after the death of a loved one—noble deeds for sure in the minds of funeral directors and their families, who did not understand why the media persistently reported the venomous attacks in publications throughout the country.

Then in August, 1963, Simon and Schuster published Jessica Mitford's *The American Way of Death*, which became a phenomenal success and marked a turning point in American attitudes toward disposal of the dead. Funeral directing in particular would never be the same again. In brief, Mitford presents a scathing indictment of the funeral industry, drawing attention to the commercialism and exploitation she saw driving the enterprise. She mockingly denigrates funeral directors and other industry leaders, questioning their motivations, integrity, and value to American society. The practice of embalming, the very heart and soul of the industry, she singled out as particularly outrageous. According to Mitford, its central position in the disposal of the dead is, in reality, based on the funeral director's ability to sell his services and impose a self-serving, and highly lucrative regimen of ritual activities invented in the early 1900s. The "art" of embalming, a figure of speech popular in funeral trade magazines and other industry publications, was at bottom a vast funereal charade in Mitford's aesthetic, foisted on the undiscriminating, senseless American public by unscrupulous, mercenary capitalists.

Without question Mitford, more than any other critic before or since, shaped the terms of the public debate over funerals in American society and the kind of coverage funeral directors receive in popular media. Indeed, the series of events that unfolded in the late summer and fall of 1963 illuminate many of the dominant issues and themes that recurred in public debates throughout the century, and raise some of the key questions motivating this cultural history of the funeral home, such as: Do funeral directors prey on the vulnerability of grieving survivors to make a profit, or do they provide a valuable service to the public? What is the psychological, sociological, and religious significance of embalming in American rituals of death? How does the funeral industry figure into larger cultural attitudes toward death and the presence of the dead? And perhaps most important, did Mitford's analysis accurately explain "the American way of death," or did she misread cultural cues about the meaning of death in the United States and misunderstand the role of funeral directors in the lives of Americans?

By early summer 1963, many within the multibillion dollar funeral industry knew Mitford's book was on the way, but did not know what impact, if any, it would have on their lives and work. Although Mitford's book came out only a year after another critical study of the American funeral, Ruth Harmer's The High Cost of Dying, some opined it would quickly disappear and be of no lasting consequence. Others were less sanguine, however, and began to speak out against the charges of exploitation, corruption, and duplicity they were expecting to hear. Still others were less concerned about the substance of her arguments and instead asked how the book could help funeral directors provide even better services to the living.[2]

In June 1963, a writer for one of the more prominent funeral industry magazines, *The Director*, responded to a preview of Mitford's book, published in the May 1963 issue of *The Atlantic Monthly* entitled, "The Undertaker's Racket." Although the author writes that "it should not be necessary" to provide any biographical material on Mitford in his piece, he wastes no time in pointing out that she "was a member of an aristocratic English family [,] has lived a many sided, often questioned and much publicized life . . . [and] is one of the most vocal leaders of the East Bay Funeral Society (San Francisco)." The writer goes on to question her methods, accuracy, and generalizations, and disparages Mitford's narrow-minded focus on the economics of death. He suggests that any rebuttal by funeral directors to her accusations "will mean little if anything to those on the outside. Some may welcome her thoughts. Others will shudder at statements [made by Mitford] such as . . . 'I'd rather be nice and rotten than covered with whiskers of mold.'" Finally, the author states explicitly what is at stake for undertakers:

> The real issue is not what she wrote but is whether or not it will be of consequence. To those to whom funeral service is the business or industry of disposal of dead human bodies—the piece may present a hard to face appraisal. However, to those who regard the funeral as an experience of value best provided as a professional service, the article loses much of its impact. . . . The difference is in the attitude of the person providing the service. If it is that of a business, then business practices prevail. If it is a professional service then trust and confidence dispel worries as to any and all transactions in most instances.[3]

For the first half of the twentieth century, most undertakers struggled to be perceived as death experts with the appropriate amount of technical training, specialized knowledge, and human dignity to be legitimately called "professionals" just like other doctors, dentists, and lawyers. This was one strategy used by the predominantly male class of funeral directors and representatives, who consistently tried to counter the public perception of their work as simply a business and therefore particularly susceptible to the capitalist excesses of greed, exploitation, and deceit. With the Mitford book on the horizon, some of those who made a living off the dead wanted to make sure that funeral directors showed a united front. In an editorial in *The Director*, simply entitled, "The Only Answer—A

Profession," the author acknowledges a surprising diversity of opinion within the industry itself about whether "funeral service is a profession, business, or an industry." If funeral directors are going to respond effectively to public criticisms and maintain their respectability in the public eye, the editorial suggests, they would have to become a "full fledged profession" by conforming to an established set of values, educational standards, and practices instead of purely market-driven principals and policies. In reality, the author notes, clients are more appreciative of "services rendered and advice given by you . . . derived from education and training which you exercised primarily in their interest"[4]—words any decent doctor or dentist would live by.

Jessica Mitford's book not only ridiculed the language of professionalism employed by funeral directors and others to authorize, and dignify, the work of disposal, it also leveled a series of charges against undertakers who claim to have the interest of others in mind when the dead are taken from the living. She skillfully skewered nearly every component of the funeral "tradition," a tradition that many inside and outside the funeral industry understood as profoundly important to maintaining social order, and which placed American society at the apex of social evolution. Yet in spite of the industry's confidence in the rituals it provided for grieving survivors, and in the face of deep-rooted, solid neighborly support for most family-run funeral homes in cities and towns throughout the country, the book struck a chord with the American public and became an immediate cultural sensation.

After its release in the summer of 1963, the book shot to the top of the *New York Times* best-seller list (displacing Lasky's popular *J.F.K.: The Man and the Myth*), and received scores of enthusiastic reviews in major newspapers and magazines. The tremendous popular reception of *The American Way of Death*, and its pervasive, profound, and politically powerful cultural afterlife into the 1990s, indicates why it is a highly significant document not only in the history of death in America, but in United States history in general. Mitford's arguments move in two directions simultaneously. On the one hand, she articulates a number of critiques and charges that had swirled around the profession from the beginning of the century. On the other hand, as a result of the way in which she frames the issues and the public outcry that followed the book's publication, Mitford singlehandedly revolutionized many critical details of the American funeral industry. Her book, in fact, permanently changed the public face of death in America.

Mitford covers a range of funeral-related topics besides embalming in her exposé, including cemeteries, cremation, relations with the clergy, and the rhetoric of professionalism. Her muckraking journalistic style, along with her wry British sense of humor, made the book an enjoyable, entertaining read even as it fueled the long-standing antipathy towards funeral directors in many quarters of American society. Most of the reviews for the book were positive; they not only "got the joke" in Mitford's harangue, but some even participated in the very serious public condemnation of the industry.[5]

One commentary published in the *Saturday Review* at the end of August was derisively titled "Ambush on the Styx." In it, David Cort sets the confrontational tone immediately and alludes to the inherent imbalance between customer and funeral director in almost every case of death. "One should certainly pass this book by if one's whole family is immortal. Otherwise, it is the most exhaustive, documented, appendixed, and indexed explanation available of the ambush you and your family are inevitably walking into, unless you are lost at sea or vanish in an atomic war. The undertakers, in short, have got you."[6] From the opening salvo to the final, insulting paragraph, Cort draws from Mitford's work to pummel undertakers and challenge the integrity of their work.

Cort mentions a variety of sobering points discussed by Mitford, including the billion-dollar status of the funeral industry in 1963, the sacrilegious nature of the funeral, the intensive lobbying efforts and political organization of funeral directors, and the complex network of associated, exploitative enterprises related to flowers, cremations, caskets, and cemeteries. Although Cort acknowledges that protest has been futile in the past, he also points to two possible remedies to the dilemma of disposal. First, Cort argues, clergy should be called upon to ensure the funeral becomes a rite with high morals and low cost. Second, thanks to "sane citizens, usually in university towns," memorial societies offering simple, less expensive funerals for cost-conscious consumers were growing more and more popular. Cort saves his most virulent attack for the end of the article, where he states that "since the majority of funeral establishments handle one body or less a week, these people are the idlest, and must be the laziest, employed men in the United States. Perhaps this is why they are so pernicious."[7]

Advertisements for the book appeared in numerous newspapers and magazines after its release, bringing public attention to the scandals unearthed by

Mitford's study. Most of these ads trumpeted the sensationalism of her charges, and reveled in breaking the cultural tendency to privatize and keep silent about the funeral experience. One ad, from a September issue of the *New York Times*, went for the jugular, evoking an immensely popular parody of the American funeral—also penned by an English-born writer— published a few years before *The American Way of Death*:

> Crackling with life, Jessica Mitford's astonishing book makes public the bizarre inner workings of America's Funeral Industry. It's just published and in its second big printing. It's a bombshell of a book—an outburst of sanity, crashing through the sanctimonious hush that has kept one of America's most hard-sell industries from public scrutiny. The grotesqueries that we glimpsed in Evelyn Waugh's novel, *The Loved One*, pale before the actuality—as Mitford discloses the curious facts behind the average American funeral coast to coast.[8]

Even major newspapers covered the social impact of the Mitford book and reported on how segments of the public were responding to the economic outrages it revealed. Some states took immediate action, with local congressmen calling for public hearings on the business practices of the industry. A few months after the book's release, the *New York Times* ran a front page article on the critical role it played in prompting the state attorney general's office to investigate "alleged price-gouging, bill-padding and fraudulent selling techniques in the funeral business."[9] Although the charges were certainly scandalous, funeral directors tried to find ways to defend themselves and their profession. The article stated that George Goldstein, acting counsel for the New York State Funeral Directors Association, had said that the "New York Better Business Bureau reported recently that it got 'practically no complaints' about price excesses by funeral directors, and that the State Health Department, which licenses the directors, got 'very few complaints in proportion to the number of deaths in the state.' [Goldstein] added that 'many of these are the result of misunderstandings.'"[10]

In September, the *Wall Street Journal* ran a story on its front page entitled, "The Funeral Furor: Top-Selling Book Spurs Expansion of Societies Promoting Simple Rites." Noting that the book was already in its fourth printing, the article discusses the "small but growing group of Americans" joining funeral and memorial societies across the nation. While these kinds of societies had been around for years in one form or another, Mitford's book brought them unprecedented publicity and created a surge in popular interest. According to the writer, funeral directors were responding to the charges against them and the traditions they upheld by increasing funds for public relations programs and publicly denouncing "Miss Mitford and the societies for advocating 'irreligious,' 'materialist' or even 'communistic' rites."[11]

Like the ad mentioned earlier, the *Wall Street Journal* article also refers to the particular cultural setting in which the public debates about funerals emerged: "Besides winning readers itself, the book has inspired a rash of magazine articles, radio discussion programs and the like, which have opened up for general public discussion a subject long thought to be taboo."[12] While there are many questions about the accuracy of the word "taboo" to describe American attitudes in the first half of the twentieth century, the author is clearly correct about the immediate aftermath of publication: Death was a hot topic in 1963, present in the popular imagination in a way that was quite different from the decades before the book. While various opinions about death and funerals were being expressed in American society, the news media pursued Mitford's sensational story, reporting on the charlatans and quacks who were callously ripping off people at their most vulnerable moment.

A prime example of this media fixation was the broadcast of "The Great American Funeral" on CBS in October, 1963. The program contained a number of interviews with clergy, funeral directors, and leaders in the industry, and Mitford herself. It also explored such topics as the high cost of funerals, the elaborate accouterments surrounding the dead, and alternative forms of disposal. At the time, defenders inside and outside the industry occasionally had their say in public, charging that Mitford's generalizations were inaccurate and focused on a relatively small group of irresponsible men. At least one U.S. congressman, James B. Utt (a Republican from California), defended the funeral business, charging that the CBS show was a "pro-Communistic documentary," and even asserted in the congressional record that Mitford was heavily involved in communist activities. But even though the show itself was clearly weighted in favor of Mitford, it also contained curious statements that were not fully explored, like the following from an Episcopalian minister: "I don't like the first thing about mortuaries. . . . I don't blame the morticians for it [extravagant expenses at funerals]. . . . The people like it."[13]

The Southern Funeral Director published an article anticipating the show in October, 1963. The author encouraged everyone associated with funeral service to watch it, and to expect the usual array of accusations. But, the author continued, while the show may be seen as a "great victory" for reformers, it should not undercut the most important pillar of funeral success, a long history of local support: "It will take a landslide of public opinion to change funeral and burial customs which have taken history many, many years to establish."[14] Although the article underestimated the social impact of Mitford's work, it correctly pointed to a strong undercurrent of popular approval for the rituals associated with the American funeral.

In addition to literary reviews, advertisements, newspapers reports, and the CBS special, many magazines around the country gave extended coverage to the book and generally presented evidence that bolstered the credibility of Mitford's allegations. *TIME*, *Newsweek*, *Life*, and a range of other periodicals ran stories about the economics of death, reiterating the same basic criticisms found in Mitford's book. In the November 1963, issue of *Changing Times: The Kiplinger Magazine*, a lead story about the "furor over funerals" states that "as Americans we are dying without dignity and beyond our means."[15] According to the article, "many clergymen, persons concerned with economic exploitation of the public (such as administrators of union welfare and pension funds), and a large number of resentful citizens" believe that the American way of death is indecent.[16]

While much of the article focuses on the charges of various reformers, it also gave champions of the American funeral a chance to voice their opinions. One unnamed "funeral industry spokesman" remarks, "In keeping with our high standard of living, there should be an equally high standard of dying"—a sentiment frequently expressed by funeral directors even today. A national funeral industry journal editorial is quoted as well: "A good funeral should be so different from a cheap service, should be so obvious in quality, that the purchaser doesn't have to exhibit the funeral bill to prove that he selected something in keeping with his sense of pride."[17] Covering the usual topics—the floral industry, cemeteries, the rise of memorial and funeral societies, religious outrage against the funeral—the piece ends with a series of suggestions for the bereaved: call a minister immediately; "reject showiness" and limit spending; consider having the funeral in a church instead of a funeral home; "minimize the period of worst anguish" by scheduling the services "as soon as practicable after death" (and "remember that you don't have to permit embalming if you don't wish it"); keep the casket closed and "let the funeral center around the spirit rather than the body"; and ensure dignity for close relations by making any graveside service private. The final point in the article shifted to Judaism, claiming that anyone "who has given sincere thought to the subject" would agree with "the Jewish decree that the funeral should be conducted with 'dignity, sanctity and modesty.'"[18]

In spite of the chorus of public condemnation raging in the media, and the often clumsy responses from funeral men in the industry, there remained signs of popular support and deep commitment to American death rituals. In the October 4, 1963 edition of *TIME* magazine, a number of letters criticized the sensationalistic nature of the charges against the industry. One indignant funeral man associated with the Erie Burial Case Company set his sights on Mitford herself, writing, "If Miss Mitford does not like our American funeral customs, let her return to the less civilized customs from which she came." Another letter in the magazine, from a leader in a Somerville, Massachusetts, Congregational Church, offered a completely different representation of funeral directors from those circulating in much of the popular press.

> It's a sad day when *TIME* gets either conned or seduced into presenting only one side of an issue. In the several communities where I have served, the funeral directors have been a most efficient and highly ethical group of businessmen. In general, they are extremely sensitive to the needs of others. We often fail to realize that they are on call round the clock, must check out more than 200 fine details for every case, have a tremendous overhead and operating expense, and usually serve the public at a great sacrifice to their personal family life.[19]

In the November 19, 1963 edition of the *National Review*, two letters responding to an article on Mitford's book decried the attacks against American funeral traditions. One writer states, "If Mr. Russell [the author of the article] chooses to dispose of his family's dead with none of the reverence that helps most people, he may do so at whatever cost he wishes." Another writer argues, "The existence of abuses among funeral directors, and American ambivalence toward death do not excuse an attack on those customs which reflect and reinforce the Christian belief in a life after death."[20] Many Christians rejected the glorification of a Jewish model—and many Jews themselves rejected the model of orthodox simplicity—as the more appropriate response among the living when faced with the task of corpse-disposal.

In the aftermath of Mitford's book, funeral directors began to believe that the best defense would be a good offense. Many now advocated a strategy that had been debated within the industry for much of the century: disclose to the public the range of duties and responsibilities that the funeral director must undertake when death strikes a family. This strategy, and other efforts to counter the raging public attacks against the industry, were discussed at the October 1963, annual convention of the National Funeral Directors Association (NFDA), in Dallas, Texas. According to the chairman of the public relations committee, people involved in funeral service "received a good kick in the seat of the pants" as a result of Mitford's work and the media coverage surrounding it.[21]

Despite the social impact of the book, the NFDA did not back down from the challenges it posed to the public. The public relations committee put forward a series of recommendations to quell the furor, hoping that a united, concerted response would help turn the tide. These recommendations included increasing the distribution of literature, films, and other NFDA-produced materials that could "tell the story of funeral service positively"; making sure that all the information the executive offices of the NFDA had about death and funerals was available to any interested parties; getting appropriate representatives of the industry on radio and television to defend the American funeral industry; and underwriting "the cost of 100,000 copies of a book being written by Dr. Edgar Jackson tentatively entitled, *Death in America* (eventually titled *For the Living*)."[22] These and other steps were discussed before the October convention ended. Funeral directors who attended the annual meeting believed that national representatives of the NFDA had a fairly coherent plan of action, and they expected to carry on their own public relations efforts at the local level in their hometowns.

By the end of November 1963, however, an event took place that sent a shock wave around the nation, and indeed around the world. The thirty-fifth president of the United States, John Fitzgerald Kennedy, was assassinated in Dallas, Texas, the same city where funeral directors from across the country had recently gathered to discuss the state of funeral service in America. Members of the NFDA had been preparing a response to still another negative article, but the editor of the magazine no longer thought it was necessary.

> When the editor was called late in November of 1963 about using the rebuttal he said his publication didn't have to because "The Great American Funeral" (the title of the CBS telecast) was played out before millions of Americans the day the world stood still—the day they paid respects to and buried J.F.K.[23]

"The Day the World Stood Still"

On Saturday morning, November 23, a day after the assassination, John F. Kennedy's embalmed body remained hidden within a flag-draped casket in the East Room of the White House, the same room where Abraham Lincoln's embalmed body had rested before its twenty-day journey to Springfield, Illinois, nearly a century earlier. An honor guard and two priests were present in the room with the body and kept a vigil over the dead president until Sunday, when his sacred remains would be transported to the rotunda in the Capitol. The president's widow requested the same solemn decorations in the room that had been used for Lincoln's funeral ceremonies. In contrast to the public spectacle surrounding Lincoln's traveling body, however, she ultimately refused to give the public one last look at their stricken leader. Kennedy's casket stayed closed, shielded from the eyes of the mourning nation from the moment the body was placed inside until it was lowered into the ground at Arlington National Cemetery.[24]

The nation's, indeed the world's, gaze remained fixed on the closed casket as it moved from the White House to the Capitol to Arlington over the course of three days. The dramatic impact of the funeral and the outpouring of grief and sorrow across the country was unparalleled in U.S. history. Although there are obvious grounds for comparison with Lincoln's assassination and funeral ceremonies, the presence of the media at the ceremonies, and the mediated presence of Kennedy's dead body in the lives of millions of television viewers, created an instantaneous sense of common suffering on a scale never seen before. When the accused assassin, Lee Harvey Oswald, was murdered by Jack Ruby on live television that Sunday—the same day the president's body was removed from the White House and placed in the rotunda of the Capitol—the drama captivated and mortified an already grieving audience.

Only a few months after the release of *The American Way of Death*, and in the midst of a raging public debate about the social value of American funerals, the nation engaged in one of the most significant collective ceremonies in its history. Since that moment, scholars, journalists, and other commentators have explored the gruesome details of the assassination, its social and political implications in the context of twentieth-century America, and the cultural repercussions of this shared experience in the life of the nation. But most have overlooked the historical coincidence of Kennedy's funeral and the public debate initiated by the publication of Mitford's work. A few people immediately placed the events surrounding Kennedy's death in the context of this debate, but most temporarily set aside questions about the funeral industry and concentrated on the business at hand: disposing of the president's body in a manner that reaffirmed national solidarity and allowed for the expression of personal grief.

One person who had Mitford on his mind just after the assassination was the president's brother, Robert Kennedy. According to Arthur M. Schlesinger Jr.'s account in *Robert Kennedy and His Times*, after the body arrived at Bethesda Hospital from Dallas, Robert realized that "there were so many details. The funeral home wanted to know how grand the coffin should be. 'I was influenced by . . . that girl's book on [burial] expenses. . . . Jessica Mitford [*The American Way of Death*]. . . . I remember making the decision based on Jessica Mitford's book. . . . I remember thinking about it afterward, about whether I was cheap or what I was, and I remembered thinking about how difficult it must be for everybody making that kind of decision.'"[25] Speaking in the third person, Mitford writes in the revised version of her book that she was "most gratified to learn that her message had been absorbed in high places," and then goes on to explain how the Kennedys were ruthlessly exploited by the two funeral directors—one in Dallas, one in Washington—who handled the president's body.[26]

In addition to Schlesinger's account, William Manchester, another close Kennedy aide, reconstructs the events surrounding Kennedy's death in *The Death of a President: November 20–November 25, 1963*, a book written at the request of Jacqueline Kennedy soon after her husband's funeral. Manchester supplies many details about the role of funeral men in the burial of Kennedy and, like Mitford, portrays them in a negative light. According to Manchester, the first undertaker contacted in the aftermath of the assassination was Vernon B. Oneal, who owned a funeral home close to Parkland Memorial in Dallas, the hospital where the president was pronounced dead. Manchester reports that secret service agent Clint Hill instructed Oneal to "bring the best" casket to Parkland. Oneal chose the "Britannia" model from the Elgin Casket Company line, which was a massive, solid bronze container weighing over 700 pounds, and placed it in the brand new, white Cadillac he had bought a month earlier at the NFDA convention.[27]

When the casket arrived at Parkland, it was immediately taken to the president's room. Before Oneal and others began to prepare the body for its journey to Washington, Jacqueline Kennedy removed her wedding ring and placed it on the finger of her dead husband, an act inspired by memories of her father's funeral, where she had felt the same impulse to leave something of tremendous value with the body before it disappeared from view forever.[28] Manchester then turns his attention to Oneal, who was "plying his craft. He was concerned about the Britannia's pale satin upholstery; it was immaculate now, but could easily be stained. . . . he made certain that there would be seven protective layers of rubber and two of plastic between the damaged scalp and the green satin."[29] Unfortunately, complications emerged in Parkland that made the removal of the body from Dallas quite difficult. Earl Rose, the Dallas medical examiner, originally refused to turn the body over to the president's key advisors from Washington, D.C. until after an autopsy was performed, a legal requirement in Texas when a homicide takes place. After a series of arguments and more serious confrontations regarding who exactly had jurisdiction over the body, the casket was loaded into Oneal's hearse and taken to Love Field.[30]

Oneal assumed that the president's remains would be left in his care for the embalming and cosmetic work, and then conveyed to a local memorial park.[31] He was disappointed when he learned that the body would be taken directly to the airport, and then sent to Washington, where another funeral director would take charge of the highly important and, considering the damage to the president's skull, challenging work of preparing the body for the funeral. According to Manchester, he was also disappointed when he discovered that the driver had failed to take the red ambulance sign from the window, which meant that "nobody would be able to identify it as a hearse."[32] After arriving at the airport, secret service agents accidently damaged the casket while taking it out of the hearse and placing it in Air Force One, something Mitford fails to explain in her discussion of the "badly damaged" casket mentioned in the revised edition of her book.[33]

Once in Washington, a new funeral directing team took over the responsibilities of preparing the body and helping to plan the funeral. Manchester interjects his own commentary about the funeral business when describing how doctors and members of the staff at Bethesda Naval Hospital, where the body had been taken upon its arrival in the nation's capital, understood the role of undertakers in these proceedings. He also notes the significance of Mitford's book in the deliberations over how to plan Kennedy's funeral.

> The funeral industry had attained a kind of metapsychic domination over all who dealt with death. They had even adopted its jargon; Metzler, Miller, and the doctors at Bethesda referred to "the remains," not "the body," and Fort Myer's Old Guard had abandoned the more dignified "pallbearers" for "casket team." All of them had been seduced by the curious myth that only licensed morticians could prepare "the remains" for burial. It was untrue. . . . But everyone at a responsible position . . . was under the impression that there had to be one. Indeed, so unanimous were they that the issue would never have arisen had it not been for the publication of Jessica Mitford's *The American Way of Death* six months earlier. Robert Kennedy had read Miss Mitford's carefully documented exposé of the gouging of bereaved relatives, and so had Dr. Joseph English, the Peace Corps psychiatrist who stood at Sargent Shriver's elbow Friday afternoon.[34]

"The decision was made that a private funeral home, rather than the government, would prepare the body. Someone recommended Gawler's Funeral Home, a prominent local establishment over one hundred years old that had been involved in the funerals of Presidents Taft and Roosevelt, as well as other government officials and wealthy citizens.[35] Although personnel at Bethesda could embalm the remains, they could not do much else. Both Robert and Jacqueline Kennedy did not want any private undertaking firms handling the body of the slain president, but others involved in planning the funeral knew it was inevitable. Manchester explains that the damaged casket would have to be replaced and that no decision had been made about whether the casket would be open or closed—"and should the coffin have been open during the lying in state, the special arts of the undertaker would have been essential."[36] There are conflicting accounts about the events surrounding the selection of the casket, but the total bill from Gawler's, which included a "Marsellus No. 710" casket made of 500-year-old solid African mahogany wood, and the most expensive vault available from the funeral home, was $3,160.00.[37]

The casket was then transported to Bethesda, where attendants from Gawler's brought it into the morgue. After the autopsy on the president's body, Gawler's men, including a cosmetic specialist, began their duties. In the words of Jim Bishop, who also wrote a detailed account of Kennedy's death and offers a more sympathetic view of the funeral team, "the function of [Gawler's men] was to restore John Fitzgerald Kennedy to an approximation of serene sleep. In a manner of speaking, this is the most tender and most difficult of services. It is normally performed in secrecy. For Joseph Gawler's Sons, it would have been easier to take the body to their establishment. . . . This was not permitted because Mrs. Kennedy did not want the body taken from the hospital."[38] According to one of Gawler's men, the cosmetician "was really under the gun. There were about thirty-five people, led by General Wehle, breathing down our necks. We were worrying about skull leakage, which could be disastrous. We did not know whether the body would be viewed or not."[39]

The procedure lasted about three hours, and even though Kennedy's personal physician, Dr. Burkley, knew about Jacqueline's request to keep private undertakers away, he let the work continue for the following reason: "I was determined that the body be fully dressed and that the face be just right in case people opened the coffin a thousand years hence."[40] According to Bishop, the people in the room who observed the work of Gawler's men were quite impressed. Using language that might be applied to religious specialists who work miracles, Bishop writes: "To the witnesses, the morticians were, in a manner of speaking, magicians. They had been given a broken shell of a man, and they had walked around him many times, whispering incantations to each other, applying the laying on of hands, and the shell began to look more and more like John F. Kennedy. The brows, the cheeks were smoothed outward and downward. The natural complexion of the President seemed to return."[41] When the procedure was finished, the attendants positioned the body in the coffin, and one of Gawler's assistants placed a rosary in Kennedy's arranged hands.

In the early morning hours of Saturday, November 23, Jacqueline Kennedy insisted to Secretary of State Robert McNamara that the coffin remain closed during the period of lying in state. According to Manchester, McNamara responded by saying, "It can't be done, Jackie. Everybody wants to see a Head of State." Jacqueline then replied, "I don't care. It's the most awful, morbid thing; they have to remember Jack alive," and expressed her distaste for a fundamental component of the American way of death: viewing the remains. Manchester notes that, at this point, Robert Kennedy was in agreement with McNamara because this was "an exceptional situation. He didn't see how a President's funeral could disregard the public; private preferences had to be set aside."[42] These men believed that the American public craved a comforting image of the president, a last look before the fallen leader's final interment.

Working from an engraving of the East Room during Lincoln's funeral ceremonies, William Walton arranged the room in the White House where the president's body would lie in state. A replica of Lincoln's catafalque was assembled and decorations were put in place. According to Manchester, Walton too was a Mitford reader, and when men from Gawler's offered their own funereal accouterments, including satin coverings, elaborate candlesticks, and a five-foot cross, he rejected them, remarking that "it's just hideous."[43] After the casket was placed on the catafalque, Jacqueline came and stood in the doorway of the East Room. Robert Kennedy then came to her side and whispered that he would settle the issue about whether or not the casket would be opened or closed. After Jacqueline left, Robert had the lid of the coffin opened and asked everyone to leave the area surrounding the catafalque. Schlesinger provides the following quotation from Robert's recollections: "I asked everybody to leave and I asked them to open it. . . . When I saw it, I'd made my mind up. I didn't want it open and I think I might have talked to somebody to ask them to look also."[44]

A few other people in the White House then went to look upon the face of the thirty-fifth president. McNamara was the only one who wanted the casket opened, even though Dr. English said he was "surprised that his appearance was as good as it was, that he looked well."[45] They were clearly in the minority; the others who gazed upon the face, including Arthur Schlesinger, Nancy Tuckerman (Jacqueline's secretary), and William Walton, all agreed that John Kennedy did not look presentable. Walton remarked to Robert, "You mustn't keep it open. It has no resemblance to the president. It's a wax dummy."[46] When the news broke that the casket would remain closed, the media was inundated with questions from the public about why they would not have one last opportunity to see and say good-bye to the president.

According to David Brinkley, who was at NBC at the time, the station was "flooded by letters and wires demanding an explanation. I was repeatedly asked to provide one, and usually I refused. . . . To me it was obvious. I feel strongly that the coffin should be closed at all funerals."[47] *TIME* magazine also reported on the closed casket, stating that "The casket . . . was never to be opened because the President had been deeply disfigured."[48] Manchester writes that this explanation was "wholly untrue. Neither wound had damaged the president's face. His features, intact when his wife examined them at Parkland, had been treated with cosmetics, and this was what gave offense."[49] A few days after the funeral ceremonies, the *New York Times* ran a short article entitled, "Mrs. Kennedy's Opposition to Open Coffin Explained." It stated that Jacqueline had "acted as many religious leaders wish that all bereaved families would. . . . They believe that it is pagan, rather than Christian, to focus on the body. . . . Priests and pastors who share this view hold that a closed coffin minimizes morbid concentration on the body, and makes it easier for the Christian funeral rites to get across the point that it is the soul that matters."[50]

The casket remained closed all day Saturday, while a steady stream of visitors, including friends, government officials, and foreign dignitaries, made their way into the East Room to pay their respects to the Kennedy family.[51] By Saturday evening, Jacqueline Kennedy realized that, although she had insisted on a closed casket for all the funeral ceremonies, she wanted to have a private moment with the body of her husband to say good-bye and leave other personal objects with him.[52] On Sunday morning, Jacqueline asked their daughter, Caroline, to write a letter to her father, and had their young son, John, mark a sheet of paper; these two letters, along with one she wrote her husband, would be placed in the casket when it was opened. In addition to the letters, Jacqueline decided to leave a special pair of cufflinks and a scrimshaw. Walking by Robert's side, the widow entered the East Room while the military guards on the death-watch turned to face the wall. The two then knelt by the opened coffin and, according to Manchester, Jacqueline thought, "It isn't Jack, it isn't Jack," and expressed relief that the coffin had remained closed during all the ceremonies. She then placed the gifts in the coffin. Robert also placed something special in the coffin: his brother's PT-109 tie pin and an engraved silver rosary. Before they left, the widow took a lock of her husband's hair.[53]

Jacqueline and Robert left the privacy of the White House to participate in the public departure of the body for the rotunda in the Capitol. The Kennedy family entered the black limousine that would transport them to the Capitol, while the casket was placed on a caisson, surrounded by the honor guard that would escort it in the funeral procession down Pennsylvania Avenue. When the casket arrived at the Capitol, Jacqueline and her two children followed it up the steps and into the rotunda, where the pallbearers lowered it onto the catafalque. Inside, three speakers eulogized the fallen leader and then, after they finished, one of the most memorable and painful scenes took place: Jacqueline Kennedy and her daughter walked to the casket and knelt next to it. Jacqueline touched and kissed the flag that draped the casket, and Caroline reached under the flag to touch the coffin that held her dead father.[54]

During the rest of the day, thousands of people entered the rotunda to see the flag-draped casket and pay their last respects. According to reports, at least 115,000 mourners passed the president's enclosed remains by 2:45 A.M. the following day.[55] Although some dignitaries were there, the *New York Times* reported that "mostly they were just people, shuffling in awed silence, two abreast, in two semi-circles around the bier guarded by military men."[56] People across the nation, as well as around the world, collectively experienced the solemn day of mourning thanks to the unprecedented, commercial-free coverage of the media. Television cameras placed within the rotunda captured the sorrow of the mourners moving past the closed coffin; NBC covered the sad procession without any commentary.

On Monday, November 25, the body of John F. Kennedy was moved from the Capitol and buried at Arlington National Cemetery. Even though many advised his widow to send the president's body to his home state of Massachusetts, Jacqueline made the final decision to bury her husband in the soil of the country's most famous national cemetery for military personnel.[57] The cortege moved slowly through the streets of the nation's capitol, with the riderless horse, Black Jack, following the casket, and hundreds of thousands of mourners lining the procession route. When the cortege stopped at St. Matthew's Cathedral, Richard Cardinal Cushing blessed the casket before the march continued to Arlington. The ceremonies at the grave site followed regular military protocols—they were formal and dignified, and before the casket was placed beneath the ground at Arlington, soldiers folded the flag that accompanied the body and gave it to the grieving widow.

The same day that President Kennedy was laid to rest, the body of his accused assassin, Lee Harvey Oswald, was buried in Fort Worth, Texas. Several newsmen acted as pallbearers because there was no one else to carry the casket. Newspapers reported that, after the religious service commenced at the grave site and before the body was lowered into the ground, the casket lid was opened so Oswald's wife and mother could kiss his face. In the presence of Oswald's mother, brother, wife, and two daughters, the plain pine coffin that held the man charged with killing the president was then lowered into the ground.[58] Even under the circumstances of these horrible events, the family surrounding this murdered body were allowed to have their ceremonial, intimate moment in a Fort Worth cemetery.

Commentators around the country celebrated the funeral observances surrounding the burial of the president of the United States. Most commended the actors involved, and praised the honor and dignity of the rituals that brought order to a chaotic, sorrowful time. An editorial in the *New York Times* stated that, "In time of sudden shock—such as that of this tragic weekend—we fall back naturally on traditional symbols and accustomed ceremonials. President Kennedy's funeral may well have been in many respects the most elaborate and impressive farewell a modern ruler has ever received."[59] While many around the nation appreciated the "traditional symbols and accustomed ceremonials," people within the funeral industry felt absolutely vindicated about the services they provided to Americans, and assumed that the splendor and success of Kennedy's funeral would silence all their Mitford-inspired critics.

In one of the first written accounts of these events published in a funeral trade magazine, psychologist Robert L. Fulton and executive director of the NFDA at the time, Howard C. Raether, extolled the funeral ceremonies associated with the death of the president.[60] Fulton and Raether described the key elements of the funeral, and then argued that these traditional elements "provided the proper climate for mourning, the healthy channeling of the nation's grief." They went on to offer the argument that had become standard in funeral circles throughout the country: Viewing the remains is a critical step for survivors to confront and then overcome the reality of death. "It is said that the family saw the body of the President in the White House after it was prepared, dressed and placed in

the mahogany casket. For obvious reasons, there could not be public viewing. This is undoubtedly why many people said and still say they cannot
believe the President is dead." At the conclusion of the article, the two
authors comment on the religious and patriotic nature of the American
way of death not only in the funeral of Kennedy, but also with respect to
the burial of Oswald: "These two events serve not only to remind us of the
oneness of our society but compel us to recognize that there is a dignity to
all men regardless of their accomplishments or their crimes. . . . In [these
burials] this country saw its unity under God and reaffirmed the dignity of
man."[61] For these and many other individuals inside and outside of the
funeral industry, the psychological value of having one last look at the
deceased, the social benefits of maintaining funeral traditions, and the
religious imperatives of ensuring a proper form of disposal, were all reaffirmed in the ceremonies surrounding Kennedy's death.

In a piece published in the December 1963 issue of *The American
Funeral Director*, editor Albert R. Kates relied on the above-quoted editorial in the *New York Times* to neutralize the cries of reformers. For Kates,
the recent television series about American funerals had gotten it all
wrong; the services for the slain president were, in fact, the perfect example of "The Great American Funeral." He continues his praise for the
American way of death by writing, "President Kennedy was buried with a
ceremony that is typical of the religious and sentimental manner in which
virtually every other American is laid to rest, regardless of rank or degree
of wealth."[62] Kates also notes that the only tradition not observed in
Kennedy's funeral was an open casket. He writes that "this apparently did
not result from any objection by the family to this custom," and then
quotes from an Associated Press dispatch, dated November 27, in which
an assistant White House secretary states that "the reasons for [no view-
ing] should be obvious. . . . Mr. Kennedy was shot in the head and neck."[63]
While Kates may have been misinformed about the behind-the-scenes
planning for the funeral, he extols the democratic, religious, and personal
virtues of American traditions, even in those cases where the embalmed
body remains concealed from public view.

Kates and others within the funeral industry thought the Kennedy ceremonies would exonerate them in the eyes of Americans; indeed, the
NFDA turned the article by Fulton and Raether into a brochure that could
be sent around the country to inform people of the value of traditional
funerals. Others outside the industry recognized the coincidental timing of

Kennedy's death and funeral. In a newspaper article published at the time in the *Buffalo Courier Express*, a Reverend Ralph W. Loew wrote:

> It is ironic that a national funeral should have interposed itself in the midst of the recent public discussions concerning the American and death. Suddenly there was played out before us the need to concern ourselves with ministering to one another in an hour of grief. It is patently true that there have been sentimentalisms and expensive actions which violate our faith. It is also true that we have a need to express our ties of understanding.
>
> The fact that hundreds of thousands of persons would want to walk past a closed casket is more than sentimentalism; it is the renewal of our belonging to a larger entity. Suddenly the drawer of our own experience was pulled open and we discovered the need to say something, to do something and to share something in the hour of our common grief.[64]

Kennedy's funeral did not ultimately quell the uproar over industry practices initiated by Mitford, but it did momentarily reveal the complex set of relations that exist between the living and the dead. In this case, as with Lincoln roughly 100 years before, private and public attachments to the dead body required its presence and accessibility to mourners participating in the final ceremonies. However, the degree of intimacy that can exist between the mourner and the corpse—a last touch, kiss, gesture, or final gaze, if the casket is open, and less intimate acts if it is closed—depends on a host of social conditions, material resources, and cultural scripts that result in acceptable, meaningful, and fulfilling ways to bring the dead to the living one last time. In twentieth-century America, funeral directors took charge of the body so the bereaved could have what they wanted most—one last private moment with the loved one. Despite Mitford's national success in the public arena, which raises a host of relevant questions about larger cultural attitudes toward death and the dead, her analysis was simply, finally, dead wrong.

The pages that follow will explore the world of death specialists who emerged on the American scene at the end of the Civil War and assumed an authoritative role in the disposal of the dead over the course of the twentieth century. American funeral directors, in conjunction with an array of specialized service-providers and public relations people, not only became the primary managers in the disposal of the dead, they also began to determine the interpretive and ritual frameworks available to many Americans facing the loss of a loved one. As the funeral industry began to expand and solidify its position in the early decades of the century, growing into a highly successful American enterprise by the 1960s, frequent attacks from many others before Mitford failed to make an impact. Although the media focused increased public attention on industry scandals and criticisms after Mitford's book, the continued stature and respect afforded local funeral directors in towns and cities throughout the country ensured their dominant role as the primary mediators between the dead and the living, and suggests that undertaking families had been providing friends, neighbors, and fellow citizens with valuable, greatly-appreciated goods and services. Contrary to the accusations leveled by Mitford and others, there is more to the business of death than simply economics—the emotional, psychological, religious, and cultural dimensions of disposal must also be taken into historical account when investigating American ways of death.

FROM HOUSE CALLS TO FUNERAL HOMES:
CHANGING RELATIONS BETWEEN THE LIVING AND THE DEAD

Get six jolly fellows to carry my coffin,
And six pretty maidens to bear up my pall,
And give to each of them bunches of roses
That they may not smell me as they bear me along.

**"The Cowboy's Lament" in *Cowboy Songs and
Other Frontier Ballads*, John A. Lomax and Alan Lomax, 1938**

Intimacy Lost

By the start of the twentieth century, the relationship between the living and the dead in America had begun to change dramatically. In many ways, the intimacy that had connected the physical remains with a community of family and friends was gradually being supplanted by a gaping social divide. Although the transition from intimacy to estrangement occurred more slowly in the South and in rural areas generally, in time the pattern was replicated just about everywhere in the United States. In large part, the divide was produced by three social factors: changes in demographic patterns, the rise of hospitals as places of dying, and the growth of modern funeral homes.

For many modern Americans at the turn of the twentieth century, it was easier to imagine the dead than to actually encounter them in everyday life, a common feature of social history up until that time. What historians have identified as a "mortality revolution" in the early twentieth century contributed to the gradual disappearance of the corpse from the lives of Americans. Mortality rates in the United States and other industrialized countries around the globe steadily and dramatically decreased during this time. (The influenza epidemic of 1917–1918 led to one of the few noticeable, and short-lived, increases in the death rate.)[1] Life expectancy, in turn, began to improve radically. According to one recent study on longevity, "The average length of life increased more during the twentieth century than during all previous periods of history combined."[2] While changes in these numbers varied according to community and region, families were stricken by the death of close relations much less frequently than ever before in human history—a point commonly made by funeral directors in trade journals and other publications throughout the century.[3]

Life expectancy, infant mortality, cause of death—these and other variables in mortality tables all point to the same conclusion: the presence of death in the early decades of the twentieth century looked quite different than any other period of American history. There are a variety of explanations for these dramatic changes in demographic patterns, with most focusing on breakthroughs in medical sciences and technologies, improvements in sanitation and personal hygiene, effective public health reforms, and healthier eating habits.[4] While the repercussions of these social transformations have been analyzed from a number of perspectives, one of the most common observations is that a completely new kind of relationship with the dead emerged in the early decades of the century.[5]

In one study, demographer Peter Uhlenberg argues that over the course of the twentieth century, declining mortality rates led to structural transformations in family relations as well: "As the experience of losing intimate family members moves from a pervasive aspect of life to a rare event, adjustments in family structure become imperative."[6] He discusses the social impact of these changes and writes that decreasing infant mortality rates produced intensified bonds of affection between parents and their children, led to fewer adults dying between 20 and 50 years old, which reduced the number of orphaned children, limited the number of deaths an individual encounters within the nuclear family, and ensured that longer life expectancy would allow children to have more time with their grandparents.[7]

The statistical details of these profound demographic changes are quite startling, even when rendered in the abstract. In the first few decades of the century, infant mortality dropped from a rate of over 125 deaths per 1,000 live births at the end of the nineteenth century to a rate of less than 50 per 1,000 by 1940.[8] The death rate for adults, aged 25 to 34, also decreased for both men and women in this period. Between 1905 and 1909, there were roughly 722 deaths per 100,000 males; by the early 1940s the rate plunged to about 275. For the female population, the decrease is also striking: 648 deaths per 100,000 in the early period, and 195 per 100,000 near the middle of the century.[9] In 1900, the journey from birth to death lasted roughly 47 years; by the 1940s, the journey stretched out to beyond 60.[10]

Another significant demographic change during this period was in the leading causes of death. The first half of the twentieth century witnessed an important shift in why people died—a transition from "the age of

receding pandemics" to "the age of degenerative and Man-made diseases."[11] In the words of social demographer Paul E. Zopf Jr., "Long-term
trends in cause of death reflect the nation's movement through the epi-
demiologic transition, from the early 1900s when infectious and parasitic
illnesses claimed many lives, to the present when the degenerative diseases take a heavy toll."[12] Dysentery, influenza, tuberculosis, typhoid—
these and other infectious diseases were replaced by heart disease, cancer,
and strokes as the leading causes of death by the middle of the century.
In addition to degenerative diseases, more violent causes of death, such
as accidents, suicides, and homicides, killed a higher percentage of
Americans than ever before.[13]

As the health of the social body began to change, hospitals became
the primary institutions to care for the sick and monitor the passage from
life to death. The dramatic rise in the number of hospitals across the
country and their increasing control over the health of the nation contributed to the separation of death from everyday life. As doctors
achieved professional dominance in the practice of medicine in this period, hospitals emerged as the principal site for the diagnosis and treatment
of patients.[14] In the words of one social historian, "Whereas doctors came
to patients in the 1870s, by the 1920s, patients increasingly came to doctors. Over this time span, the American hospital changed in size and
clientele. An 1873 survey counted 178 hospitals, about 50 of which were
institutions for the mentally ill. A 1923 tabulation listed 6,830, or an
increase of about 3,800 percent."[15] While this change was most dramatic
in the urban landscape, it also occurred gradually in rural areas. It should
be no surprise that one consequence was an increase in the number of
deaths away from home, the traditional place for end of life scenarios.

In the first half of the twentieth century, medical professionals rapidly assumed the power to define death, to record the pathological details
of its appearance in once-living bodies, and to control the living bodies
surrounding the dying, often lonely, patient—in effect, hospitals began to
have "a local monopoly on death."[16] The medicalization of death not only
established the doctor as the crucial professional figure in charge of the
dying process, it also shaped public attitudes about the meaning of
death.[17] As medical institutions grew in stature, technological advances
revolutionized treatment, and health care became accessible to more and
more people, a new perspective on death began to take hold in the
United States: Life must be sustained at all costs, with death viewed as a

devastating defeat. In the words of historian Philippe Ariès, "Death . . . ceased to be accepted as a natural, necessary phenomenon. Death is a failure, a 'business lost.' This is the attitude of the doctor, who claims the control of death as his mission in life. But the doctor is merely a spokesman for society. When death arrives, it is regarded as an accident, a sign of helplessness or clumsiness that must be put out of mind."[18]

The cultural implications of this environmental shift from death in the home to death in the hospital were profound, and contributed to the literal displacement of the dead from the everyday social worlds of the living. Dying in the isolated space of the hospital room institutionalized the experience as a passage requiring scientific, and increasingly technological intervention, rather than prayers and the presence of the community. In this setting, even though nurses often mitigated the impersonal treatment of patients, a clinical gaze emanating from an assortment of doctors redefined the existential status of the dying individual into one that emphasized the triumphs of science and diminished the spiritual needs of the patient about to pass out of this life.[19] The dominance of a medico-scientific framework for monitoring, interpreting, and responding to signs of death transformed the ways in which Americans spoke about the process of dying, and replaced the human family drama surrounding the deathbed so common in the home of the nineteenth century with a professional performance at the hospital bedside that depended on equanimity, rationality, and a detached commitment to saving the life of the dying patient.

Decreasing mortality trends, increasing longevity, and the rise of the hospital system are a few of the crucial early twentieth-century social developments that allowed the funeral industry to take root, and flourish, in American society. The success of the funeral industry was a product of the radically changing conditions of modern life, and modern dying, in this historical period. The number of funeral homes around the country grew rapidly in the wake of these significant social developments and fundamentally altered the relations between the living and the dead. Funeral directors achieved an air of authority in mortal matters, and became the primary managers of the corpse and the ceremonies to dispose of it. With the blessing and patronage of the public, these funeral men— and most, though not all, were men in this period—took the dead out of the hands of living relations and performed all of the necessary, increasingly complicated, and for many Americans, deeply unpleasant tasks associated with the death of a loved one.

At the end of the nineteenth century, most communities had under-takers who would go to the home of the deceased and take care of an assortment of responsibilities, including locating a casket, notifying friends and relatives, arranging the funeral service, contacting the appro-priate religious leader, coordinating the burial with the local graveyard, and preparing the corpse. Like many men with middle class, professional aspirations in this period undertakers began to build associations, publish journals, and found schools devoted to establishing their credibility as trustworthy and knowledgeable experts.[20] The linguistic innovation pro-posed at the first national meeting of undertakers in 1882 reflected a new self- and class-consciousness about the public value of their work. They began to see themselves as "funeral directors" who attended to the details of death, and, like other essential experts who had cultural authority in confusing, often highly stressful experiences in life such as sickness or legal action, could charge for their services accordingly.[21] Unfortunately, for the future social standing of the industry, early methods for charging customers were highly irregular, and raised serious questions about ethi-cal standards that have persisted to this day. In spite of dogged criticism of their business practices (a subject to be addressed more fully later), families welcomed funeral directors into their homes to handle their dead, organize the final ceremonies, and usher the deceased out of the living community. Most Americans simply did not want to care for the corpse, but they still desperately desired its presence during the funeral rituals.

A variety of institutional and structural shifts in modern America also contributed to the removal of the dead from the home. For example, liv-ing quarters for many families began to change, which affected the avail-able suitable space for the dead in the home. In the nineteenth century, middle and upper class houses often had included a family parlor that served as a place to display domestic identity and, more importantly for this discussion, to enact significant life rituals, including the funeral. By the early twentieth century, however, changing tastes in home design, new practical considerations in planning domestic space—especially in urban settings—and shifting attitudes about family life led to the disap-pearance of the parlor.[22]

Given these kinds of social and cultural changes, the dead were begin-ning to lose their traditional familiar place in the world of family rela-tions. But another factor in this process of dislocating the corpse from the home is perhaps the most critical: the standardization of embalming in the preparation of the dead for disposal. As the bedrock of the emergent industry, embalming required specialized knowledge, technical training, and professional service—qualities undertakers assumed would legitimate their enterprise and win them public favor. But the reliance on embalming, emanating from both funeral directors and their customers, led to the invention of new American traditions that transformed the rituals of disposal and the architectural space of death, as well as the visual, tactile, and olfactory experiences in the presence of the dead body.

Resistance to embalming remained strong in many segments of American society at the turn of the century, primarily because of persistent fears that the procedure entailed bodily mutilation and grisly surgical tactics. It had been employed primarily in medical schools, usually in secret away from public awareness, to preserve cadavers for instruction in the middle of the nineteenth century. But after the Civil War, when northern soldiers were embalmed and transported home, and especially after the funeral journey of Abraham Lincoln's embalmed body from Washington D.C. to Springfield, the procedure slowly gained legitimacy. As more and more undertakers became versed in the delicate process of arterial embalming, and produced inoffensive, well-groomed, and appealing corpses, the public embraced the practice as an integral component of a successful funeral. This should not be surprising since the public viewing of the dead had become a desired moment for many Americans over the course of the nineteenth century. The expectation that survivors would have a last look at the deceased before or during funeral services, a meaningful ritual act in the struggle to make sense of death, had significant symbolic weight in the American imagination before embalming appeared on the scene.[23] Indeed, embalming increasingly made sense not only because of this persistent desire to gaze at the remains, but because modern conditions seemed to demand it. Undertakers justified preserving bodies for other reasons, compelling at the time, that had to do with public health concerns about sanitation, and in response to the highly mobile quality of social relations—embalming bodies allowed invited guests the time to travel great distances to attend the funeral.

There are no statistical data for the number of bodies embalmed in the early decades of the century, but according to many second and third generation funeral directors, embalming rapidly became a standard feature of the undertaking work performed by their fathers and grandfathers. Even before many undertakers had their own funeral homes, embalming was often practiced at the home of the deceased. More and more funeral men began to acquire the necessary knowledge and skills to be certified as embalmers of the dead from the rapidly growing number of mortuary schools around the country. Between 1900 and 1920, schools devoted to training embalmers—students often entered a class without much college or even high school education—appeared in such cities as Minneapolis, Los Angeles, and Cleveland. Initially, courses would last roughly six weeks, but as curriculum requirements became more rigorous, state boards began to examine and license prospective embalmers and funeral directors, and the overall appearance of serious educational training became more critical to professional legitimacy, the length of each term increased. In this era of experts, scientific training particularly in such areas as anatomy and chemistry became crucial components of an education. By 1934, around the time these schools were assuming the more professional sounding title of colleges of mortuary sciences, courses lasted 9 months.[24]

Undertakers in rural areas had to rely on traveling instructors, or use educational texts that covered the basics of anatomy, physiology, and embalming techniques. Silas Ross, who became a funeral director in 1914 and went on to become Reno City councilman and a member of the Board of Regents for the University of Nevada, recalled methods of instruction in the West at the turn of the century.

> There were no embalming schools in the early days. One learned from practical men or proctors, who had learned from peripheral men who became undertakers after the close of the Civil War. In the late '90's and the early 1900's, short courses were offered by men well versed in mortuary practice as learned from those who served during the Civil War. These courses were offered over a period of one month or six weeks. Then compends . . . were prepared and printed for reference for the beginners, and it covered anatomy and a lot of things like that.[25]

In a relatively short period of time, embalming became the enduring signature of the nascent funeral industry, a practice at the center of the economic, cultural, and religious funereal universe taking shape. The appearance of the body in the open casket, an element of death rituals in nineteenth-century America, was judged according to a new, thoroughly modern set of criteria by both embalmers and the public. Most of the journals and trade magazines proliferating in the first few decades of the century, supported by such integrally related industries as casket manufacturing and the production of new and improved embalming fluids, championed the displayable body as the crucial factor for a funeral director's success or failure. Falcon Products placed an advertisement for their embalming fluids in a 1929 edition of the *Southern Funeral Director*. In bold, capital letters, the ad asks the funeral industry reader: "What's the verdict?" It then explains, "On no point is the public more critical than in the matter of embalming. 'The body looked well' is the highest praise a layman can bestow on the mortician. . . . Are you doing all you can to earn a favorable verdict? The uniform quality of FALCON Products will help you to keep your embalming to a high standard."[26] The appearance of the body began to matter deeply to modern Americans, and to an industry that coalesced around the practice of embalming.

Make Way for Modern Embalming: The Myth of Origins and the Spread of Funeral Homes

Embalming was the lifeblood of the American funeral industry from the beginning of the twentieth century. Without this procedure, funeral directors would have had a difficult time claiming that they were part of a professional guild, and therefore justified as the primary mediators between the living and the dead from the moment of death to the final disposition. Their increasing authority over the corpse, and the simultaneous rise to dominance of the funeral home—a confusing space of business, religious activity, corpse-preparation, and family living—forever changed the social and cultural landscape of death in the United States. As we have seen, these changes were also shaped by a variety of contemporary trends and tastes, as well as deeper-rooted, long-standing desires in American social life. More and more people began to rely on this emerging class of ritual specialists to dispose of their dead rather than do it themselves. Americans no longer died in the familiar surroundings of the home, but in the sequestered, frequently inaccessible space of the hospital, where another class of specialists cared for the body not yet dead. Finally, in the midst of the fast-paced, technologically driven changes in modern society, more and more Americans continued to long for a fixed, permanent image of the deceased at peace.

Prescient undertakers in the first few decades of the century understood what their friends and neighbors wanted at a funeral, and embalming fit perfectly into the aesthetic, religious, and practical concerns of both consumer and expert. With a growing number of specialists and professionals available to steer Americans through the hazards and rewards of the expanding consumer marketplace, the determined organizational and institutional efforts by funeral men to standardize embalming and claim expertise in this and other disposal-related areas dramatically transformed their own self-perceptions and self-worth. Many within the industry also engaged in innovative linguistic strategies that encouraged embalming in the lives of Americans. Embalming was presented as a thoroughly modern practice, yet part of a new American tradition; it was a scientific procedure that also had religious value for the living; and it was a highly technical, hygienically-beneficial intervention that required the delicate skills of an artist.

Indeed, Jessica Mitford was on the right track when she identified a "new mythology" emanating from industry rhetoric to legitimate business and ritual changes in the details of modern American funerals.[27] But in her determined efforts to skewer rather than clarify, denigrate instead of appreciate, she misses a compelling mythic narrative that undergirds the logic and self-understanding of the new class of death professionals. In particular, a myth of origins, based on a combination of historical, anthropological, scientific, and imaginative resources, placed embalming in a larger cosmic framework, and propelled the industry forward.

Funeral industry journals, magazines, booklets, and newsletters from the first half of the century, published by casket companies, chemical manufacturers, professional associations, and individual entrepreneurs, present the history of embalming and the historical relation of modern practices to ancient methods, as well as more general, encyclopedic views of funeral customs around the world. These historical narratives contain religious language and logic—indeed they offer a truly mythic account of both the origins of embalming and its place in a transcendent order of truth and meaning.[28] They also place the American practice within a much longer historical trajectory and provide a detailed explanation of how modern mortuary developments differ from older models. On the other hand, many texts highlight specific similarities between new and old methods of embalming and find common human impulses to preserve the dead and treat them with dignity. Whether establishing a point of origin for embalming or arguing for the superiority of modern American techniques, this genre of funereal literature helped shape the mind-set of first- and second-generation funeral

directors who were trying to acquire professional respectability in these critical early years of institutional formation.

The lineage of embalming, understood primarily in evolutionary
terms, is recounted in the literature circulating within the emerging
funeral industry at large, and was read more specifically by students
enrolling in the growing number of mortuary schools and by funeral
directors who had attained the professional responsibility and resources
to keep up with developments in their field of expertise. Funeral directors
were keenly interested in the historical background of the practice for the
entire twentieth century, suggesting that familiarity was critical to the
requisite knowledge of students and the collective memory of the industry. These increasingly common historical narratives made the appearance of embalming on the American scene seem meaningful, and perfectly natural, to the nascent industry. Not surprisingly, the mythic
accounts of embalming and its place in the larger panorama of human
funeral rituals demonstrate a fascination with a specific point of origin in
a civilization far removed from modern America: ancient Egypt.

The funeral industry was not alone in its fascination with ancient
Egyptian culture at this time, of course. This exotic civilization appealed to
many Americans thanks to the colonial expeditions pilfering, and then displaying, cultural artifacts—often dead bodies, from this time forward popularly identified as "mummies," snatched from their eternal resting places.
One particularly revealing expression of this fascination at the time
appears in early cinema, which conjured up peculiar images and sensations
linked with ancient Egypt, both in terms of the architectural design of early
movie theaters and the content of the films themselves. In the words
of film historian Antonia Lant, "There was an association between the
blackened enclosure of silent cinema and that of the Egyptian tomb. . . . a
perception of cinema as a necropolis, . . . an understanding of cinema as a
silent world that speaks through a pictorial language, as hieroglyphics
revealed by light . . . a noted parallel between mummification . . . and the
ghostliness of cinematic images . . . a link between the chemistry of mummification and that of film development."[29] Americans were especially
drawn to the highly popular mummy films of the early twentieth century,
such as The Egyptian Mystery (Edison, 1909), The Mummy and the
Cowpuncher (1912), and The Egyptian Mummy (1914).[30]

Early funeral industry publications fixed their attention on the mummies of ancient Egypt and the ritual specialists who cared for them for

different reasons than thrill-seeking Americans venturing into the mysterious darkness of stygian movie houses to watch the dead magically return to life. These texts look to the past and around the world to explain the wonders of contemporary American funeral rituals. Most industry overviews begin where they end, with embalming. The wonders of ancient Egypt set the conceptual stage for the subsequent enlightened discussion of world death rituals. Writers inevitably emphasized certain themes in the earlier cultural context that would return to frame the exposition of modern American practices generally, and embalming in particular: religious sensibilities behind mummification, practical public health benefits of the procedure, technical expertise and craftsmanship in the special arts of preservation, the social as well as cosmic standing of death specialists who stay close to the dead for the good of living communities, and similar cross-cultural considerations.

The Evolution of the American Funeral Director, published in 1934 and dedicated to "the Ethical Funeral Directors of America," examines the relation between ancient Egyptian practices and the modern "science" of embalming.[31] This author, like most writing for the industry at the time, has faith in the miracles of modern science to cleanse, preserve, and present a dead body. Like their professional kin in the medicinal arts, undertakers are involved in a special calling, a calling that requires them to remain in close, but scientifically-distanced, contact with cadavers, and to recognize that their professional knowledge and actions have implications far beyond local respectability. The book's introduction begins with the following statement: "Embalming in this country is now a recognized science, and Funeral Directing has attained the dignity of a profession. This short sentence tells the story of a nation's progress, for from the dawn of history, in all lands, the advance of civilization and culture has been measured by the degree of respect paid to the dead."[32] Under these explanatory conditions, the ritual experts who bring the dead home play an extraordinarily crucial role in the progress of human society. Modern embalming sets American funeral directors apart from their ancient predecessors, and serves as a clear marker of distinction and advancement.

The authors identify the ancient Egyptians as originators of embalming, but contrast the religious sentiments behind Egyptian practices with the efficiency of modern, technologically-advanced ones: "Modern embalming has for its purpose the preservation of the body, to repair the ravages of sickness and disease, to restore the effects of disfiguring acci-

dents, and to give the body as close a semblance as possible of its appearance in life. . . . To compare present day embalming with that practised
by the Egyptians is like comparing electric light to that of a tallow candle."[33] Despite these differences, there were also significant common
impulses driving ancient and modern procedures, including love,
respect, and a desire to honor the dead in the final passage. The authors
even point out that, economically speaking, embalming was a much
better deal in 1934 than in ancient Egypt: "In the days of the Pharaohs
it cost about three hundred dollars in our currency to embalm the body
of a commoner, a person of small importance; a king cost several thousands. Today the proper preparation of a body for burial does not cost
one-fifteenth of the smaller sum."[34] A critical element of these narratives
is precisely this advantage: royal treatment available to all citizens. Or,
in other words, the democratization of what was once an exclusive,
highly valued, ritual for important personages. For most funeral directors, this realization only reinforced the deeply patriotic commitment to
American funerals—the nation's position at the pinnacle of human
evolution depended on their ritual vigilance and stewardship over the
newly dead.

Learned textbooks rehearsed the myth as well, passing on to students
the wisdom of the past, the promise of the future, and the achieve-
ments—scientific and technical for sure, but also aesthetic—of the present. Simon Mendelsohn, consulting chemist for the industry in
Cincinnati, Ohio, began his text, *Embalming Fluids: Their Historical,
Development and Formulation, From the Standpoint of the Chemical Aspects
of the Scientific Art of Preserving Human Remains* (1940), with an overview
of the history of "the embalming art." The first section, entitled "The
Ancient Period," defines embalming as the "art of preserving the human
body after death," and names ancient Egypt as the likely place of origin
in human history. But rather than conjure up mysteries of the dead and
other religious wonders, Mendelsohn assumes a confident, scientific posture about mummification: "With the exception of a few minor details,
there is but little about the ancient craft that is not at present well-
known."[35] Embalming is not a secretive, inscrutable practice whose
origins are beyond the grasp of moderns. For modern undertakers, a careful look at the history of embalming and its fulfillment in American
methods illuminates the truth of death like nothing else.[36]

Funeral trade magazines, journals, textbooks, and other publications from the first half of the century offer a dizzying amount of historical and cross-cultural information on how humans treat their dead. This careful attention to what people do with their dead was perhaps equal to the interest exhibited by scholars within the growing fields of archaeology and anthropology, who identified death rituals as particularly valuable for understanding and explaining distant cultures. After covering the ancient Egyptian mortuary arts and crafts, narratives generally take a comparative turn, describing funeral customs from around the globe. Death rituals in African, Native American, Chinese, Indian, and other cultural settings are discussed in some detail. Inevitably, the story turns to the two additional pillars of the triumphant American way of death: Judaism and Christianity. In the collective imagination taking shape in the formative years of the profession, these two traditions comfortably rest at the foundations of the industry. Jewish customs are often highlighted because of their simplicity, deep respect for the body, and attention to mourners; most writers, however, also respectfully note past and present aversion to embalming within Orthodox communities.

More important for the self-understanding and social standing of funeral directors in the twentieth century were early Christian practices. The reason for this interest is obvious: In order to legitimize their enterprise and counter the accusations from some church leaders that modern funerals represented a perpetuation of pagan rites, funeral men had to find ways to link themselves to distinctly Christian ways of treating the dead, especially at the origins of Christian culture. In one early booklet entitled *Funeral Customs Through the Ages*, produced by a Saint Louis casket company in the late 1920s, early Christian burial customs are described as a blending of Jewish, Greek, and Roman influences. No cremation and no embalming but, the author notes, "ancient Christian custom was to perfume the body in commemoration of the spices in which the body of the Saviour was wrapped."[37] In later years, the author continues, specific functionaries under the supervision of the church took charge of preparing the procession, carrying the bier, lifting the body, and digging the grave, making sure that even the poorest of the poor received some kind of consideration.[38] Christian charity and respect for the dead, as well as biblical references to the reverent treatment of Christ's body, established a general framework funeral directors could rely on to sanction their control of the funeral in a deeply religious, broadly Christian country. But Christianity alone did not have the symbolic, ritual, and textual resources to justify embalming.

Industry mythic narratives really pick up chronological steam with the waning of the Middle Ages, when embalming became aligned with the field of medicine and the need to preserve the human body for dissection and anatomical study. Despite its long European history, embalming truly comes of age, for these authors, in the United States in the early decades of the twentieth century, as the following quote from 1940 makes clear: "The American method of arterial embalming is . . . more sanitary, more satisfactory and more scientific than that of any other kind. It adds but another laurel to the crown of inventiveness, ingenuity, and scientific research which the world universally accords to us. . . . In fact, there is no profession on record which has made such rapid advancement in this country as embalming."[39] While some might question this claim, embalming's spectacular rise and its position as the cornerstone of the rapidly growing funeral industry is undeniably a great American success story.

For most authors of funeral-related publications, the Civil War is the dramatic turning point in the history of embalming. It was the first American war to make provision for the return of the dead to families, primarily Northern families, who wanted control over the final disposition. Also, embalmers on the battlefields and in some cities began to manufacture their own embalming fluids, an enterprise that would eventually bring economic life to the industry in the modern era. Finally, a future generation of funeral directors would learn from the experiences of these early battlefield embalmers such as Dr. Thomas Holmes, considered to be one of the crucial "founding fathers" because of his competence and creativity with embalming fluids during the war.[40] Holmes's early experiences as a doctor and coroner's assistant in New York City during the 1840s and 1850s led him to begin experimenting with various embalming fluids for the purpose of preserving bodies. Instead of using the dangerous preservatives that were then often injected into the body, including arsenic, zinc, and mercury, Holmes tried a variety of alternative substances and avoided any cavity work that required the removal of internal organs. He is also considered one of the earliest merchandisers of embalming chemicals and the inventor of an injection pump for the arterial method of embalming.[41] But it was his trial by fire during the Civil War that made him the legend who helped turn a nation to embalming.[42]

In the words of one of these early textbooks, "Modern embalming belongs exclusively to the United States of America, and had its beginning with the period of the . . . Civil War."[43] After the war, embalming did not immediately find a place in American deathways. By the early 1880s, however, it began to grow in popularity among undertakers, thanks in large part to the business of manufacturing and selling preservative fluids and efforts by chemical and casket companies to educate practitioners about these fluids, efforts that eventually contributed to full-fledged educational institutions for an expanding field of recruits.[44] Companies that manufactured embalming chemicals sent out salesmen—early pioneers in these mythic accounts of the immediate past—who taught "courses," usually lasting only a few hours but which led to the acquisition of a "certificate" or "diploma." Before the end of the nineteenth century, schools established exclusively for the training of students in the fine arts of embalming appeared in various parts of the country. The Clarke School of Embalming (later renamed The Cincinnati School of Embalming), considered to be the first, was established by Joseph H. Clarke, a traveling casket salesman for an Indiana company.[45] Other key individuals who figure in many mythic accounts of modern embalming include Hudson Samson, identified as the first funeral director to incorporate embalming fully into his ritual repertoire after 1875,[46] and Dr. August Renourd, another early pioneer credited with writing the first embalming textbook and opening an embalming school in Rochester, New York, in 1882. The first national meeting of the NFDA took place in Rochester that same year, and Renourd was able to demonstrate embalming techniques to the undertakers in attendance.[47]

The history of embalming and of funeral customs around the world has been a critical educational component in the training of funeral directors. This hallowed body of knowledge provided individuals in the industry with more than a reservoir of facts and data—it also gave a class of self-designated, and constantly scrutinized, professionals a greater sense of purpose and orientation in the larger scope of human history. The narrative structure of these sacred, deeply meaningful histories, starting with the earliest embalmers in ancient Egypt and ending with the important forefathers and innovations during and after the Civil War, placed funeral directors at the summit of an evolutionary trajectory. It also contributed to the legitimacy of embalming as a uniquely American way to dispose of the dead and the transference of near complete control from family and community members to members of a professional class who charge for their expertise and services. With a firm understanding of this history, those within the funeral industry could transcend the attacks of funeral reformers and tap into a deep wellspring of knowledge that justified their chosen vocation as society's ritual experts in matters of death.

For the public to fully relinquish control over the dead body, lose the traditional familiarity with it in everyday life, and embrace the entire range of services offered by the funeral director, however, another mortuary innovation would have to appear: the American funeral home. The rise of funeral homes in towns and cities throughout the nation created a new social space for preparing, displaying, and communing with the dead. This new space of death both institutionalized embalming and reinforced the widening gap between the living and the dead. Though these establishments eventually dislodged the corpse from the familiar residential surroundings of the deceased, funeral directors did everything they could to maintain the domesticity of death in a home away from home.

In many parts of the country at the turn of the century, embalming the dead body became part of the undertaker's repertoire when visiting the home. Indeed, most funerals took place in the home of the deceased, so undertakers would make house calls when news of a death reached them at their place of work—often the livery or a furniture store, or their own home. The undertaker would either work alone or with an assistant. If family members had concerns about leaving the corpse alone with the man, it was not uncommon for someone to stay and watch him work. Operating in a secluded room of the house, the undertaker would assemble the tools of his trade, which, according to one description, might include "a portable 'cooling board' on which to embalm the body and an embalming cabinet and dressing case containing essentially a hard rubber pump with check valve, arterial tubes, trocar, needles, forceps, scalpel, scissors, eye caps, razor, granite cap for shaving, combs, brushes, shaving soap, chin supporters, surgeon's silk, a piece of oiled muslin, a package of court-plaster, a paper of pins, a dozen collar buttons, cotton sheet, whisk broom, and two one-half gallon bottles."[48]

During the visit, the undertaker assumed a detached and impersonal demeanor geared toward promoting efficiency and demonstrating respect for the dead. He also wanted to ensure customer satisfaction with the services rendered—which meant good "word-of-mouth" and the promise of more business. As care for the dead evolved into an industry, institutionalized through the creation of trade and professional journals, schools, and local and national organizations, more and more energy was focused on convincing the public that modern funeral experts lived by professional, virtuous guidelines.[49] Printed regulations about how to behave when going to the "funeral house" to prepare a body and organize the ceremonies can be found in numerous textual materials, including mass-produced funeral record books, often entitled *A Ready Day-Book for Undertakers* in early versions. For example, in a record book covering the first decade of the century, the following suggestions can be found in the preprinted section under "Funeral Ethics": "In all things use good judgment and cool deliberation in performing your work, and remember that you are not called upon to console the bereaved, but to take care of the remains, and do that in the most competent and least ostentatious way."[50] It goes on to advise the traveling undertaker to avoid being intrusive at the family home, to speak quietly when talking with family members, and not to be afraid to recommend the purchase of good, solidly built caskets. By organizing a funeral that is "conducted in a quiet, well-ordered and dignified manner," the undertaker will reap future success as a trusted, reliable community member.[51]

Reminiscing about the challenges faced by his father when embalming in the home, third-generation New York funeral director Thomas Kearns describes some of the difficulties as well as sense of dignity found in these early house calls:

> The body was embalmed on the bed. . . . Just to make things more effective the embalmer would sometimes bring his own folding board. The embalmer had to work very, very neatly embalming in somebody's bedroom. Opposed to the modern embalming room if you had a problem or an accident it would be easy to scrub down a porcelain table. You had to be a neat worker like a surgeon. They didn't work with a surgical gown. My father embalmed generally in his high button shirt and tie as a gentleman and not as some type of worker. . . . He'd put a wide rubber sheet under the body and over the wooden board he brought along, and embalmed the body. . . . You could lay the body out in the best room they had which was generally the front room in the flat where kids didn't go unless it was Christmas or their birthday or something like that. It had the best furniture and very often [was] not used for weeks at a time.[52]

The fact that the undertaker entered the private home of the grieving family to prepare the body for its final viewing, arrange the funeral services that would take place there or, less frequently, at a local church, and be paid for his labors created an especially delicate situation. It should not be surprising that an emerging class of men seeking professional standing and social legitimacy in the early-twentieth century made public pronouncements about ethical behavior and codes of conduct in their chosen field. As more and more funeral homes began operating around the country, and the dead body was severed from the intimate ties of family residence, a new set of professional guidelines—primarily, though not exclusively devoted to moral responsibility in commercial practices— emerged from within the industry.

An institutional code of ethics was established at the third national convention of the newly formed NFDA. This national organization, created in 1882, responded to a call by undertakers who had begun to form numerous state organizations around the country. On a purely economic level, the efforts of this central bureaucratic agency brought national order to a varied and dispersed set of activities and transformed the burial of the dead into big business. But on another level, funeral directors also understood the religious duties and social obligations associated with this vocation, and their code of ethics became one of the crucial vehicles for conveying this sense of mission and solemnity. In the original text of the code, the closing section states: "There is, perhaps, no profession, after that of the sacred ministry, in which a high-toned morality is more imperatively necessary than that of a funeral director's. High moral principles are his only safe guide."[53] Although details of this code change over time, commitment to such American virtues as public honor, professional decorum, and personal decency have remained critical to the industry's self-image and won the confidence of millions of Americans who trust their local undertaker.

At the turn of the century, some undertakers began offering the use of their own "parlor" when the deceased's family could not provide a space for preparing the body and hosting the funeral. But as a result of the social changes discussed earlier—the shifting space of dying, architectural modifications in living arrangements, and the institutionalization of embalming—many funeral directors saw the need and financial promise in building a new home for, or opening their own dwellings to, the dead. Funeral men invested in freestanding establishments that would serve as a single location for the treatment of the physical remains and their public presentation before or during a funeral service, as well as a retail outlet for all the goods and services required by the family.[54]

By the 1920s, establishments identified as funeral homes, or less frequently, funeral chapels, parlors, or even churches, became the primary location for carrying out the responsibilities associated with burial in many larger populated towns and urban areas—a trend that would gradually occur in most regions of the country in time. According to one industry explanation, there were numerous reasons for this trend, including new forms of illness ravaging dying bodies, structural changes in home design, and general difficulties associated with planning a funeral in the home at a painful and chaotic time for surviving family members. In addition, many no longer wanted to contaminate the sanctity of living space reserved for the affections of the nuclear family with the pallor of death: "Perhaps most appealing of all is the desire to keep the home free of the atmosphere a funeral inevitably leaves, particularly if there are small children in the family."[55] Modern America, industry insiders believed, was temperamentally well-suited for the emergence of separate mortuary facilities to manage the intimacy between living relations and dead bodies.

The proliferation of funeral homes in towns and cities around the country was parallelled by an upsurge in the number of men working exclusively as funeral directors. In 1927, at the 46th annual convention of the NFDA, the executive secretary communicated the tremendous changes taking place: "The undertaking parlors of old have been replaced by the funeral home. The rolling stock of the funeral director has been changed from hideous monstrosities to veritable palaces on wheels. . . . The astounding part of this funeral service business is the mushroom growth of funeral directors and funeral homes. In 1890 there were 9,891 funeral directors, while in 1920 there were 24,469. This is in spite of the fact that the death rate per year has dropped from 19.6 per 1,000 population in 1890 to 12.1 per 1,000 population in 1920."[56] The "mushroom growth" took place during a critical period of modernization in American society; many of the technological revolutions that were transforming other industries and public life in general also were having an impact on the American funeral. The introduction of the automobile, expansion of telephone lines throughout the country, and advances in public sanitation all contributed to the viability and efficiency of separate funeral homes that cared for the dead.

In *The Confessions of an Undertaker*, Charles W. Berg offers more personal reflections on some of the changes that were taking place in the first two decades of the twentieth century. Although he had a decided bias against modern elements of the funeral developing in America, he is clear about the growing centrality of embalming for funeral homes throughout the country: "The undertaking business took a decided leap forward when embalming was made practicable for the average undertaker to perform. The practice of embalming had much to do with placing the undertaker in the professional class."[57] He also identifies many of the social functions associated with these new establishments. Besides the embalming room, office, stock room, and chapel, the funeral home also included rooms to lay out the dead after they had been embalmed, extra rooms that could be used by family members from out of town attending the funeral, and living quarters for employees working at the home. Additionally, Berg remarks that many funeral directors owned one or more hearses to move bodies and other automobiles to transport funeral necessities like caskets. Occasionally, these automobiles also served as ambulances to convey seriously injured community members to a local hospital.[58] Before ambulance service was taken over by hospitals, it had been a particularly important source of pride for funeral directors, who began to understand their work in broader terms than simply caring for the dead.

Despite the panoply of activities taking place within their walls, the new American mortuary establishments primarily functioned as living quarters for funeral families now exclusively in the business of death and disposal. Many older, second generation funeral directors fondly remember growing up in these homes, and identify early memories of helping Dad as critical in leading them down the mortuary path. Trevino Morales, a funeral director from Texas, was born in the 1930s and raised in his father's funeral home, where he "learned to walk and crawl under caskets." Morales believes that every individual has a special purpose in life, and that he realized early on his purpose is to take care of the dead: "I remember when I was 7 or 8 and I used to stand holding on to the dashboard of the old hearse helping my dad pick up the body. I used to look back when we were driving and you could see the body back there. It didn't bother me. We used to live upstairs and I'd go in and tell my Momma that 'we brought the body in.'"[59]

The domestic atmosphere was a significant factor in gaining the public's trust that the corpse indeed belonged in the funeral director's hands and in his home. The fact that the public did entrust local, and often civically active, undertakers with deceased relations reinforced the social divide between the living and the dead. The expertise possessed by these aspiring professionals, which sanctioned their control over the dead, was only reaffirmed with the emergence of the funeral home, which consisted of private, usually unseen rooms where chemical embalming and body preparation took place, public showrooms where funeral directors could dispense advice about casket selection, and chapels where the ceremonies, organized in large part by funeral directors themselves, would take place before the procession to the grave.

In one 1920 commentary, the Reverend G. B. Carpenter praised the funeral director for assuming more responsibilities and suggested the living were better off because of his interventions. Thinking back to how drastically the funeral has changed in his own lifetime, Carpenter wrote, "Your service is of high order to the community, and I want to offer my testimony that you are lifting the standard of that service. . . . Twenty years ago you know we used to stand around the grave, the people themselves would take those awful straps—I just have a cold chill when I think about it—but now you lower the body, just to the level of the ground, then get the people home, and they get through their difficulty so much better."[60]

Another commentary, written by a funeral director in 1929, underscores the growing diversification of professional obligations and the ultimate goal of those who serve in this vocation: "It is the aim of the man of this profession today to specialize in the supervision of every conceivable phase of the planning of funerals, to be that specialist who can be depended upon to carry out to the fullest measure every desire of those who call upon him, and to do all this toward the end that, in the final analysis, his helpful service will help those who are left behind to 'Remember with consolation.'"[61] No longer looking to be as unobtrusive as possible in the home of the deceased, small businessmen who owned, worked at, and lived in funeral homes began to insert themselves more forcefully into the disrupted lives of mourners struggling to do right by the deceased.

As funeral directors found their niche in early twentieth-century American society, the age-old familiarity of the living with the dead was replaced by a new alienation. Combined with the mortality revolution taking place and the growing presence of medical institutions that sequestered the dying from the living, new ritual patterns for disposing of the dead founded on the practice of embalming relieved living relations of traditional duties. Dead bodies, in effect, disappeared from the everyday world of twentieth-century Americans. When they reappeared in the living world, social mediators often controlled the terms of the encounter—but not exclusively. The public desire to confront the corpse and say good-bye to the deceased in a meaningful way shaped the ritual innovations taking place at the beginning of the century.

Intimacy Regained

Funeral directors took the dead out of the homes of living relations; but living relations wanted to find a way to be "at home" with their dead—if only for a short period of contemplation and emotional release. Funeral homes provided the space for this intimate ritual moment. Preparation rooms, where washing, embalming, and cosmetic work were carried out, transformed the corpse into a suitable ritual object of devotion. Indeed, the increasingly common criticism from the first half of the century that, with the advent of embalming, the American funeral had turned into a form of pagan body worship, was on the right track. The body had become something more than simply a container for the spirit, dust that returns to dust with no religious power to transform the experiences of the living. Under the loving gaze of mourners, the corpse acquired a sacred status that was decidedly material rather than spiritual, and comforting rather than horrifying.

Despite objections from some religious leaders, viewing the body was an integral and long-standing tradition that brought order and meaning to the encounter with death in America—and embalming made the presentation of the dead more appealing. For many funeral directors, offering a simulation of life, of a body at peace in comfortable surroundings, brought the reality of death home to mourners who wanted a chance to say good-bye to a familiar face. The goal of creating a "natural" or "lifelike" appearance did not encourage the denial of death, as more and more critics began to publicly assert; instead, it domesticated death, giving close friends and relatives one last opportunity to commune with their dead and, according to a growing number of people in the industry, create a therapeutic "memory image." For Americans in a variety of communal settings, the growing popularity of postmortem and casket photographs taken by hired professional photographers or family members themselves supported the industry's instincts about the role of memory images in dealing with loss.[62]

An important early funeral director who presented a psychological argument for embalming and viewing the body was Edward A. Martin. In a 1940 article entitled "Psychology for the Funeral Director," Martin stresses the emotional value of gazing upon the embalmed body of a close relation and the instrumental presence of this body for the entire funeral service. The key to alleviating the suffering of the bereaved, according to Martin, was a pleasing "memory picture" produced during the final, intimate moments with the body. He writes that the appearance of the body is of utmost importance and can serve as a vehicle for eliciting tender, soothing memories of the departed. American ceremonies of "respect and reverence . . . lavished on the physical form," which Martin identifies as an attitude handed down through the generations, depend upon modern professionals who care about the well-being of their clients: "The final appearance of the dead body is the foundation upon which is based the success or failure of every funeral establishment. . . . It is this final memory picture which remains with family and friends as long as they live, that can be a comfort to them or a source of horror. The embalmer holds the key to success or failure by the results he obtains through the application of his knowledge and skill in preparing the body."[63] The development of a psychological line of reasoning to support embalming and the continued mediating role of funeral directors depended on the therapeutic logic of viewing the dead in a safe, intimate, and temporary setting.

Embalming, however, was only one of a series of duties performed by the undertaker. According to *Funeral Customs Through the Ages*, the "modern funeral director" had one primary responsibility when carrying out the myriad tasks associated with the disposition of the dead: "To give comfort to the bereaved family by handling the numerous details relative to a funeral which under the circumstances would prove distressing." No longer a detached undertaker awkwardly making house calls, the twentieth-century funeral director required a modern, all-purpose funeral home to do most of his work—for the living as well as the dead. "The high-grade efficient mortuary establishment of today is equipped to perform an infinite variety of such services to families in distress. Up-to-date methods, scientific equipment, and a sincere, intelligent mental attitude combine to serve the needs of the bereaved better than they have ever been served before."[64] The needs of the bereaved, increasingly framed in emotional and psychological terms rather than simply practical terms related to public health and convenience for the mourners, assumed prominence in the public justifications of new American funeral traditions.

In one NFDA pamphlet distributed to the public, the rise of funeral homes was seen as a great relief for the bereaved, who could now entrust the body to the caring, knowledgeable proprietor of the local funeral home. Although the corpse was moved out of the home, the funeral director would ensure the opportunity—for a price—of meaningful, healing closeness with it:

> Maintenance of a beautiful funeral home in which the body of the departed may lie in state in appropriate surroundings is part of the service rendered by your funeral director. It is worth what it costs, however, in the elimination of all the worry to the family so often attendant upon other arrangements.
>
> Every facility for the proper conduct of the funeral is available to the family in the modern funeral home. The atmosphere is one of peace and reverence but without sadness and gloom. To it can come the friends and relatives and there find every convenience for their privacy and seclusion. This is why a constantly increasing number of funerals are being held from funeral homes and chapels rather than from private homes as in the past.[65]

According to early industry literature, the success of a funeral home depended on fashioning a domestic and religious ethos that promoted intimacy with the dead—and thus perpetuated what had been an integral dimension of the experience with death in American history. One article on public relations, which asserts that in 1929 between 90 and 95 percent of all funerals in the United States took place in a funeral establishment, suggests that, "a funeral home in general might be termed a place designed to serve as a temporary home for those who call upon a funeral director for service. . . . A funeral home is an establishment that in appearance, surroundings, and atmosphere closely resembles a private residence."[66] But imagery associated with funeral homes also called upon another sacred American institution to evoke feelings of trust, respect, and honor: the church. Despite the fact that business transactions occurred there, and body preparation took place in secluded rooms, the ideal ethos produced in a funeral home was characterized as "reverential," "church-like," or "sacred." As a domesticated space of death, the funeral

home upset conventional boundaries between the religious and the pro-
fane, commerce and spirit, private and public.

A number of factors contributed to producing the appropriate ethos.
The family of the funeral director often lived in the funeral home, which
automatically imbued a sense of domesticity, especially with children
around the house and sons following their fathers into the business. More
important than the presence of children was the increasing participation
of women in the day-to-day operations of local funeral homes. Although
gradually more and more professional training became available in the
first half of the century, women rarely enrolled in mortuary schools and
generally did not own their own funeral homes. In the early years of
industry growth, funeral directing was a male profession with only limited career opportunities for women. However, with the rise of funeral
homes as places of both business and residence, wives of funeral directors
assumed a variety of responsibilities, including bookkeeping, planning
funerals, applying cosmetics to the face of the deceased, and giving special attention to the funerals of children. Their involvement, along with
a growing number of hired female assistants, soon came to be an accepted aspect of the profession, with "women's clinics" offered at state and
national conventions.

Mabel Hamlin, from the Hamlin Funeral Home in Moose Lake,
Minnesota, wrote of her attendance at one of these clinics in 1940. In
the article, entitled "A Woman's Viewpoint on Children's Funerals;
How to Achieve an Effective 'Memory Picture' Which Will Assuage
Parents' Grief and Build Good Will and Profit for the Funeral Director,"
she emphasizes the financial benefits of organizing a well-planned funeral and indicates the authority many women had in matters of embalming and cosmetics:

> In endeavoring to show a woman's place in the funeral profession—a
> place which I consider highly important—it is, obviously, fitting that
> a discussion on 'Infant's and Children's Funerals' is assigned to a
> woman, who knows motherly instincts and who has been active in
> professional service. . . . Children's funerals can and should be made
> profitable, and merit careful study and maximum attention on the part
> of every funeral director and embalmer. . . . In the preparation of the
> body of a child it does not seem well or fitting, and with proper
> embalming it should not be necessary to use as much cosmetics, as on
> an adult, if any.[67]

In addition to the nurturing presence of women, the interior layout of
the funeral home helped create a domestic atmosphere and responded to
mourners' desire for closeness with the body. Funeral homes often had a
separate room where the bereaved were allowed to spend time with the
corpse in private, usually before the public funeral service. Funeral directors arranged these rooms, designated "slumber rooms," so they resembled
a typical bedroom. In fact, they served as a place where the deathbed scene,
a traditional component of death in private homes, could be reintegrated
into funeral rituals at this home away from home. Far from inventing an
association between death and sleep, funeral directors redesigned the space
of their establishments in response to a long-standing deeply-rooted religious understanding of death as sleep.

Beyond slumber rooms, the chapel was the most important architectural
innovation for encouraging the use of funeral homes as a one-stop, all-purpose establishment. Within the first few decades of the twentieth century,
the funeral home chapel replaced the church and the home in many
Protestant and some Jewish and Catholic communities as the primary location for holding the religious services at the time of death. Funeral directors
designed the chapel to inspire a combination of religious sentiment and
domestic comfort. According to one commentary, the "atmosphere of reverence is the predominating note which is popularizing the chapel. . . . A better word than reverence would probably be churchly, though reverence is the
desired end. . . . On the other hand, however, there is a slight tendency in
chapel architecture to evolve a home atmosphere, meeting the demand of
those who formerly desired funeral services in the home."[68]

Although it was a confused and complicated space intermingling
religion, domesticity, economics, and nostalgia, the chapel took on significant cultural value for the mourners as a place to experience communal
ties, reexamine primary identifications, confront the sacred, remember the
dead and, most importantly, take their leave of the body. Many discerning
funeral directors understood the social power of and profound need for this
addition to their buildings and, in the increasingly competitive marketplace, chapels became a critical "selling point." They came in a variety of
shapes and sizes, with interior design and external aesthetics often receiving great care and attention from both husband and wife, whose main concerns were decorum, morality, and respectability.

Another new strategy for establishing the appropriate mood at the
funeral was the introduction of music; funeral directors began to install

organs to help mourners feel at home before, during, and after the service, and to send a religious message about the sanctity of the space. One advertisement in a trade publication for a Chicago firm that made pipe organs exclusively for funeral homes asked, "Has Your Funeral Home a Soul?" Next to a picture of their product, the text reads: "What the Soul is to a human so is a Pipe Organ to the mortuary. Without the enthralling presence of its solemn music the service lacks that vital quality—sacred atmosphere."[69] The aural sensation evoked by the organ, along with the visual stimulation of the interior design, aimed to create a safe, comforting, religious environment for guests attending the funeral service and confronting the principle ritual object in these services: the embalmed corpse.

While funeral directors tried to encourage a supportive, intimate, domestic view of death for survivors—one that tapped into deep-rooted cultural scripts and responded to modern social conditions—they also understood the value of good public relations. Rather than discourage public scrutiny and close themselves off from their neighbors, many funeral directors either opened their doors and invited the public to become familiar with the new space of death or they went out into the community and spoke in various public settings. Funeral directors participated in open houses, educational evenings, community presentations, and other forums to inform the public about their calling and, no doubt, convert potential customers in an increasingly competitive and highly criticized market.

One industry article notes that close to 1000 people visited the opening of a new mortuary in El Paso, Texas, in 1929. "Throughout the day there was a steady stream of visitors going through the building to see for themselves one of the newest and most beautifully equipped funeral establishments in the section."[70] In a speech given at an educational evening in 1932, Reno funeral director Silas Ross declared that public exposure to the intimate details of running his funeral home, including the persistent questions about charges for items and services, will alleviate any suspicions or fears associated with the modern business of death: "We hope that your visitation here tonight will in a small way help to break the spell of gloom that is associated with 'walking thru the valley of the shadow' . . . . In planning this mortuary we have grouped the institution around the family, always bearing in mind that the comfort and tranquility of those in bereavement is paramount. You will note that we have arranged privacy for the family before, during and after the service."[71]

Representatives of the growing funeral industry often drew attention to the services funeral directors provided, the setting in which the funeral would take place, and, in many cases, the need to be informed before death strikes within the family. They also, of course, emphasized the psychological value, social utility, and technological benefits of embalming. In an address to the rotary club in Springfield, Ohio, a sales director for a major supplier of embalming chemicals stressed the technological strides made by the late-1920s in arterial embalming: "Do you know that there is no mutilation in embalming, merely the tiniest incision in which the fluid is injected? The bodies you have seen throughout the years past have been hard and curb-stone like—have been cold and forbidding. They have risen like nightmares out of the casket for months after a funeral. They have not been a consolation to those who remembered. Now he is able to restore the bloom of youth that has faded in wasting illness."[72] The combination of striking poetic images, confident psychological posturing, and detached scientific rigor in this short passage indicates something of the complex and varied perspectives on embalming and its role in early twentieth-century American funerals.

The public face of embalming was championed in other ways as well; display of embalmed bodies—sometimes for a fee, other times as a public relations tool to demonstrate the quality of work in local funeral homes—offered the community another opportunity to see a dead body and witness the wonders of modern funeral care. In 1911, for example, an enterprising Oklahoma undertaker exhibited the embalmed body of a train robber killed by a posse—purportedly for five years.[73] Another example comes from the early history of a funeral home in rural Georgia, where the politics of race as well as commerce entered into the public exhibition of an embalmed corpse. Jimmy Fletcher entered the funeral business in 1956 after marrying a woman whose family had owned a funeral home for some time. He remembers hearing a story about a black man hanged in the town square for a crime that sealed his post-mortem fate as a real-life example of the wonders of embalming for one small, Southern funeral establishment:

> At that time the funeral home served both black and white. This man was black and his family came and asked [the owner of the funeral home] if he would take care of him after the hanging and he said he would. Because embalming was so new they used every opportunity they had to do it and they asked if they could embalm him because

they weren't sure how long it would take to get arrangements made. Several days later the family came back and said the people who owned the cemetery would not bury him there. . . . This went on and after five or six months the family disappeared and the funeral home was left with this black man. He was placed in a casket in a back room in the funeral home. The family never came back and during the years people knew that a man who had died several years ago was still presentable so people came by to see him. Sometimes they had to change his clothes every now and then because of changes in style . . . . It also made known the value of embalming.[74]

Embalming was publicly acknowledged in other, more civically-redeeming ways too—usually in times of disaster and destructive violence. Floods, industrial accidents, explosions, and other instances of tragic death often demanded funeral directors take the lead in the necessary, often gruesome task of gathering and then preparing bodies. Their actions usually received high praise in newspaper reports and publicized letters. When local morticians in Texas responded to an explosion at a local school building that killed numerous children and teachers, Clarence E. Parker, commanding officer of the military district of New London, wrote of his deep gratitude for their civic, cooperative, and charitable spirit. He also states that, "I think particular attention should be brought to the fact that each of the children who was killed in the catastrophe was thoroughly embalmed and that each was placed in a casket and buried in an individual grave. Military authorities were at no time confronted with any menace to the public health, by virtue of the operations of the funeral directors and embalmers."[75] Although rare, public demonstrations of support and gratitude for their difficult work did comfort undertakers, especially when it came from socially respectable figures in the military, the church, or other valued American institutions.

Unfortunately for funeral directors, many segments of American society did not hold embalming, indeed many modern aspects of the funeral, in such high regard. Instead of praise for services geared toward the reduction of stress at a painful time, the improvement of public health, and the psychological needs of survivors, many undertakers received criticism for their work as unnecessary, unnatural, and un-American. It came from a variety of quarters, including writers within the industry itself, dissatisfied customers, special reports submitted to the public by a variety of organizations, and popular presses and local newspapers. Evidence against the funeral industry was compelling to many, and popular media representations often relied on this evidence to characterize the entire profession. But it is important to note a common element in most of the public indictments against the industry: Intimate matters surrounding death, including treatment of the body, personal responses to the funeral, and, most important in these attacks, cost to consumers, were provided in detail.

In spite of the growing social divide between the living and the dead, the topic of death did not disappear from public culture in the first half of the century. The growth and public presence of funeral homes kept the topic alive in the public arena. But while funeral directors worked diligently—and successfully—at the local and national level to establish the ritual and symbolic language to help Americans make sense of their experiences with death, their voices were often drowned out by others who challenged the composed, sentimental, and comforting rhetoric. A more detailed examination of this public criticism will take place in the next chapter, but its presence in popular consciousness—indeed, its formative influence on standard media representations for the rest of the century—is an important characteristic of public discussions of death in the 1920s, 1930s, and 1940s.

In the final chapter of his *Confessions*, undertaker Berg criticizes some of the changes overtaking the business of funerals in the first decade of the century. He laments, "Why is it, when we are growing more and more enlightened on other phases of rightful living, that we still persist in making such gruesome affairs of funerals?" For Berg, many social customs of the time, such as large funerals, elaborate processions, and floral displays, were "barbarous," "a farce," and "pretentious." Particularly offensive to him was a central social act in the funeral services: "viewing the remains."

> In our rural districts, the out-pouring of a heterogeneous mass of folk from every point of the country-side is a farce that cannot be too soon abolished. A funeral is essentially a time for the meeting of the family and relatives and the closest friends, and the fewer the number of outsiders present, the better. Nor is there anything quite so barbarous as the present custom, in town and country, of 'viewing the remains' by a motley collection of persons, many of whom never knew the dead in life, or if they did, never thought enough of him to come and see him. The vulgar curiosity that prompts a 'last look' at a loved one

and incites comment on the conduct of the 'mourners' and the number of 'floral emblems,' cannot be too strongly denounced.[76]

Criticism from undertakers and others within the industry occasionally made it into print. But far more significant were the numerous outsiders who sought to reform, if not destroy, the blossoming business of
death. Another important book from the 1920s—perhaps second only to
Mitford's 1963 exposé in its impact on public perceptions of the industry—was a study commissioned by the Metropolitan Life Insurance
Company, *Funeral Costs: What They Average; Are They Too High? Can
They Be Reduced?* In it, author John C. Gebhart describes the results of
an investigation requested by representatives of the New York company,
who wanted to protect their industrial insurance policyholders—primarily urban laborers in a variety of ethnic and religious communities—from
overcharging by unethical undertakers. These undertakers, one vice president charges in the text, "made their bills sufficiently large to absorb all
of the [industrial] insurance money available" to the family.[77] The major
factors cited as encouraging more expensive funerals? A combination of
demographic changes and increasingly competitive conditions in the
market. According to the insurance company, a decline in annual death
rates and a growth in the number of funeral homes meant that funeral
directors were resorting to desperate measures to bring in money.[78]

In this comprehensive and informative study, Gebhart highlights the
tremendous financial growth of the industry and describes questionable business tactics among funeral directors. He begins with a lengthy discussion of
the "social origins of burial customs" in which, like the industry mythology in
funeral literature, he covers a variety of cultures in human history. Gebhart,
however, turns the myth on its head in his overview of disposition in
America. Rather than celebrating culturally-inspiring accomplishments of
the present, he immediately remarks on the capitalist spirit that has "gradually invaded a field which was once largely a neighborhood function." The chief
reason behind the commercialization of death: Embalming. Gebhart continues, "Embalming was introduced about 1875 and has spread until it is now
almost universally used. With embalming has come a demand for more elaborate and expensive merchandise—caskets, grave vaults, burial clothes and
funeral paraphernalia."[79] The emphasis on consumer demand for goods and
services that periodically creeps into his report is a characteristic that surfaces
in numerous studies, though it is never addressed in any substantive sociological or historical detail.

The peculiar nature of the funeral business—"funeral transactions usually take place in an atmosphere in which ordinary trading motives are almost entirely lacking"[80]—creates a climate fraught with emotion, suspicion, and ambivalence. Gebhart explores a number of questionable strategies that developed in these early, formative years, including advertisements for a "complete funeral," high-pressure sales tactics in an increasingly competitive field, and the tendency to inflate the cost of the casket to offset a variety of other expenses. Gebhart examines these—and other issues relating to law, class, race, and ethnicity—to present a startlingly exhaustive account of the business of death in 1928. Gebhart's work may not have been widely read, but it provided a great deal of ammunition for critics and reformers of the funeral industry who were shocked by his revelations.

Many newspaper and magazine articles drew on the material collected by Gebhart to publish sensational and disturbing reports that embarrassed funeral directors and kept the topic of death in the public eye. In one 1938 magazine article that worked directly from Gebhart's book, entitled "Can You Afford to Die?" the writer begins with a hypothetical account of a grieving widow trying to arrange the funeral of her husband. The initial meeting between the funeral director and the widow, the hard sell by the director, the visit to the casket room—these and other elements in the interaction are satirized and condemned. A series of shorter vignettes followed, each highlighting the fact that the total bill for the funeral barely fell under the amount of life savings or insurance coverage for middle and lower class families. The writer looked to the past, when "the matter of disposing of a dead body (since it was dead and therefore not much good to anybody) was done without fuss and as rapidly as custom would permit," and characterized present trends as "a return to the old pagan cult of body-worship and mortuary pageantry."[81]

One of the most publicized stories in the first half of the century exposed the business tactics of W. W. Chambers, a flamboyant, highly successful, Washington, D.C., funeral director. In 1939, the Federal Trade Commission ordered Chambers to stop misleading the public with inaccurate advertisements.[82] The FTC found that, contrary to ads claiming free services and reduced prices for customers, Chambers engaged in deceptive charging methods—he, like others at the time, would hide charges under the price of the casket or other merchandise. The FTC directed Chambers "to discontinue representing as customary and usual certain prices and values which in fact are fictitious and greatly in excess of the regular prices; to cease advertising certain prices as constituting a saving or discount to the purchaser when in fact they are the usual prices; and to desist from employing the word 'free' to designate articles or facilities regularly included in a combination offer with caskets or other similar merchandise."[83] Newspapers picked up on the story, and began covering these and subsequent government reports and hearings on the state of the funeral industry. In time the independent-minded Chambers, who had started in the livery business before becoming immensely successful in the funeral trade testified in congressional hearings against his fellow funeral directors and their shady practices. The popular fascination with the sensational charges against the industry contained in news reports covering Chambers' testimony illustrates an abiding public attention to matters of death and the dead.

Entertaining Death: American Obsessions in the Popular Imagination

The rise of funeral homes, the local presence of funeral directors, and numerous critical reports and news stories on the economics of funerals ensured that death was not denied or evaded in public culture. Indeed, the evolution of the ritual moment with the embalmed body, various social interactions between undertakers and their community in public settings, and media coverage of the rapidly growing funeral business, show that in the first half of the twentieth century, Americans were engaged and familiar with the realities of death, although the dead and dying were being increasingly managed out of sight from the living. The public presence of the dead, did not only depend on the work of new professional mediators. While life was becoming increasingly dominated by science, technology, consumer culture, urbanization, and other modernizing forces, Americans continued to be enamored with death and attached to the dead keeping them firmly in the public imagination as a way to reflect collectively on their social, cultural, and religious meanings. Three strikingly different cultural phenomena from this period—Rudolph Valentino's death and funeral ceremonies, Thornton Wilder's play *Our Town*, and early animated films from Walt Disney such as *The Skeleton Dance* and *Snow White and the Seven Dwarfs*—speak to these deep-seated desires to maintain some degree of intimacy and identification with the dead.

When international film sensation Rudolph Valentino died on August 23, 1926, of complications arising from a perforated ulcer, the passing of the thirty-one year old "Latin Lover" aroused a wave of public grief and provoked desperate acts of mourning. The handsome and athletic Italian immigrant whom many identify as Hollywood's first screen legend had starred in such early films as *The Four Horsemen of the Apocalypse* (1921), *The Sheik* (1921) and *Blood and Sand* (1922), before his untimely death. At the time of his death, Valentino was one of the most popular and celebrated entertainment figures in the world. Millions of fans who adored the screen star and faithfully paid to consume images of that face and body in exciting, often romantic cinematic predicaments, desired full, unmediated access to his private life as well. Valentino came to life on film, but he also came to life for his fans as tabloid fodder. He was one of the early entertainers to inspire both religious devotion among star-struck followers and profit-driven fervor to give those followers as many intimate details of his life as possible. His death only fueled these passions among many Americans stunned and grief-stricken by the news, with some reportedly committing suicide in the days following. These deep and powerful emotions also erupted among New York fans, who knew exactly where to find that highly desirable body and, many hoped, see it one last time.

Like many dead bodies at the time, Valentino's corpse was securely in the hands of a local funeral director who ensured it arrived safely home— in this case, one of New York City's best-known funeral establishments, Frank E. Campbell's Funeral Church—before it was given over to the tender gaze of his loving family, friends, and fans. The days following its arrival were marked by genuine feelings of loss and sadness for many Americans who had very little in common except for their common participation in a vital, community-forming social phenomenon that was taking shape in the early years of movie-making: celebrity worship. But solemnity and decorum did not prevail among many who desired the kind of personal access they were used to in the darkness of the movie theater or the clarity of a gossip column. As newspaper reports, eyewitness accounts, and documentary film footage make perfectly clear, pandemonium erupted at the public ceremonies for young Valentino, where tens of thousands of people gathered to pay their respects to an unforgettable star whose face would now and forever be permanently fixed in the popular imagination as the celluloid prototype of male sex-appeal.

The events surrounding Valentino's death were simply spectacular, including the riots at the public viewing in New York where hundreds were injured; the appearance of fascist Black Shirts to serve as honor guard at Campbell's; publication of altered photographs in some tabloids, depicting Valentino in the hospital, funeral home, and the great beyond; a cross-country journey for the embalmed body by train to Hollywood, California; additional funeral celebrations there that included Hollywood's hottest stars and most powerful studio executives; and the final entombment in a Hollywood mausoleum, where all expected him to remain in perpetuity. These events added significantly to Valentino's enduring legendary status in American popular culture and made his life story a fixture of Hollywood mythology.

In 1967, screenwriter and novelist Irving Shulman wrote a popular biography of Rudolph Valentino, simply called *Valentino*. The star's life made for interesting biographical research because he was an "authentic socio-cultural phenomenon," a point driven home in 1950 when, according to Shulman, he visited a "little apartment-temple to the memory of Rudolph Valentino." He wrote: "The temple was the private property of a lady not at ease in this world. The holy place, its artifacts, and the dithyrambic declamation of its curator, which alternated its verse praise of Valentino with a violent fishwife's denunciation of all the false high priestesses who dishonored the memory of the Great Lover with their fraudulent claims of election to his favor, so impressed me that I incorporated this visit and a description of the shrine in my novel *The Square Trap* (1953)."[84] This description appears in Shulman's "Author's Note," immortalizing a peculiar, if not downright pathological ritual display of continuing devotion to a long-dead Hollywood legend on the part of an irrational woman "priestess."

Rather than begin his biography proper with the infant Rudy's family and communal life in Italy, the author perpetuates this morbid attention to the dead by titling the first section "Act One: United Artists Presents a Frank E. Campbell Production: The Great American Funeral."[85] Undoubtedly informed by the post-Mitford cultural awareness of funerals in the 1960s, Shulman starts with Valentino's dead body and the energetic work of funeral director Campbell, journalists on the entertainment beat, and movie studio executives at United Artists looking to profit from two as-yet unreleased Valentino films, *The Eagle* and *The Son of the Sheik*. In "Act One: Scene Two" of this drama, Shulman describes the mortuary work taking place at Campbell's on August 24, 1926, to produce a magnificent funeral. Proprietor Frank Campbell offered his services for free, though welcomed any form of compensation from United Artists or the Valentino estate.[86]

Shulman's narrative of these events is not only organized as a Hollywood screenplay, it reads like one too—dramatic, fast-paced, with heroes and villains, and a fabulous leading man. Most of the first act of the biography takes place in the funeral home, where Shulman spends a good deal of time describing the well-documented scenes of chaos the day after Valentino's body arrived. By the morning of August 24, hundreds of fans began to line up outside on Broadway, where a carnival-like atmosphere very quickly spread among the throngs waiting for the doors to open at 6:00 P.M. so they could have their last glimpse of the Great Lover. Scuffles broke out in the line and police from all over Manhattan were soon notified that a mob was forming at the funeral home. The first to arrive on the late-summer day were women and girls, but the gathering became increasingly unusual as men began to enter the scene: "The average age of the boisterous mob seemed under thirty-five and reporters remarked on the increasing number of men sporting bolero jackets and gaucho hats. Many also wore balloon trousers, spats, and the slick hair and long sideburns made popular by Valentino. As mourners they presented a strange assembly."[87] Strange for the times, but clearly a popular expression of allegiance to the dead megastar who, the newspapers alleged, wanted his body to be on display for his loyal fans.

Police, some on horseback, tried to control the crowd and bring order to a rapidly deteriorating and potentially dangerous situation. They were asked to clear an area just outside the funeral church for the growing numbers of reporters and photographers. By two in the afternoon, Shulman reports, over fifteen thousand people stood on the surrounding streets waiting to enter the funeral home; some began to chant for the doors to be opened immediately. Shulman brings a dramatic rhetorical flair to his characterization of the intricate historical reality lived out by the people lining up to see the dead star: "Psychologically blind, emotionally drunk, intoxicated by steamy human contact, increasingly defiant of the impotent police force—the mob, transformed into a human juggernaut, stormed the doors. It shouted and screamed and cried out in a masochistic ecstasy that transmuted pain into joy. Step by step, three of the policeman gave ground until with a mighty surge the mob trapped them against the large plate-glass window. Then, as if it were a giant wave, it paused, gained a crest and broke against the policemen until the glass shattered, raining razor-sharp shards over the struggling policemen and the screaming mob."[88] Like the mysterious woman the reader meets in the "Author's Note" at the beginning of the book, the crowd is possessed by inscrutable, irrational religious desires that lead to aberrant, destructive forms of behavior. All inspired by a mere mortal the public had turned into a god.

In the ensuing bedlam, the crowd rushed into Campbell's, trampling the injured underfoot and causing disorder and damage inside the usually tranquil funeral establishment. Police, funeral employees, and even journalists helped to restore order and get the frenzied fans back outside, some of whom carried with them mementos, such as a petal from a flower or a tassel from a garment, lifted from the funeral home. While Valentino's body was removed to a better protected room, more and more people arrived outside to pay homage to their fallen hero. Later in the afternoon, Campbell's opened their doors, and mourners were allowed to pass by the open-casketed, carefully positioned, embalmed body and see, for one last time, Valentino's face, slightly turned in the direction of anxious visitors waiting to file by. Order prevailed for only a short time, according to Shulman, before the "rowdier elements in the crowd" started to rush the police, leading to even more chaos in the streets.[89] Shulman then quotes from a press release written by the disbelieving police captain in charge of the scene, who claims that he had never seen anything like this in his twenty years on the force: "This crowd has the real mob spirit. . . . So many of them are morbidly curious that they won't go home."[90] More and more people arrived by six that evening, all determined to make their way past the catafalque with the open casket.

For most of the night, police maintained a semblance of order in the line—estimated by some at upwards of thirty thousand people—that wound its way through the streets of Manhattan. People continued to walk respectfully past the body while shedding a tear or looking sadly on the star's features. Some, however, had other responses in the presence of the body. Shulman writes of young girls kissing the casket and the burial cloth accompanying it, and even of one "bolder, more imaginative soubrette" who mounted the catafalque and kissed the glass lid covering the Great Lover's face.[91] The tremendous outpouring of grief continued in the following days and the deceased star remained in the public eye, thanks to a remarkable series of media events tied to his highly visible, embalmed body. One particularly strange occurrence was the Black Shirt incident—one of many theatrical touches apparently conceived by a Campbell Church employee who arranged for Black Shirts from a fascist group in the United States bearing a wreath with condolences from the Italian dictator, Mussolini, to enter the premises and temporarily serve as additional protection at the bier. There were also two funeral services with Valentino's body present on both coasts, a star-studded Hollywood production following the New York ceremonies. The arrival of Valentino's devastated lover, Pola Negri, who claimed they had just become engaged, only fueled the press's sense of public responsibility to report on the private life of the dead man. All in all, Valentino's death, and particularly the popular attachment to the embalmed body while it remained accessible, caused quite a stir in the 1920s, one of many examples from the first half of the century demonstrating the powerful hold of the dead on the American imagination.

Another example from this period can be found in Thornton Wilder's Pulitzer Prize–winning play, *Our Town*, first performed in 1938, in the midst of New Deal politics at home and the rise of fascists abroad a year before the onset of World War II. At the beginning of the third act, the actors sit in chairs arranged in rows on the stage. The chairs represent graves in the local cemetery. Actors play the dead who return to have a conversation with the newly-arrived Emily, one of the main characters in the previous two acts who has died in childbirth. According to Wilder's stage direction, "The dead do not turn their heads or their eyes to right or left, but they sit in a quiet without stiffness. When they speak their tone is matter-of-fact, without sentimentality and, above all, without lugubriousness."[92] The first act depicts a typical day (May 7, 1901), in less stressful, complicated times in Grover's Corners, and the second act, also focused on one day (July 7, 1904), is simply called "Love and Marriage" by the narrating Stage Manager. The third and final act, which takes place in summer, 1913, completes Wilder's dramatic contemplation on daily life, family and community relations, and religious truths at work in the mysterious universe.

At the core of Wilder's play is the reality of death. This reality, as basic to human experience as birth, enters into the dialogue immediately after the Stage Manager says, "So—another day's begun."

> There's Doc Gibbs comin' down Main Street now, comin' back from that baby case. And here's his wife comin' downstairs to get breakfast.
>
> Doc Gibbs died in 1930. The new hospital's named after him. Mrs. Gibbs died first—long time ago, in fact. She went out to visit her daughter, Rebecca, who married an insurance man in Canton, Ohio, and died there—pneumonia—but her body was brought back here. She's up in the cemetery there now—in with a whole mess of Gibbses

and Herseys—she was Julia Hersey, fore she married Doc Gibbs in the Congregational Church over there.

In our town we like to know the facts about everybody.[93]

The first character to speak, Joe Crowell, Jr., has a short discussion with Dr. Gibbs, and then exits the stage. At that moment the Stage Manager interjects the following information:

Want to tell you something about that boy Joe Crowell there. Joe was awful bright—graduated from high school here, head of his class. So he got a scholarship to Massachusetts Tech. Graduated head of his class there, too. It was all wrote up in the Boston paper at the time. Goin' to be a great engineer, Joe was. But the war broke out and he died in France. All that education for nothing.[94]

As these opening excerpts suggest, the dead are a vital dimension of life in *Our Town*. Their presence is immediately invoked and inserted into the story before any of the characters actually die. For Wilder, a dramatic examination of everyday life reveals universal truths—one being that death cannot be separated from life or the search for meaning in life. The third act explicitly relies on the dead and the centrality of death in life to make a larger religious point about human time and a sacred timelessness. After describing the cemetery itself, the scenery of the surrounding landscape, and the textual history of the town found inscribed on the tombstones, the Stage Manager becomes quite philosophical about the meaning of death:

Yes, an awful lot of sorrow has sort of quieted down up here. People just wild with grief have brought their relatives up to this hill. We all know how it is . . . and then time . . . and sunny days . . . and rainy days . . . 'n snow . . . We're all glad they're in a beautiful place and we're coming up here ourselves when our fit's over.

Now there are some things we all know, but we don't take'm out and look at'm very often. We all know that something is eternal. And it ain't the houses and it ain't the names, and it ain't the earth, and it ain't even the stars . . . everybody knows in their bones that something is eternal, and that something has to do with human beings. All the greatest people ever lived have been telling us that for five thousand years and yet you'd be surprised how people are always losing hold of it. There's something way down deep that's eternal about every human being.[95]

Wilder allows the audience to see the universe through the eyes of the dead, and it is a dark, unsentimental vision of their relations with the living. The dead, the Stage Manager explains, lose interest in the living—including surviving husbands, sisters, et cetera—and, in time, any meaningful connection to or memories of their life: "They get weaned away from earth."[96] The Stage Manager then discloses a fact about the relations between the living and the dead that is strikingly similar to what anthropological literature tells us about death in primitive societies: "And they stay here while the earth part of 'em burns away, burns out."[97] In other words, the dead remain close to the living until their bodies have completely disintegrated, even in Grover's Corners.

After the Stage Manager finishes his reflections in the cemetery, he pauses before introducing the living characters in this Act. The first one he mentions is Joe Stoddard, "our undertaker, supervising a new-made grave."[98] Although in the scene for only a short time, he is clearly not like the other undertakers depicted in popular culture in the first half of the century—representations to be discussed in a later chapter that contributed to the stereotype of the conniving, callous, suspicious, often bizarre outsider profiting from the pain of others.

Wilder's undertaker is clearly an exception to the emerging stereotype, a throwback to a disappearing, rural image. Stoddard interacts easily with Sam Craig, who has returned to town to attend his cousin's funeral. He is depicted as an individual who has mixed feelings about his work: "Very sad, our journey today. . . . I always say I hate to supervise when a young person is taken."[99] He is also a family man in a family-run business: "My son's supervisin' at the home."[100] His intimate knowledge of the town and its inhabitants is clear in his short conversation with Craig. But Wilder has the undertaker exit before the dead begin to educate the recently-deceased Emily and the audience about the irretrievable past, the immensity of the universe, the minuscule status of any one particular human, and the eternal part of every individual life.

The initial response to the play was quite negative, not only because of its experimental, modernist staging and tempo, but also because of its content.[101] When it opened in New York, however, some reviewers raved about its haunting, evocative, and moving atmosphere, and praised the unconventional production choices. Although reviews continued to be mixed at first, the play went on to win the Pulitzer Prize that year, and it eventually became one of the most popularly-performed plays of twenti-eth-century America.[102] As an innovative, highly original, and profound dramatic work, *Our Town* has lasting cultural power in America largely because of its third act—the intimacy with the dead opens up new perspectives on time, identity, and cosmic meaning. The undertaker plays only a marginal role in this act, but his proximity to the dead in rural, turn-of-the-century Grover's Corners is neither derided nor satirized; given the context of his appearance, he is a rather comforting, humane bridge between the living and the dead.

Another popular and innovative artist of this period also focused on death in his works to transmit moral, universal messages about the mean-ing of life—and entertain the masses at the same time. Walt Disney's cul-tural productions, including films, television shows, and theme parks, left an indelible mark on the life of the nation. His works and his life story have assumed mythic proportions in American culture because they con-vey many fundamental tenets of an American way of life.[103] But if Disney was a mouthpiece of an American way of life, the force of his voice depended on a curious obsession with death—an obsession that can be found in both his personal life and the early animated films he pro-duced.[104] These films were immensely popular with the American public, and rather than being hidden from sight, death and death-related themes are front and center. Like many fairy tales and other forms of children's literature, his animated films demonstrate a fixation on the presence of many unpleasant human realities, including death.[105]

Just before the stock market crash in October, 1929, and on the heels of Steamboat Willie—which introduced Mickey Mouse to the world and secured "Uncle Walt" a place in American popular culture—Disney pro-duced the first of the *Silly Symphonies*, an animated short called *The Skeleton Dance*, which contained haunting, though hilarious, images of death. In this short, four animated skeletons—awakened by a fight between two tomcats in a moonlit cemetery—emerge from out of their graves to perform a modern and playful dance of death. Originally called "The Spook Dance," Disney expressed his enthusiasm for its commercial prospects in a letter to his chief animator, Ubbe Iwerks, stating, "I am glad the spook dance is progressing so nicely—give her Hell, Ubbe—make it funny and I am sure we will be able to place it in a good way."[106]

Many of the theater managers who previewed it early hated the macabre piece, with one purportedly saying to Walt's brother, Roy, "What's he trying to do, ruin us? You go back and tell that brother of yours the renters don't want this gruesome crap. . . . What they want is more Mickey Mouse. You go back and tell Walt. More mice, tell him, More mice!"[107] According to another account, one exhibitor "visibly shivered after he had seen it and said it would give his customers goose bumps."[108] While many were shocked by Disney's thematic choice, the first *Silly Symphony* finally had a showing in Los Angeles, where critics and patrons raved about it, turning the "gruesome crap" into the national hit Disney expected.[109] Disney returns to the space of the haunted graveyard in a darker, more menacing vision, in the last sequence of *Fantasia* (1940), but his films contain no representations of funeral men serving as a bridge between the living and the dead. Instead Walt Disney, like other creative artists preoccupied with and inspired by death, acted as another kind of ritual mediator who brought mortal matters home to modern Americans.

Some of his films do bring the audience into the intimate moment when the living confront the face of death, or what appears to be the face of death, to extol moral messages about honor, virtue, and family. What is most striking about Disney's early animated films is that death, or the threat of death, is the motor, the driving force that enlivens many narratives. In *Pinocchio* (1940), the wooden puppet boy has to die in order to be resurrected as a real boy; in *Bambi* (1942), the little fawn becomes a mature deer in the aftermath of his mother's ruthless killing by the hunters—one of the first and most memorable scenes of death for many children. Disney's first, full-length animated film, *Snow White and the Seven Dwarfs* (1938), is a retelling of one of the tales collected by the Grimm brothers, and conveys the story of a queen's desire to kill an innocent young girl.

The evil queen is convinced that after Snow White eats from the poisoned apple, she will be "buried alive," and no longer a threat to her own status as the "fairest of the land." Perhaps because of his own obsession with death, Disney avoided funerals in real life, but he clearly understood the dramatic, and commercial, possibilities of the artfully illustrated deathbed scene—that familiar, deeply-rooted cultural script encouraging an intimate moment when life is finally extinguished, and loved ones surround the fresh corpse.[110] Transcripts from story conferences for Snow White capture Disney's awareness of these possibilities, as well as his energy and dominance in the creative process of producing films. Imagining the conclusion of the film, Disney envisions Snow White's encoffined body, and the dwarfs' reactions to it:

> Fade in on her in the glass coffin, maybe shaded by a big tree. It's built on sort of a little pedestal, torches are burning, two dwarfs on either side with things like guards would have, others are coming up and putting flowers on the coffin. It's all decked with flowers. The birds fly up and drop flowers. Shots of the birds; show them sad. Snow White is beautiful in the coffin.
>
> Then you hear the Prince. The birds, dwarfs, everyone hears him off-screen. As they turn to look, here he is silhouetted against the hill with his horse. As he walks down the hill singing the song, cut to Snow White in the coffin. As he approaches, everyone sort of steps back as if he had a right there. He goes up to the coffin and finishes the song. As he finishes the song, he lifts the glass lid of the coffin and maybe there's a hesitation, then he kisses her. From the kiss he drops down and buries his head in his hands in a sad position, and all the dwarfs see it and every dwarf drops his head.[111]

The dwarfs' foil the queen's plans by not burying the young woman. Like many Americans at the time, the dwarfs were fixated on being close and seeing the beautiful body in repose, too entranced by it to say good-bye forever, but unencumbered by professional managers whose job is to ensure the final, unbridgeable separation between the living and the dead.

Although the dwarfs eventually have to say good-bye to the revitalized Snow White after the reanimating kiss from the handsome prince, the vision of their ascent to a castle above the clouds conveys a central message in Disney films: The happy ending comes after death has been overcome, or vanquished, by virtuous actions that reconstitute the integrity of an eternally-loving, transcendent family unit. In most of his films, Disney ends the story with the promise of domestic bliss, a ray of light in a dark, dangerous world. Without his preoccupation with death, Disney would not have created the modern day fairy tales that had the cultural impact they did in the twentieth century; and if Americans did not have similar preoccupations, and like-minded strategies for imagining meaning in the face of death, his films would not have garnered so much public interest. Early Walt Disney films, like many early Hollywood productions in general, exhibited an enduring fascination with bringing the dead back to life, an imaginary exercise that resonated with modern Americans transfixed by the reality of death.

In more immediate, personal ways, the funeral industry controlled the public face of death for many Americans in the first half of the twentieth century. The language funeral directors used in their line of business, and the rituals they invented to say good-bye to the dead, contributed to the cultural and social meanings of death available to those who had to make sense of losing a close relation. The dead were being uprooted from the home and sequestered in institutional settings for professional care, often by strangers with no intimate connection with the deceased. But Americans refused to completely give up control of their dead and their fascination with death. As we will discuss, they maintained a sense of intimacy with the dead and integrated the realities of death into their daily living in a variety of ways. During these early years, a simultaneous alienation from and attraction to the dead was manifested across the cultural and social landscape. In addition, during these years the triumph of embalming as an American practice and the funeral home as an American institution were secured—developments that led to increasingly public and popular challenges to the growing economic prosperity and cultural legitimacy of funeral directors.

2

EXPLAINING THE AMERICAN FUNERAL, 1918–1963

I'll hire a black Cadillac, to drive you to your grave,
I'm gonna be there baby, throw that mud in your face,
I'm gonna ride at your funeral, Daddy, in a black Cadillac
Oh yeah, you think you won, Oh baby, but you can't come back.
"Black Cadillac," Joyce Green, 1959

The Will of the People? The Case of World War I

The funeral industry was generating billions of dollars for funeral directors, casket and vault manufacturers, cemetery owners, florists, embalming-chemical companies, and other burial-related businesses in the early 1960s. Receipts for funeral services rendered during the first half of the twentieth century give some indication of the reach and range of transactions taking place in the name of the dead. On the other hand, receipts also misrepresent some of the details of these transactions—especially in the early decades of the century—making them highly questionable as accurate records of labor, pricing, and profit.

By the middle of the century, funeral directors had become acutely aware of the need to account for their time. The escalating public attacks and calls for reform ensured that undertakers learn more sophisticated methods of detailing every step taken in the burial of the dead. Interestingly for this domesticated business arrangement, it was often the children who passed these accounting skills on to the father. For example, in a letter from 1946, Eugene Baxter provides his dad, Alex, with a list of funeral services and the average number of hours for each service. The younger Baxter, an associate in a separate branch of the family business, is trying to help the elder run a more efficient funeral home. He offers an itemized accounting of the 30 hours needed to prepare a typical, Schenectady, New York, funeral.

Service call (2 men at 1 hour)	2 hours
Embalming	5 hours
Arrangements and sale	1 hour, 30 minutes

Cosmetics including hair dressing	1 hour
Dressing and casketing	1 hour
Arranging flowers	1 hour, 30 minutes
Open house [receptionist for incoming calls]	3 hours
Office (calling in notices, obituary, billing, etc.)	3 hours
Delivering box and/or equipment to cemetery	1 hour
Service (4 men at 2 hours) (per previous page)	8 hours
Certificate and permit	1 hour
Music (organ only)	1 hour
Cleaning (after service)	1 hour

Eugene mentions later in the letter that the numbers are subject to revision, depending on the circumstances of the particular case. For example, "it may take only two hours to do the embalming, and take three hours to make the necessary arrangements and the sale." But this approach to charging the bereaved has been highly successful, according to Eugene: "The plan is . . . receiving much favorable comment from our clientele, not only from what they have told us personally, but from replies we have obtained so far from our follow-up letters. The plan is paying its way just as well as the old pricing system." Although the method for determining the costs of these services is not outlined in the letter, this list covers many of the basic components Americans paid for when they buried their dead.[1]

Over the first half of the twentieth century, the national effort to organize a credible, upright, self-regulated, and profitable enterprise led funeral directors to argue that these basic components had significant social value for the living, and were important enough that their vocation deserved to be called a profession. Some segments of American society, however, grew increasingly suspicious about the undertaking and wondered publicly why funerals produced so much revenue. Even as distrust translated into public hearings and official condemnations, the people continued to bring their dead to the local funeral director and pay for his services—though many were not exactly sure prices were fair. For most inside the industry, the increasing commodification of the American funeral was a perfectly natural development in one of the most powerful capitalistic nations in the world. Indeed, the entrepreneurial spirit animating the network of commercial activity surrounding the funeral was experienced in patriotic terms, and any threats to its standing in the free market denounced as an attack on American democracy.

The funeral home evolved into an American institution during a tumultuous period of social change: industrialization brought the "machine age" to life; consumerism introduced new relations between people and objects; and faith in science and technology undercut even further the relevance of institutional religion to everyday life. The values beginning to energize the social body in the modern era contributed greatly to the shape and texture of the American funeral, and the final appearance of the embalmed body safely cared for in the funeral home. Nevertheless, the dramatic appearance of this new home for the dead in the first half of the century became a source for much public debate and led many individuals both inside and outside the industry to scrutinize the business of burial.

At the end of the First World War, questions about repatriating the remains of soldiers killed overseas forced national leaders and family members to express their views about burial and responsibility toward the dead. A reformist zeal aimed at transforming American funerals—ostensibly motivated by concern for the spending patterns of the poor—began to emanate from insurance companies, universities, and public presses. A variety of publications challenged the value of contemporary practices and the integrity of neighborly funeral directors, and raised difficult ethical questions about the "myth of progress" cherished by men and women involved in the final rite of passage. Charges of corruption—both financial and spiritual—issued from religious leaders as well. Indeed, from the early part of the century to the 1960s, Christian denouncements, usually framed in a fairly standard series of arguments, were commonly referenced in media coverage on the topic.

All of these public debates about the virtues of the American funeral pivoted on a series of highly contentious questions: What do the people want for their dead? What should the people want for their dead? And, how much should it cost—if anything at all—to give the people what they want? Although many entered the debate to right economic injustices and purify corrupt business practices, critics of the funeral industry and its supporters ultimately relied on moral and religious justifications to secure their respective positions. Disagreement over relations with the dead had as much to do with differing religious sensibilities about the meaning of death as with the costs associated with burial. The moral ambiguities many Americans faced when they visited their local undertaker did not stop at the bottom line of the funeral bill; the moral seriousness and sacred

standing projected by the high-minded undertaker, on the other hand, did
not detract from his pursuit of wealth.

One of the earliest and most important moments of public debate
about the treatment of the dead occurred after the First World War. In
this war, as in most American wars, soldiers who fought and died for the
good of the country achieved a special standing in society. Their remains,
sacred to both the nation and family members an ocean away from the
fighting, became the responsibility of federal government officials, who
tried to make sense of the carnage to American citizens and provide for
the appropriate rituals to dispose of the dead. At the beginning of
America's involvement in the war, the War Department planned to
maintain the policy followed in both the Spanish-American War and the
Philippines Insurrection: repatriate the remains of soldiers and hand
them over to grieving families. In spite of the rapid advances in embalming technologies sweeping over the industry at the time, the War
Department declined the services of the Purple Cross, a volunteer organization created by patriotic morticians who insisted that they could
secure the return of the war dead "in a sanitary and recognizable condition a number of years after death."[2] Instead, military leaders thought it
best to leave the dead to the undertaking branch of the military, the
Graves Registration Service.

American losses were significantly less than those of other Allied
countries, but the Graves Registration Service did not have much success
burying the dead during the conflict. Conditions in France did not allow
for the satisfactory care of the dead, so General John J. Pershing ordered
individual units to assume this obligation, with the Graves Registration
Service providing essential bureaucratic support for record keeping and
some physical assistance in establishing military cemeteries.[3] Even
though the war dead were hailed in the United States as martyrs to the
cause of liberty, it became clear that repatriation was simply out of the
question. The War Department made its position clear to the people of
Pittsburgh, who had requested the body of Private Thomas Enright, one
of the first Americans killed in combat, in November, 1917. Contrary to
earlier statements, complications on and near fields of battle led the government to decree that the return of fallen soldiers would have to wait
until the war ended.[4]

At the conclusion of the war, the battle over the remains of American
soldiers flared up immediately. Many political and military leaders

advocated the creation of national cemeteries in European countries that would maintain the presence of honored American dead. The vast majority of civilians, however, wanted family members brought back to the United States for burial. Ralph Hayes, assistant to the secretary of war, produced a document in May, 1920, entitled "A Report to the Secretary of War on American Military Dead Overseas," that identified the differing opinions about repatriation. After visiting Europe to see firsthand the treatment and locations of the military dead in early 1920, Hayes writes about his own perspective on the war dead: "I do not hesitate to say that the sight of actual disinterments, however reverently made, and the vision of the Fields of Honor have left me with the fervent hope that the proportion of parents preferring to have their sons rest overseas will be large."[5] Still, he continues, the government must ultimately fulfill the vow it made at the beginning of the war: to leave the fate of the dead to family members.[6]

After these preliminary statements, Hayes turns to public opinion, and describes the increasingly hostile debate over repatriation. Those who favored keeping American dead in overseas cemeteries relied primarily on two arguments. First, practical considerations in France made the return of corpses particularly difficult. The devastation of war had hit transportation lines hard and they were already stretched to serve the needs of inhabitants trying to recover from five years of battle. Sympathy with their plight "should make us unwilling to place the further burden on the morale of this brave people that would be caused by the continual sight of endless funeral trains passing through the country."[7] In addition, Hayes writes, "the gruesomeness of the operation is insufficiently appreciated by those who demand it."[8] Disinterring bodies that have been buried for years, and then adequately organizing and paying for their shipment to American soil, was a tremendous, highly problematic undertaking for the War Department, as well as the French government.

Advocates of American cemeteries in France further argued that reverence for the military dead compelled American families to offer a second sacrifice for the good of the nation: Their close relations died fighting for a just cause, and now their bodies could continue to serve as a potent reminder of America's contribution to saving the world. For those families who were willing to make this sacrifice, the new military cemeteries, designated as "Fields of Honor" by a powerful coalition of supporters, including former presidents, labor leaders, military officers, chaplains, and members of the American Legion, enhanced the sacred status of the dead resting there. Hayes quotes from a resolution passed at the Minneapolis convention of the American Legion which stated that only those family members who desire repatriation of soldiers' remains should get their dead. As a policy, fallen soldiers should stay in foreign cemeteries, established and protected by the United States government so "those who made the supreme sacrifice may be maintained as a fitting memorial of America's unselfish service to humanity."[9]

Supporters of the "Fields of Honor" attempted to persuade families who lost close relations that the dead were better off across the Atlantic, cared for by local French authorities and the American military. After the fighting ended, General Pershing sent a cable to the War Department stating what he believed to be the wishes of the dead: "[C]ould these soldiers speak for themselves, they would wish to be left undisturbed, where with their comrades they had fought their last fight. . . . The graves of our soldiers constitute, if they are allowed to remain, a perpetual reminder to our allies of the liberty and ideals upon which the greatness of America rests."[10] Pershing and others who emphasized the glory of overseas cemeteries did not mention the fact that black soldiers performed most of the lugubrious labor of producing these "Fields of Honor"—they scoured the battlefields for corpses, disinterred buried bodies, and reinterred them in these now-venerated spots.[11] While these supporters avoided any discussion about who actually handled the bones of soldiers, they were quite vocal about who they did not want involved in this operation: profit-minded undertakers.

As Hayes points out, many believed that funeral men were stirring up support for the return of the dead to American soil: "It has been alleged that the motive behind the proposal for the return of bodies is 'the propaganda of the undertakers and coffin makers.'" Although Hayes acknowledges that insufficient data existed to prove these charges, he also alludes to the questionable actions of a "group of embalmers" who distributed leaflets and advertised their services. "But," he continues, "there was a repudiation without delay from the recognized association of reputable funeral directors."[12] Still, many people charged undertakers with placing capitalism above nationalism, exploiting the sorrow of grieving citizens, and engaging in a conspiracy to sway public opinion. In spite of the patriotic, civic participation of funeral directors in community life, and their strengthened institutional position as mediators between the living and the dead, opponents of repatriation were outraged at their involvement in the public conversation over the final disposition of fallen soldiers.

The funeral industry responded vigorously to these charges and any attempt to prevent the return of sons, brothers, and fathers to their families. Funeral directors were strongly in favor of repatriation, a position that resonated with the majority of Americans who did not want to be separated from their dead even if they died fighting valiantly for a noble cause an ocean away. Indeed, a national organization called the "Bring Back the Dead League" was formed in 1919 to fight for the return of bodies and make sure they remained securely under the control of family relations. Supporters of repatriation argued against overseas cemeteries for several reasons. Traditional military policy, as well as the stated policy at the beginning of the war, was to bring the dead home. Also, the distance between Americans and their dead impeded, in the words of the Hayes report, "reverential pilgrimages to the graves" and protection of these sites might lead to future wars.[13] Some felt the French could not be trusted with maintaining these sites. And, contrary to General Pershing's views, the soldiers themselves look homeward at the time of death, and would want their bodies brought home after they pass from this life.[14]

The evidence of strong public support for repatriation did not temper the suspicions of those who targeted the funeral industry as unscrupulously manipulating the will of the people. Numerous funeral industry publications printed articles and letters protesting their innocence in the face of these charges, as well as their patriotic views about supporting what most Americans want for their martyred heroes. In a front page article of a leading funeral trade magazine that appeared in January, 1920, a writer for *The Casket* responded to the accusations of Congressman Charles Caldwell, who claimed that this journal in particular was a chief source of propaganda in the debate over the repatriation issue. The lengthy lead-in to this article exclaims that the congressman has stated his support for bringing bodies home, but then boldly retorts:

> In That Case They Must be Buried and Funeral Directors Must Do the Work—Does Mr. Caldwell, or Any Other Excited Member of Congress, Claim That This Should be Done Gratis and Without Legitimate Profit—Are We Not All Living Under the Capitalist System Whose Chief End Is Profit—Has Not Our Government Said Over and Over, That It Is the Business of Business Men to Make Profit—Is the Undertaker Alone Excluded?—If Not What Becomes of Our Critic's Crocodile Tears for The Families Who Are Perfectly Willing to Pay for Services Rendered?[15]

Near the end of the article, the author states that the United States "missed its opportunity to give the world a new object lesson in the humane treatment of our heroic dead" immediately after the war, and *The Casket* therefore held the position that return of the dead was indeed a governmental decision.[16]

This edition also reprinted a newspaper letter to demonstrate the strong public disapproval of overseas military cemeteries and the refusal to scapegoat funeral directors as grand conspirators in a scheme to profit from the vulnerability of family members—views, it is suggested, especially close to the heart of grieving mothers. In the introduction to this letter, *The Casket* author asserts, "No one human—not even such a flint-hearted monster as the undertaker is pictured by certain honorable members of the House of Representatives—can read this mother's appeal for all that is left of her boy without a catch in his throat and a suspicious moisture in his eyes."[17] The letter, which was written in response to the recommendation of Episcopal Bishop, Charles H. Brent, senior chaplain of the American Expeditionary Force, that the dead remain in Europe, is then printed in full:

> In reply to Bishop Brent's letter . . . I would like to ask him has he a son lying in a foreign grave, where he may never have a chance to visit?
>
> I am a broken-hearted mother with my only dear son lying in a foreign grave, and have waited one year and six months for the return of my son's remains. Our government promised us their return, and why do they not keep their promise? It was all right to rush our boys over there, and it is just as right to bring them back promptly. There has been ample time.
>
> All the camouflage against undertakers and the glory of the so-called American field of honor in a foreign country cannot alter the determination of American mothers to have their loved ones' remains brought back to America and buried in American soil, where they themselves can tenderly care for their graves day by day.[18]

In a subsequent issue, *The Casket* responds to claims in the "Yellow Press" that freedom-loving, patriotic—and capitalist, for sure—funeral industry leaders and representatives were behind various forms of legislation to spend millions of dollars to pay for the return of the dead. Speaking for "funeral directors' organizations" and "individual members of [the] profession," the article offers readers evidence from a number of congressmen who declared in writing that undertakers had nothing to do with the congressional bills stipulating the government return the dead to American families. For example, Pennsylvania Representative Thomas S. Cargo writes that he "was besieged by many of my personal friends in Pennsylvania who had lost sons in France and who were anxious above all things else to have their bodies returned."[19] Cargo himself feels it would be better to leave the dead in France but, he admits, throughout the war military officials had led people to believe that the dead would be brought back to national soil.[20]

Ultimately, the majority of American military dead were returned to the United States. National overseas cemeteries were established for the remainder, though the symbolic power of these distant sites was overshadowed by the controversial, hallowed bones of one particular figure, the Unknown Soldier, who was laid to rest in Arlington National Cemetery in Washington, D.C., and who fulfilled a national duty as a surrogate body for the grieving social body.[21] In the end, Congress acted on the desires of families who wanted to be close to their dead, and turned to civilian funeral specialists—the very people who offered to form the volunteer Purple Cross unit at the beginning of America's involvement in the war—to assist in the process of identifying and shipping the bodies home. In postwar America, however, charges of profiteering, deception, and corruption continued to haunt the funeral industry. Although the First World War had demonstrated that Americans wished for some form of control over the fate of the dead, funeral directors continued to have a great deal of difficulty explaining their role in this process, and that the services they provided ensured the appropriate amount of interaction between the living and the dead.

The Public Battle Over Funeral Reform

Calls for reform of the American funeral came from many quarters of society from the 1920s to the 1950s. These public attacks argued that America's funeral homes were built on lies and deceit rather than trust and sincerity, and contributed to the troubling public image of funeral directors circulating in popular consciousness. In many ways, the rhetoric and publications set the tone, established the storyline, and provided ammunition for the majority of popular press reports and articles exposing the business of death as a sham. Writers covering the funeral beat sometimes implicitly, often times explicitly, joined the chorus of critics digging into America's growing class of ritual death specialists.

In 1921, the University of Chicago Press published *Funeral Management and Costs: A World-Survey of Burial and Cremation*, written by the Reverend Quincy L. Dowd. The preface of the book states why Dowd felt compelled to write it: "To awaken your interest in certain significant and heart-moving facts brought out by this investigation, which, while setting forth the efficient municipal management of burial and protective provision made by European states and cities for people bereaved, plainly show the urgent need in America for similar municipal control and public protection on behalf of all citizens alike."[22] Dowd proposes "treating burial as a public utility" and strongly argues for an alternative form of disposal that was only beginning to appear on the American scene, the "enlightened choice" of cremation—"a beautiful and economical, not to say Christian, practice."[23] He also includes some discussion of funeral practices in other cultures. Contrary to the mythic language at work in the evolutionary story produced by the industry, Dowd describes the management of burial in America as backward rather than advanced, and desperately in need of rehabilitation. But his emphasis on the economics of death, and particularly the financial burdens placed on the middle and lower classes, raises significant questions about popular desires in the disposal of the dead.

Many similar published studies of funeral costs in the first half of the twentieth century contained the same basic message: The masses are making the wrong choices at the time of death. Instead of following the more "enlightened," rational path of simplicity, refinement, and austerity during the funeral ceremonies, most Americans, and particularly the poor who are "especially given to making a show at funerals," succumb to foolish consumer impulses and misplaced concern about social status.[24] In Dowd's economic and class analysis of the cost of dying, which includes sections on "burial expense," "burial among the poor," "last-sickness bills," "mourning apparel," and "the florist's bill," the typical American encounter with death had the potential to be financially devastating—with the exception of expenses associated with mourning clothes, the use of which declined dramatically after the war. In the section on flowers, which in Dowd's estimation cost the public $84,000,000 annually (1,680,000 deaths per year, and $50 spent on flowers for each one), the incomprehensible spending patterns of Americans is portrayed as not only tasteless, but sacrilegious: "This wastefulness is not encouraged by religious teachings, nor does it go without rebuke by the church. This misuse of flowers, this misplaced love of display at burials, vaunts itself in spite of the discountenance thrown upon it by church leaders. . . . Only wider intelligence, purer artistic taste, a finer example on the part of social leaders, and united influence on the part of ministers can bring in a better and more economic conduct of burial, eliminating the vulgar desire for display and omitting useless waste."[25]

For Dowd and other reformers, of course, the real culprits who cultivated and exploited these "vulgar" sensibilities were unethical funeral directors and other unscrupulous capitalists running wild and unregulated in American society. Dowd's charges do not mean, however, that everyone associated with the business of death was guilty of heartlessly gouging the bereaved. Most of these surveys and reports were careful to avoid condemning the funeral industry en masse. Dowd, for example, wrote that although "repugnance" was felt by some toward undertaking, "most undertakers are esteemed now for their work's sake and for personal qualities. Therefore . . . ample justice should be done to men and women whose professional duties require skill and peculiar aptitude for ministering in bereaved homes."[26] With this qualification in mind, Dowd goes on to detail numerous instances of overcharging, deception, and pure greed rampant in the industry.

In addition to the outrageous costs associated with flowers, vaults, and cemetery plots, Dowd also names the church as an institution frequently in cahoots with undertakers and profiting from expensive funerals: "But proof comes that churches in certain districts and remote parishes lay 'heavy burdens and difficult to be borne' upon their members by connivance with some undertaker. A correspondent wrote from North Dakota charging that priests of Polish parishes share in excessive profits of the undertaking trade. . . . Perhaps undertakers may take comfort from instances of this kind, showing that the pot should not call the kettle black."[27] The first few decades of the century did not see many distinctions between urban and rural undertakers—in these years critics were suspicious of them all.

In the matter of funerals, Dowd slams the capitalist logic of supply and demand undergirding this particular, peculiar business: "In truth, undertaking is not excusable, as other trades may deem themselves to be, in respect to charging all that the trade will bear; for funeral and burial charges are in a class by themselves, i.e., are dire, forced necessities, are

involved in 'class' sentiments and ecclesiastical ceremonies which make
the utmost demands on the family purse already emptied by medical, nurs-
ing, and drug bills."[28] To counteract the rising fortunes of the funeral business, Dowd called for a series of reforms, focusing on municipal control,
education, more public examples of simple, inexpensive funerals for prominent figures, acceptance of cremation, and local committees and academic
studies to investigate funeral costs. Religious leaders in particular needed to
do more to teach "people a better, less costly way of funeral necessities and
rites." Dowd continues with his own recommendations, which include dis-
couraging funerals on Sundays, eliminating funeral sermons, and forbidding "the promiscuous showing of the corpse in public."[29]

In his important 1928 report for Metropolitan Life, *Funeral Costs: What
They Average; Are They Too High? Can They Be Reduced?*, John Gebhart
also analyzed competition among funeral directors. After examining thousands of funeral bills from around the country, and following detailed
investigations of estate settlements in New York City, Chicago, and
Pittsburgh, Gebhart wrote, "Competition in the undertaking business is
not extensively on the basis of price. Competition among undertakers, to
put it bluntly, is chiefly for the possession of bodies. Once the undertaker
secures possession of the body, he can usually charge all that the traffic
will bear."[30] He points out that the stiff competition produced by a small
volume of business and a crowded field of undertakers was a powerful
motivation for "gouging and overselling." (Based on the ratio of annual
number of deaths to number of undertakers, he estimated that the average
undertaker had to earn his wages on one funeral a week.) Unfortunately,
Gebhart reminds his audience, because a small number of successful funeral homes do more than one funeral a week, the majority have to survive
on less.[31]

But Gebhart is hesitant to indict everyone involved in the funeral trade,
and even mentions that the six funeral directors placed on the
Metropolitan-sponsored Advisory Committee on Burial Survey moved
from an "attitude of suspicion and antagonism" about an independent
investigation of the costs of burial, "to one of cooperation and support."
According to Gebhart, "the more enlightened and progressive funeral
directors" understand how such studies, despite the initial fallout, will ultimately benefit their enterprise.[32] After all, he continues, this particular
business is fraught with difficulties that do not occur in other industries,
and the temptations to make easy cash off of someone who is not in a

"rational frame of mind" are strong. It is in the best interest of undertakers, Gebhart explains, to act ethically and discourage "undue extravagance."

> We often hear of the funeral director who makes it a point to ascertain the value of the insurance or other savings which the family may have and who makes his bill large enough to absorb most of the money available. Such abuses, as we shall see later, do frequently occur. It is only fair to point out, however, that the ethical funeral director, who is at the same time a good business man, does not want to encourage undue extravagance for two perfectly good reasons: He wants to avoid bad debts and he wants to keep the good will of the community. . . . Moreover, families who purchase extravagant funerals are likely to regret their extravagance when they are in a more rational frame of mind and may even blame the funeral director for overcharging them.[33]

Gebhart's study, like Dowd's, was principally motivated by concern for the poor, who sometimes inappropriately spend beyond their means because of their mistaken, popular beliefs about how properly to demonstrate care for their dead. Funeral directors may then prey on victims with these distorted, unenlightened views. If the poor paid for a funeral that corresponded to their "station in life and to the value of [the] estate," Gebhart argues, no problems with burial costs would exist. The wealthy may indeed pay for a lavish funeral—"conceivably a form of economic waste," according to Gebhart—but the hardship and distress for survivors would be much less than for lower-income families.[34] The numbers made a clear statement about the costs: "Funeral expenses among the poor and middle class are out of all proportion to those prevailing among the well-to-do."[35]

Spending patterns also suggested that a different set of values was operating in the upper classes compared to the middle and lower classes. The rich were less interested in the funeral itself—that is, the rituals surrounding disposal of the body—and spent much of their money (rationally, Gebhart implicitly contends) on extra charges for merchandise, like monuments, and for services, like perpetual care of the cemetery site, to preserve the memory of the family name.[36] According to Gebhart, funeral bills express class tastes: "Among wealthy groups the 'family complex' is at work. This is expressed in a desire to perpetuate the family name in stone and in well-cared-for burial plots. The funeral, while dignified and by no means cheap, is relatively of less importance than among lower-income groups. With poorer groups the interest is perhaps most ephemeral and is centered in a 'fine funeral' to show respect to the dead and to impress curious neighbors."[37] In a subsequent exploration into the experiences of family-welfare societies, Gebhart admits that it is difficult to state why the poor spend so much of their money, but the choices were obvious: Either the lower classes have an "unreasonable desire" for extravagance at funerals, or they are the victims of "extortion" and deceptive selling practices by local undertakers.[38]

At the end of his investigation, Gebhart is just as incredulous about the popular tastes and values of the spending public as he is about the sincerity of profit-minded funeral directors. He concludes that the dramatic rise of the burial industry in the early years of the century can be explained by the following factors: "(1) The public has no sense of values and is not trained to shop, so that price is not an important consideration. (2) Because of insurance and other savings, all but the most destitute or improvident families have ample funds with which to defray burial expenses. (3) To a certain extent, however, it is doubtless true that the demand for more elaborate and expensive caskets and funeral services has accompanied the general demand for more expensive goods of all kinds."[39] On the basis of his analysis of funeral costs, he recommends two principle steps to curb the rising costs of funerals. On the one hand, the industry must work with representatives from insurance companies, civic and welfare agencies, and other interested parties to reform the business of death and ensure that competition is not the driving force motivating people who work with the dead. On the other hand, the public must be better educated about what is appropriate for the disposal of their dead. Religious leaders are especially important in this effort because they can instill the correct values, related primarily to "simplicity and economy," in church-going consumers.[40]

Dowd and Gebhart are only two examples of early efforts to shed light on, and indeed "enlighten" the public about, the economics of the American funeral. The class biases that informed their interpretations of why funerals cost so much, and why the poor display such irrational forms of wastefulness for the burial of their dead, placed a great deal of responsibility on ignorant consumers who do not understand the appropriate financial and ritual limits of death. Although the authors express some ambivalence about indicting the entire industry, their studies demonstrate many cases of abuse and dishonesty, and attack the business practices, ethics, and motivations of those who capitalize on the tragedies of others. They recommended some form of industry or governmental regulation in the disposal of the dead, and suggested that the newly-formed class of professional ritual specialists should not be solely in charge of corpses. Another common thread: Embalming must go if Americans want to put dignity back in their funerals.

These critical texts varied in focus, and were published in a broad range of public forums, including books, newspapers and magazines, and academic journals. In 1934, for example, Times-Mirror Press published F. A. Manaugh's book, *Thirty Thousand Adventurers: An Informal Disclosure of Observations and Experiences in Research in the Funeral Industry*. Manaugh was a business counselor who worked for many funeral homes and spent years researching the industry. Although he wrote about the "many morticians of high ideals and practice," what he labeled the "right wing" of the industry, most of the book exposes the "left wing," where "the long dark shadows of moral corruption and commercial deviltry" led to unethical, and downright criminal, business practices.[41] Newspapers around the country also covered the testimony of W. W. Chambers, the hugely successful Washington undertaker who publicly asserted that the business of funerals was a "highly specialized racket." Newspaper articles geared to sell papers often highlighted some of the more unusual, sensationalistic angles of the funeral story. In an article on Chambers from the March 8, 1945, edition of the *Washington Times Herald*, the lead-in to the story quotes the talkative Chambers as stating: "To Embalm Elephant Would Cost $1.50."[42]

Others besides newspaper reporters began to mine the funeral business for insights into American social life and often to advocate for reforms in the middle decades of the century. University of Pennsylvania sociologist William M. Kephart, for example, wrote an article for the *American Sociological Review* in 1950 that described the costs associated with death and the importance of class in attitudes toward the funeral. In his study of the city of Philadelphia, Kephart found a number of crucial differences between the rich and the poor. Public viewing of the body was more prevalent in poorer families, lower-income groups usually participated in processions to the cemetery after the funeral service, and cremation rates were increasing among the rich.[43] In an effort to educate its readers about funeral costs, the June 1959, issue of *Good Housekeeping* explained that "What's spent [on the funeral] is in part a matter of personal choice, and families are often so carried away by emotion that they spend more than they need to. Advance knowledge about prices, and about what you are and aren't obligated to spend, can help reduce needlessly high costs." The piece goes on to cover prices for cemetery lots, explain the increasingly popular advertisements for "complete funerals," discuss whether cremation is actually cheaper than burial, and argue that, however burial costs are rationalized, they are often a tremendous financial hardship for families.[44]

Most of these critics emphasized the economics of death, and concentrated on spending habits to make sense of the American funeral. But many religious leaders, following the recommendations of Gebhart and other concerned citizens who advocated enlightening the masses, spoke out publicly against the funeral and the funeral industry during this period. Along with their outrage over the simple economics of the funeral exchange and the exploitation of the vulnerable mourner, they identified a more insidious and abominable threat appearing in American mortuary practices: paganism, or the misdirected religious glorification of the body during the funeral. The two-pronged charge of paganism and profiteering—both, in many respects, principally concerned with the symbolic and commercial values of the physical body—had cast a shadow over the funeral industry from the beginning of the century. Religious critiques of the American funeral, an integral element of most reform-minded publications, generally relied on a common set of arguments to educate their congregants about the dangers and demons, threats and temptations lurking in their local funeral home.

White Protestant leaders and Catholic priests—the dominant religious voices in American public culture in the first half of the century—took the lead in publicly denouncing the aberrant values behind contemporary American death practices. Like the reformers they worked with, many of these church leaders focused on the plight of the poorer segments of society and the costly extravagance displayed at their funerals. But many outspoken religious figures—especially social gospelers and others from socially active, liberal congregations—addressed the problem from the altar and in various church publications, arguing that the economic waste was only a symptom of a deeper spiritual crisis.

One of the most widely-reported religious challenges to the growing funereal "empire" came from a committee of ministers in Middletown,

New York. The Reverend Hugh Stevenson Tigner described the events surrounding the publication of the committee's final report on what constitutes a "decent Christian burial" in an October 13, 1937, article in *The Christian Century*. He begins by explaining the reason Middletown ministers banded together to take on local funeral directors doing business with their congregants:

> It was not, as one would naturally suppose, the economic aspect of current burial customs that drove us members of the Minister's Association of Middletown, N.Y., into a mood of rebellion, but the esthetic and moral aspects. We were not blind to the economic angle; we were irked at seeing a small empire of business interests fattening on death. But we were incensed at the funeral customs which cause every John Doe to view death with the eyes of an ancient Egyptian pharaoh. . . . The moral (or immoral) nature of the whole elaborate process of corpse disposal impressed us far more than the single incidental item of dollar cost.[45]

Tigner goes on to make the important point that most public attacks included—that not all undertakers are dishonest. Middletown ministers thought that, overall, they were "a decent lot of conventionally scrupulous businessmen."[46]

Not surprisingly, everything that "irked" the ministers was essential to the professional duties assumed by the funeral director. First, ministers were tired of the increasingly secondary role they played in funerals, complaining that, at the time of death, family members immediately called the local undertaker, who made all arrangements for the funeral before contacting the religious figure to officiate at the service. They argued that the institutional presence at the funeral was "too obviously a trapping"[47]—in other words, while ministers were performing a spiritual and largely otherworldly function during the funeral, too much importance was being given material, this worldly concern having more to do with broken social and professional relations and the imminent disappearance of the body than with whether the deceased was right with God.

Second, ministers interpreted the funeral scene as a pagan rite centered on worshiping the body rather than the soul. Clearly, they were operating within a distinctly separate mythological system from funeral directors. For these religious leaders, traces of ancient Egypt in American funeral

customs did not evoke a noble evolutionary schema detailing the originating point of contemporary death rituals, but instead conjured up fears
of heathenism, idolatry, and barbarism. As Tigner exclaims, "What made
us definitely sick, however, was the fact that we found ourselves continually acquiescing in a cultus of indecent barbarities, indecent and barbaric
despite the fact that it was known as 'decent Christian burial.'" Regardless
of how mourners experienced the funeral, Tigner and other displaced
ministers in Middletown understood the bottom line of these cultic
vulgarities: "ends in themselves," "triumphs of family pride and mortuary
art," and without "dignity or integrity." The most sickening aspect of
the funeral, they complained, was the presentation of the corpse itself.
Although he implicates funeral directors in the public's veneration of the
displayed corpse, Tigner acknowledged that, "a morbid desire to cling to
it" emanates from beyond the institutional reach of churches.[48] Indeed,
this desire also emanates from beyond the walls of local funeral homes,
even though it may find its fulfillment there. Its source is not the funeral
home, but the living families, where popular, religious attachments and
concerns for daughters and fathers, mothers and sons, sisters and brothers,
shapes ritual choices and ritual objects of domestic devotion not always
appreciated by the church.

The young ministers from New York decided to take matters into their
own hands and establish a committee to bring Christian decency to the
American funeral. Their recommendations, which strove for simplicity
and dignity in the disposal of the dead, called for the end of extravagance
in funeral ceremonies, excessive demonstrations of grief, and public exposure of the deceased. According to their eight-point statement, a
Christian should do the following to ensure a decent funeral: Dispose of
the body as quickly as possible ("We regard the disposition to cling to the
corpse of a loved one as something to be discouraged"); hold large funerals outside the home (preferably at the church or local chapel); close the
casket, and keep it shut for its entire public display (visitation with the
corpse should be either at the family home or funeral home before the ceremony); avoid music and singing (inconsistent with "quietness, simplicity and dignity appropriate to Christian burial"); the family should have
only one set of funeral rituals authorized by the clergy or fraternal order
("Two or more separate rituals being unnecessary, unseemly and bordering
on vainglory"); avoid scheduling funerals on Sundays, which are particularly busy days for ministers; let a friend follow the casket to the cemetery

to assure proper burial (processions and committal services are expend-able); and finally, ending on a strong pedagogic note, remember "'respect for the dead' and 'fine funerals' have no connection whatsoever"—no one ought to purchase expensive caskets, floral displays, fine burial clothes, or costly grave markers.[49]

While the document itself is significant—many eastern newspapers covered the story, bringing national attention to these religious criti-cisms—even more amazing was the public's reaction to the Middletown ministers. Tigner describes the local controversy as "red hot lava running down the sides of several craters," and remarked that "if an anarchist plot to blow up half the city had been uncovered there would not have been more hysterical talk."[50] Indeed, the "bitterly hostile" response reported by Tigner suggests an overwhelming popular repudiation of their version of a "decent Christian burial."

> Out-of-town clergy men were called in for funerals wherever the family would allow it. . . . others threatened to boycott the local ministers. 'What's the matter with you ministers?' the cry went around. 'Don't you want to bury the dead? . . . The omission of committal services—hmmmph! I don't want to be buried like a dog . . . Things were all right here until these young men came to town. . . . What do you want to do: drive all the people out of your churches?'
>
> Least of all did we foresee that the general business community would regard our action as bordering on the subversive.[51]

In this dark world where barbarism triumphs over true spirituality, where commerce is held as a sacred value, and the physical remains glori-fied over the future destiny of the soul, Tigner insisted, the light of the true Christian faith is absent.[52]

The effort at religious reform of the funeral in Middletown was not an isolated instance. Numerous religious calls for ritual modification were heard throughout the first half of the century, including a highly publi-cized statement from the Federal Council of Churches in the 1940s con-demning the commercialization of American funerals.[53] Catholics also voiced their concern about the state of American death rituals. In 1960, the Catholic magazine *Jubilee* published an article on the funeral business, reporting that "the morticians of America have given death a face-lifting such as it hasn't had since ancient Egypt."[54] The authors describe the typ-ical pattern that keeps funeral directors in business: The dead body moves from hospital room to morgue, then from the morgue to the funeral home, and from the funeral home to its final resting place at the cemetery. They also note more recent innovations in modern funeral homes of the 1950s, including the appearance of counselors to help the bereaved, the proliferation of bureaucratic forms requiring the funeral director's authorization, and of course, the omnipresence of that notoriously irreligious object, the embalmed corpse. "Modern embalming, featuring 'that alive look,' has enabled corpses to look more and more like window-display mannequins, and visitation with them has become quite popular."[55] The net effect of all these changes on Catholics and society at large? The claim was that Americans no longer really knew death, and they had certainly lost their fear of it.[56]

In the cacophony of voices claiming to explain American funerals, religious critics played an increasingly authoritative role. National magazines like *TIME* and *Newsweek* reported on public statements from various religious leaders and institutions, all expressing the same basic message to readers: The costs of funerals do not add up, a group of businessmen are profiting from the grief of others, and the religious sentiments behind contemporary American funerals are either misplaced forms of reverence or entirely absent.[57] One of the most important corrective steps they suggested to ensure the desired simplicity, quietness, and dignity, was not to wait to call your local priest or minister, but to include them from the beginning in the management of the ceremonies. Apparently, very few Americans followed this advice, and religious figures continued to play a marginal role in the details of disposal. Their critiques, like those of economists, academics, and other so-called authorities, got quite a bit of play in the media, but fell on deaf ears in local towns and neighborhoods throughout most of the United States.

The Empire Strikes Back

Despite the public challenges to their profession and their professionalism, funeral directors managed to insinuate themselves into the fabric of everyday American life. They were able to do this, in the end, because most Americans wanted the services they offered. Alternative perspectives on the place and status of the dead body—whether emphasizing the value of the corpse to the national family, advocating municipal control over bodies and the virtues of cremation, or glorifying the invisible life of the spirit over the visible remains of the deceased—did little to slow the impressive entrepreneurial spirit and downright religious sense of vocational duty inspiring individuals involved in the funeral industry. Indeed, the failure of their critics to change the details of funeral service or inhibit the national rise of funeral homes made people within the industry even more confident that the traditions they invented and maintained were pleasing to the American public. But they did not turn away from these challenges, nor did they attempt to cloak their professional duties behind a veil of secrecy. Whether they were reacting to national headlines or simply engaging in private conversations on the streets of their communities, funeral directors were able to establish lines of communication and civic participation that convinced neighbors and acquaintances they could be trusted to act responsibly, properly, and in the best interests of the bereaved when death struck a family.

This level of trust could not have developed without some degree of cooperation between the funeral director and local religious representatives, a critical institutional fellowship that rarely received attention in the media coverage more interested in scandalous funerals. While Tigner and many other Christian leaders experienced a profound sense of disempowerment as the mortician assumed total control over the organization and performance of the funeral in the first half of the century, local relations between clergy and funeral directors were also amicable and based on mutual respect and appreciation for their respective duties. In most funerals, both worked together to assist the family and each assumed their appropriate authoritative position over the body (funeral director) and soul (minister). While the media picked up on the very real animosity that existed between some religious leaders and funeral directors, when the local undertaker established his funeral home as a place of business, most church leaders were either complacent or actively supportive of the new venture. Evidence for a more harmonious relationship between religious institutions and funeral homes can be found in a variety of sources.

For example, throughout the early twentieth century numerous "funeral manuals" were published for increasingly busy clergymen who had precious little time to prepare religious services after receiving notification of death. These manuals brought suitable materials, such as scripture readings, prayers, famous quotations, and themes for reflection—often arranged according to age of the deceased—together in one practical handbook to help religious leaders provide an organized, appropriate, and respectful service without much extra work. They also often identified the division of labor during the entire funeral, and were clear about the centrality of the local undertaker. In one 1910 manual, *Pastor's Ideal Funeral Book*, Arthur H. DeLong writes in the section on "funeral etiquette": "The minister should understand that he has absolute control over the religious part of the services and that alone. The undertaker has charge of all other matters."[58] A 1918 funeral handbook for ministers covers a range of topics, such as "the language of door crepes," "notification," "the Sunday funeral," and "directing a funeral in the absence of a director," and clearly demonstrates who was in charge of America's funerals.[59]

Princeton theology professor Andrew Watterson Blackwood wrote in the 1942 publication, *The Funeral: A Source Book For Ministers:* "In matters relating to funerals the minister defers to the mortician as an expert in his art. As for morticians of the baser sort, the writer has had little experience. Those of the profession whom he has known best have been Christian gentlemen. Each of them has been glad to co-operate with any minister who is worthy of his calling. In his own sphere the pastor should be as skillful and careful as the mortician."[60] Blackwood was well aware of the controversies and scandals that engulfed the funeral industry by the early 1940s, and presents a completely different view on the undertaking profession than contemporary media coverage and more outspoken members of religious institutions.

In the religious publication, *Michigan Christian Advocate*, Pastor J. Douglas Parker wrote in his 1950 article, "How Pagan Are Our Funerals," that funeral directors are getting a bad rap in both the religious and secular press. Parker called for restraint in church criticisms of the profession, and even claimed that institutional interference in funereal affairs outside the religious service "borders on the dictatorial."[61] If paganism was an element of the modern funeral, Parker argued, it was not the fault of the funeral director. Funerals simply reflected larger cultural realities that ruled American lives. The failure to recognize these realities was a sign of corrosive church hypocrisy:

> I once heard a minister decrying the use of expensive caskets. His righteous indignation was considerably weakened, however, by the fact that he took great pride in encasing his own corpulent body in a new Buick for his work and pleasure. Expensive caskets and more expensive automobiles are simply a sign of our gadget-studded and materially dependent culture. Families take pride in caskets.

Granted that is the wrong emphasis, but so is our whole culture. When all Christians agree to take the chrome and luxuries off their automobiles, then we shall have a right to plead for simpler caskets.[62]

Parker is very clear about the division of labor in funerals, having served as a minister for 12 years and having buried his own daughter with the help of the local undertaker. Funeral directors do not preach immortality, but take care of the details of burial. According to Parker, cooperation, rather than "indulging in self-righteous criticism," is a more appropriate attitude for the clergy when participating in funeral ceremonies.

Writers within the funeral industry also became increasingly attentive to religious diversity and relied on authorities to speak for their traditions in various "funeral manuals" published for the consumption of morticians. Although morticians did not encounter much religious variation in the communities they served—Protestants buried Protestants, Catholics buried Catholics, and Jews buried Jews—crossovers did occur. Before the 1960s, the extent of this concern for diversity really covered two religions, Christianity and Judaism, and funeral directors made it their business to become knowledgeable about the internal variations in each. A complicated matter, but early twentieth-century religious leaders and representatives consistently provided intimate details for the improvement of mortuary services to the living. Funeral directors in large cities and fast-growing towns especially had to be prepared for a diverse clientele, and these manuals served as a quick reference guide.

In 1947, the State Board of Funeral Directors and Embalmers for Florida published *Funeral Direction and Management*. In 1935, the board had hired Anne Hamilton Franz, who had worked in the field of vocational education, to write, in effect, the primary textbook for the new state licensing examination, providing mostly young men brought up in funeral homes with an accessible overview of the mortuary field. Members of the state board indicate in the foreword that they believe, like many others attentive to the increasingly national, patriotic self-identity of America's funeral specialists, the mortuary information conveyed in the text is not really limited to state or region, but "applicable to the profession throughout the Nation."[63] In addition to sections on professional ethics, applied psychology, preplanning, cremation, shipping, and the intricacies of maintaining a funeral home, Franz describes "types of funeral services," which include the following headings: Catholic, Jewish, Protestant, and Protestant Episcopal.

In the acknowledgments, Franz thanks certain associations and individuals who provided substantial material for the book. In addition to various funeral directing organizations, advertising and marketing specialists, individual funeral directors, and accountants, local religious leaders receive thanks from the author for offering crucial information about their respective traditions. In each of the sections on the more ritually-rigorous Jews, Catholics, and Episcopalians, funeral directors are strongly encouraged to seek the guidance of a religious representative in the preparation of the funeral. But they are also placed on the same ministerial footing as the institutionally-recognized religious figure. The section on the Episcopal service explicitly states that the funeral director "too is a minister." The calm, sturdy demeanor of the mortician is a factor that can "bring about the peace so earnestly sought for in time of bereavement."[64] According to one of the rabbis quoted in the book, the mortician and he share "the sacred opportunity to bring solace to the grief-stricken."[65] In the face of greater and greater scrutiny of the industry, amicable relations and mutual support between religious institutions and funeral homes in this and other ventures signaled multiple levels of generally unreported communication and collaboration.

Many funeral directors today will speak with great admiration and genuine appreciation for the warm and considerate relations their fathers had with local clergy. Cordial friendships based on trust, common purpose, and admiration made for often pleasurable interactions. As the experience described by Tigner suggests, funeral directors had a great deal of popular support from local communities whose members had often known the funeral home family for a longer time than the increasingly mobile ministers moving from location to location. Bill Monday, a second-generation New Jersey funeral director, has fond memories of growing up around clergy and remarks at how relations have changed recently between the two local, generally trusted, social institutions: "We've had a wonderful relationship with the clergy. Our funeral home is next door to the parsonage of the Methodist church and we belong to the Presbyterian church a half a block from the home. Many of the ministers I knew had been there for many years. Today there is a transition—a minister might be here for four years and then is gone. In the past the minister I grew up with was in my church for thirty years."[66]

Wayne Baxter, a funeral director in Queens, New York, echoes these sentiments when reminiscing about differences between his father's relations with church leaders and his own today: "[In his father's day] the ministers at the two local Protestant churches were lifetime appointees. . . . The clergy would stay for twenty years so the relationship between the funeral directors and the clergy was great—they became friends. It is not quite the same today. Many churches encourage the clergy to move. I believe there is a seven-year rotation at the Catholic diocese in town. The local Catholic Church used to have six priests but now they only have three. They don't have time to go to lunch after a funeral anymore."[67] In the early and middle decades of the century, the funeral industry thrived in part because of implicit and explicit support from local religious professionals and institutions relieved from attending to the more corporeal aspects of death and disposal.

Personal letters from religious figures to individuals working in the funeral industry also suggest the potential for deep, trusting relations. One 1934 letter from Rex C. Kelly, General Secretary of the Young Men's Christian Association in Glendale, California, expressed gratitude to Hubert Eaton, owner of Forest Lawn Memorial Park, for covering the cost of a recent burial. Unable to get funds from the Glendale Community Chest, the "destitute widow" received an all-expense-paid American funeral. Kelly writes, "Please let me as a citizen representing our entire community . . . express our heart-felt thanks and appreciation for the manner in which you assisted this destitute widow in her time of bereavement. I could not think of a detail you left undone to be of service for this occasion."[68] Although serious fiscal abuses were found to exist among many undertakers, particularly in larger cities, numerous instances of charity—by adjusting prices, failing to collect unpaid bills, and simply not charging—were also evident, and endeared them to local religious representatives and church-going neighbors.

Along with religious leaders, the funeral industry promoted close, cooperative relations with two other critical professional groups who could have a real impact on American lives at the time of death: lawyers and government officials. The wide-ranging and complex legal issues surrounding disposition of the dead, and the strong institutional desire for as much self-regulation as possible, led to careful legal maneuvering and collective lobbying efforts by a variety of individuals and funeral-related interest groups. In Percival E. Jackson's intricate and comprehensive book,

The Law of Cadavers and of Burial and Burial Places, published first in 1936 and then revised in 1950, the "table of cases" contains a list of primarily U.S. legal decisions that is over 50 pages long.[69] Indeed, Jackson wrote the book originally to advocate the creation of a separate branch of American law, a branch exclusively focused on the increasingly complicated social definitions of, and responses to, death. Although covering a great deal more than funeral matters, Jackson devoted a considerable amount of time to the history of mortuary law and, in turn, the social standing of undertakers in America.

From the beginning of the century, the public rhetoric of this emerging class of self-proclaimed professionals relied on both a mythic sensibility and a modernist vocabulary. Most funeral directors argued that the necessity of their services was based on a variety of scientific, religious, and psychological facts of life. Many state laws and legal cases of the period, however, focused on one particularly disturbing fact of death: Corpses were dirty and dangerous. While embalming has never been compulsory, mortuary laws and state regulations generally recognized that undertaking—and the work of embalming—bears on the health of the social body. Quoting from one court ruling, Jackson writes, "The care of dead human bodies and the disposition of them by burial or otherwise is so closely related to the health and general welfare of a community that the business of caring for and disposing of such bodies may be regulated by license and special regulations under the general police power of the state." In many of the rulings, the corpse stands out as an unsanitary, polluted object that, from the prevailing scientific standpoint of the time, menaces the safety of the living community. Given this perception, the need for intervention from the "police power of the state" is not surprising.[70]

A number of newly-created state boards of embalmers and funeral directors—separate from the early state boards of health—began to appear in the first half of the twentieth century as well, paralleling similar kinds of professional requirements emerging in medicine and law. Many members of these boards were funeral directors, chosen by government officials because of their good standing in the community and their knowledge about ethical funeral practices. Their chief duty, however, was to administer examinations and grant licenses for undertakers and embalmers. The proliferation of mortuary schools in this early period, and the establishment of state and national associations of licensed funeral directors, led morticians to impose higher standards of knowledge and skill on those wishing to enter the funeral business. But even as more states began to require a license to treat and prepare a dead body for disposal—and most funeral directors and embalmers voluntarily abided by these increasingly complex regulations—numerous legal actions were filed against undertakers by dissatisfied clients. Shipment of the wrong body, breach of contract, negligent treatment of a corpse, underhanded pricing methods—these and a wide variety of other charges damaging to the undertaking enterprise naturally led to increasing interactions between lawyers and the funeral industry.

It was during this period that lawyers began to play an important role in the work of rehabilitating, on both local and national levels, the public image of the American funeral director. Indeed a lawyer from Wisconsin assumed the position of executive director of the National Funeral Directors Association in 1948 and served until 1983, an extremely tumultuous, but ultimately successful period for the industry. Howard Raether had been practicing law only six months when his professional life became entangled with the business of death in the late 1930s. Raether recently recalled how he made it to the leading position of the oldest and best known funeral industry association. As a drum major in a legion band, Raether got to know the group's manager, who was a funeral director, and his brother-in-law, also a funeral director and involved in the state association. A short time after opening his practice, Raether got a call from the state association: "More a public relations matter than a legal matter—and I handled it in Madison. That was in late 1939 and by December of 1939 I was hired as executive director and general counsel of the Wisconsin Funeral Directors and Embalmers Association. I've done nothing except work with funeral directors except for a four-year stint in the navy."[71] This professionally savvy, formidable lawyer became a crucial authoritative voice in the public debate over the American funeral. He played an integral role in crafting the national image of America's funeral directors and finding ways for the industry to explain to the American people the meaning and purpose of the final ceremonies.

Raether and other industry leaders worked diligently to convince the public that, when it came to death and disposal, local funeral directors knew what is best for Americans, and they were only giving the people what they wanted. With the help of professional allies in the fields of law and theology, many funeral directors found new and effective ways to explain their services to the American public. But funeral directors were often called upon to explain to state and national representatives why the American funeral did not require government interference, and persuade them that, in spite of some bad press, they worked in the people's interest. Although concerted lobbying efforts from people within the funeral industry would grow more complex and powerful in the second half of the century, intimate knowledge of government action bearing on their vocation led civically active funeral families, as well as state and national organizations like the National Funeral Directors Association, into the political arena.

Interaction with numerous levels of government increased over time, though by the 1940s the necessity to respond to the constant barrage of complaints and criticisms intensified collective lobbying efforts. Repatriation efforts in both World Wars also brought funeral industry representatives into contact with a variety of government agencies. The extent of this political involvement is suggested in one postwar report from the 1949 annual convention of the National Funeral Director's Association: "Realizing the importance for NFDA and its membership to the Federal Government, the officers and members of the office staff established and maintained close relationships with such governmental agencies as the Army War Memorial Division, the Mortuary Operations Division of the Veterans Administration, the Bureau of the Census, Selective Service, the Office of Civil Planning, the Social Security Administration, and the Small Business Division of the Department of Commerce." The report also acknowledged that the executive secretary's office examined nearly 9,000 congressional bills introduced that year, looking for titles that indicated any interest in the business of death.[72]

On the local level, funeral directors also demonstrated a keen awareness of any congressional activity related to their work, and lobbied hard when they saw their livelihood threatened by governmental intrusions. For example, in 1955, Sheboygan County dairy farmer and Wisconsin state Senator Louis H. Prange received letters from undertakers vehemently opposing a bill that would place limitations on funeral costs—for them a shocking betrayal of American democratic principles. George L. Wittkopp, proprietor of the Wittkopp Funeral Home in Plymouth, wrote against the bill, and implored Prange to make sure it did not succeed. "Knowing you personally we know that you would not support such class legislation, but we are writing to ask not only you to oppose the bill but to use your influence wherever possible to oppose it. . . . Bill 248-S is an unjust bill, not in the interest of the people and another step towards socialism."[73] Another funeral director expressed why the senator should oppose the bill: "We are definitely opposed to Bill 248-S, because it is entirely un-American, limiting one's choice to what the state feels is proper and just. . . . I am certain the public would be very much against such a law, in fact, those I have spoken to about it said it was ridiculous in this country to attempt anything like that."[74] In this case, as in many other cases when funeral directors expressed their wishes to congressmen across the country, the senator was persuaded by the arguments against controlling funeral prices.[75]

While funeral directors understood the importance of maintaining critical professional relations with local and national representatives, lawyers and judges, and religious leaders—relations that depended in large part on their ability to persuade them of their expertise in mortuary matters—most of their endeavors in the increasingly important arena of public relations focused on winning the confidence of potential clients who have a corpse on their hands. Indeed, from its earliest years, the funeral industry has devoted a great deal of time and energy to public relations, and much of the industry literature is replete with advice about how to reach out to the bereaved, understand the dynamics of grief, and provide mourners with a satisfactory, therapeutic funeral. By the second decade of the century, many industry publications began to regularly include articles on managing the public image of undertaking, focusing on everything from the layout of a casket showroom to personality tips for interviewing clients. Whether articles were specifically related to improving public relations or not, the publications arriving at funeral homes around the country provided a wealth of material for funeral directors to draw from in their drive to shape public opinion about why American funerals are valuable and legitimate.

These articles went beyond pocketbook issues, and covered complicated matters of the heart, head, and spirit, providing psychological explanations for the particularities of the American funeral for funeral directors to use in their interactions with potential clients. The psychological needs of the mourners became the primary concern, and began to overtake all other considerations in the profession's public rhetoric. Around mid-century, psychological factors also began to figure prominently in advertising, a point made clear in the 1950 article, "The Aim of Advertising." In an address before the American Institute of Funeral Directors, public relations specialist Dabney Otis Collins gave his advice on how undertakers might consider selling their services. (He begins with the stark truth of his field: "The objective of all good advertising is to sell.") Among other pointers, such as giving people facts, avoiding advertised quotes, and the value of restraint, Collins gets to the heart of the matter:

> Mortuary advertising, by its very nature, is most effectively done with emotional appeal—the appeal to the heart. Think of yourself—not as selling a funeral service—but as a giver of genuine friendliness and helpfulness. Picture your place of business—not as just a funeral home—but as a place where people come to you for solace in their hour of darkness.[76]

A variety of texts beyond industry journals gave funeral directors the language, rationales, and theories to legitimize their presence in the community and, more broadly, their integral place in American society. In spite of the dominant media narrative highlighting corruption and abuse in the industry, funeral directors developed their own "channels" for the dissemination of what they considered more accurate, truthful, and careful information about their work. For example, the Public Relations Committee of the National Funeral Director's Association began to produce pamphlets and brochures that were distributed to men and women working in funeral service who, in turn, were encouraged to pass them out locally. These publications were understood as helpful public relations tools that not only contributed to uniformity within the industry, but also institutionalized a shared language funeral directors could draw on to explain the values to be associated with American funerals.

One brochure called *Speaking Frankly: A Plain Talk about Funeral Service* (1940), is dedicated to the "earnest men and women" who have "conquered any distaste they might have felt and have endeavored to consider [death and burial] with the attention which so important a subject deserves."[77] In addition to the funeral director's Code of Ethics, this brochure attempts to provide the public with all relevant information about the modern funeral. When death strikes, it advises, call the funeral director right away, for he is best equipped to handle all the various responsibilities. It informs readers that individual families, not their local funeral director, should make the final determination about how elaborate the final ceremonies will be for the deceased. But it encourages the use of the funeral home for these ceremonies because of the distinct advantages it affords as an appropriate space to honor the dead.[78]

This brochure also addressed the question of costs head on. Indeed, it asserts that funeral directors are quite willing to explain prices to their clients.[79] In a section entitled, "What Determines Funeral Cost," an outline of some of the services included in the price of a funeral is presented to the reader. Details associated with death, such as filling out paperwork, meeting with family members, planning the funeral itself, finding casketbearers and making floral arrangements are specified. The preparation of the body is described as exceedingly complicated and requiring a range of resources and personnel. Rather than explicitly detail the embalming procedure, the brochure succinctly indicates why the dead are embalmed: "preservation, restoration of lifelike appearance, and compliance with sanitary and public health requirements."[80] The thoroughly modern nature is emphasized with and framed in technical, scientific language:

> The skilled embalmer of today, master of the science of derma surgery—a science similar to plastic surgery—is an artisan whose accomplishments far exceed those of the ancient Egyptians. Your funeral director will have a modern preparation room especially planned and equipped for its purpose. It bears a close resemblance to the modern operating room of a well-equipped hospital. It is immaculately clean and sanitary and those who serve within it maintain a professional attitude comparing most favorably with a modern hospital.[81]

Once again, readers are invited to compare their local funeral director with other professionals in the surrounding community who are trusted, valued, respected, and wealthy. In addition to the costs associated with treating the body, the brochure also informs the reader that managing a funeral home and maintaining the facilities also bears on the price of any funeral.

Finally, and perhaps most important, in a section describing the 24-hour availability of funeral directors, the brochure notes their philosophic and religious disposition, which could confuse the division of labor between clergy and mortician: "Your funeral director is a philosopher, who, because of his calling, has caught a glimpse of the Force which is responsible for existence and the Plan through which it operates. He is never an unbeliever because no man in such intimate contact with the experience of death can be an unbeliever." This intimacy with death, and with those who must contend with the loss of a cherished loved one, is said to imbue the funeral director with special qualities that make his position as the ritual specialist

managing the final exit of the body indisputable—at least for the authors of
this brochure. Like a physician or a lawyer, the brochure concludes, a client
must consult with her local funeral director, who will enter her home soon-
er or later to assist in the proper, respectful, indeed religious task of disposing of the physical body, and who will lift all of the burdens associated with
this task from those most affected by its painful reality.[82]

Another important channel for funeral industry public relations was
an expanding range of textbooks and manuals for mortuary school
students. These texts, read primarily by students and graduated funeral
directors, gave concrete information about the profession and the underlying justifications for the current state of funereal affairs in America. In
Successful Funeral Service Management (1951), Wilber M. Krieger discusses numerous facets of funeral service and, as the title suggests, how to
succeed in the business. Krieger states the peculiar predicament faced by
people involved in providing funerals: "Can you imagine entering a life's
work in a field of endeavor that no one (not even you) wants to think
about? That is exactly the situation in funeral service, because no one
wants to think about death."[83] But in spite of this cultural assessment,
Krieger makes it clear that by following certain managerial steps, a funeral home can attract business and become a pillar of public trust and admiration in any community.

In a chapter entitled, "How to Attract Business," Krieger asks the reader to remember four important points on the road to success:

1. No one wants to buy a funeral;
2. There is no way to have a sale to boost your business;
3. The best advertising program that anyone can design will not
create demand;
4. Funeral service is a personal service.[84]

In spite of the third point, Krieger moves on to a chapter devoted exclusively to advertising, a crucial medium for educating the public about the
integrity, value, and dignity of American funeral services. In addition to
newspapers, singled out by Krieger as "the most versatile of all advertising
media that are available to the mortician," other options for public promotion include visitations, billboards, radio, television and bus cards.[85] Krieger
emphasizes that visitations are the most productive form of advertising,
because bringing in organized groups, such as the PTA, local churches, and

various fraternities and lodges, will educate guests about the running of a modern funeral home. While the time lag between beginning visitations at an establishment and concrete financial results may be six years, according to Krieger, the value of showing guests everything in the funeral home, "even the broom closet," is instrumental in achieving success.[86]

Although television never ultimately achieved the role in funeral service advertising that Krieger had predicted for it, it would greatly affect the perceptions of the American people. Overall, television coverage has highlighted the sensational stories of greed and deception, and celebrated popular cultural representations of ghoulish undertakers entertainingly contaminated by their contact with the dead. But, occasionally, television has proven to be an ally in the cultural battle over popular perceptions of the funeral industry. In 1956, for example, the Los Angeles–based public-affairs program, "Dan Lundberg Television Show," devoted an entire episode to the cost of death. The June issue of *Mortuary Management* published a transcript of the show, which consisted of a half-hour discussion between Lundberg and five local funeral directors. In the introduction to the transcript, the editor writes that the program has a "fine reputation for the honesty and impartiality of its search into matters of public interest," and that everyone involved should "be congratulated for the exemplary manner in which they handled their subject, and for the fine job they did in presenting the true facts of funeral service as a dignified, essential and moderately-priced service to the public."[87]

The interview begins historically, with one undertaker remarking that American practices have changed drastically since the Civil War—principally because of embalming. Lundberg then clumsily tries to compare current costs to the economics of death in ancient history—a critical mythic trope in the funeral literature of the early century, but clearly not a topic on the minds of these image-conscious undertakers:

> Lundberg: We know, of course, that the Egyptians spent, nobody knows how many millions of whatever the unit of currency was, to inter and to glorify their dead and fix it so that the mummy would be in a great state of preservation to receive the spirit of his gods and thus the population itself went very, very hungry. . . . Are we spending per capita as much as the ancient Egyptians did?
>
> Llewelyn (one of the funeral directors): I have no idea of how it compares with what the ancient Egyptians did, Dan.[88]

Instead, these talking funeral heads focused on a range of issues, including a recent state legislative report—encouraged by funeral directors themselves—that rebuts recurring media attacks about the supposed high cost of dying. They also discuss the psychological and religious dimensions of funeral service, the educational value of advertising to spread fair information about funerals, the roughly 75 steps involved in planning a funeral, the importance of involving family members in these plans from the beginning, with open discussions of costs and the fact that the funeral business is like any other American business, grounded in the free enterprise system.

Patriotism, Not Paganism

At its core, the message funeral directors wanted to convey was simple: The funeral services they furnish respond to American sensibilities about propriety, respect, and honor in the face of death. In the course of developing this message, the industry invented what came to be known as "the American way of death." The true anchor of the American way of death was the visible, embalmed body, put on display either before or during the religious service. According to morticians, the people wanted to see their dead relations one last time, and they were the only ones qualified to give them what they wanted. From early in the century, funeral directors and others in the industry offered a variety of explanations for the presence of embalming in American death rituals. Most agreed on one central point that inspired the mythic imagination of funeral directors: Embalming is the bedrock of the industry, and secures America's place as the greatest nation on earth. If there is a religious impulse motivating the glorification of the embalmed body, it emanates from patriotism, not paganism. Its status as an inviolable, sacred object had as much to do with love of country as with the fine artistry of the embalmer or the popular sentiments flowing from the will of the people.

The Second World War provided another moment of public reflection on death, and on how the living understood their obligations to the dead. Even though the bodies of fighting soldiers were symbolically linked to the spiritual life of the nation—a process found in every American war—families demanded final control of the physical remains. The May 29, 1944, issue of *Newsweek* spoke directly to this demand. In a short piece called "The Soldier Dead," over 70 percent of the letters sent to the Memorial Branch of the Quartermaster General's Office were reported as sharing "the same note of painful uneasiness" in the questions they pose: "When is my son (or husband) going to be brought back home? . . . Can we bring him back ourselves?" The piece then informs the reader that, in fact, no bodies will be returned until the end of the fighting. In addition, the task—"worldwide in scope"—would be much greater than in the First World War. Noting several "facets of the delicate problem," the writer indicates that costs are presently being considered by Congress, that Arlington National Cemetery has limited space, and that Hamilton Fish, a New York representative, had introduced legislation to construct a "twin tomb" for the unknowns of this war. On the other hand, it is reported that means of identification have been improved with techniques borrowed from the funeral industry: "Means of identification and preservation are better in this war than in the last. An example of the latter: Soldiers killed in the Southwest Pacific are being buried in sealed metal containers, and in some cases even embalmed."[89]

But not in all cases. Ralph Turner, an Atlanta funeral director whose father established a funeral home in 1903, remembers when bodies from The Second World War began being shipped back to the states and cared for by his father. Unfortunately, many family members would not get to see what they hoped to when they received news of repatriated remains. The military "wrapped them up in a blanket or two and made a nice little package out of it, sealed it tight in a casket and brought it back home. The problem was that the families wanted to open the casket to recognize if it was him. They thought the bodies would still be recognizable."[90] Family members may have been disappointed by the state of the remains, but at least they secured domestic control over their final disposition thanks to the mediation of the funeral director who worked with the military and local families.

As in the First World War, support of repatriation was not universal, and a focal point for American suspicions about the program was once again the funeral directors involved in the "delicate problem." Public concerns regarding the true motivations, and profit margins, of local funeral directors received a great deal of attention, and led the funeral industry to respond with their version of the "true story" in the postwar years. In "To Each His Own: The True Story of Repatriation," published in a 1948 issue of the NFDA-sponsored journal, *The Director*, J. A. Shaidnagle Jr., and emerging industry-leader, Raether, argue that most of the money spent on disposal will go towards the purchase of a lot and cemetery expenses. Additionally, the government will provide the casket, so "funeral directors' charges will consist principally of those items incidental to the funeral service, such as delivery, newspaper notices, palm decorations, et cetera." More important to the profession's sense of pride and dignity, however, was the implicit challenge to a fundamentally American sensibility, that Americans do what they want with their dead. According to the authors, "We in America have certain traditions and customs which make up our American way of life. One of these is to have our loved ones buried on the family lot in the hometown cemetery or at a cemetery within visiting distance."[91] In other words, Americans want, indeed choose to be close to their dead.

Funeral directors saw themselves as ritual specialists who provided this service, and they have taken pains to justify their duties as representing deeply-held, unmistakably American values, such as individualism, democracy, freedom, and free enterprise. Over the course of half a century, their patriotic fervor raged in the face of criticism and calls for reform—and, of course, during warfare. Before the Second World War, W. N. Tumlin Jr., wrote in his essay, "The American Way," that a "pseudo-sophisticated school of philosophy which attempts to cast the black shroud of maudlin morbidity about funeral service" has begun to appear in numerous publications. Compared to the sentiment behind current funerary practices, he continues, the mechanized, systemized, regulated, insensitive proposals bandied about by these critics "is only a very few steps to the collectivist regimentation" overtaking half of the world. "Call it communism, naziism, fascism, or what have you, it all adds up to the fact that in these countries the desires, needs and wants of the individual—whether they be material or spiritual—command practically no consideration." Tumlin wonders if, considering "the tide of human events the world over riding the shores of the collectivist doctrine," the United States too might fall victim to this scourge.[92]

During and after America's involvement in the Second World War, the country became preoccupied with preserving the social body and keeping it free from corrosive political ideas. This concern translated into a culture-wide preoccupation with permanence, with making products that last and that consumers can count on. Milford, Michigan, funeral director, and well-known author and poet, Thomas Lynch recalls this era and the similarity of marketing strategies in the funeral business and the larger consumer culture at the time: "I can remember the notions of permanence and protection. I suppose this had to do with the postwar generation. Because war reminds people of impermanence, in the 1950s and 1960s most things were sold on permanence and protection [and] durability. Diamonds were forever. A piece of the rock. There were a whole set of marketing initiatives based on protection. Underarm deodorant, good life-insurance policies, good defense budgets. Sealed and protective caskets fit into this."[93] A 1944 advertisement for the Galion Metallic Vault Company vividly demonstrates this point. The illustration shows an American soldier peering out of a foxhole with bombs exploding all around him. The reader can only see his eyes and the helmet covering his head. The text explains: "Millions are learning that metal is the best protection."[94]

In much of the literature of the 1940s and 1950s, the fate of the nation and the protection of the dead were intertwined. For writers in the funeral industry, the easy slide from democracy to socialism to totalitarianism begins when funeral customs and other essential services, like health care, are considered worthy of state control. The tenor of their language depended on the political spirit of the times. The *Southern Funeral Director* published one of its "Editorial Outbursts" immediately after the election of Harry S. Truman in 1948. It reads, in part:

> The turn of our national election can mean only that a lot of unthinking and nonvoting people will be asked to accept a voters' 'mandate,' interpreted by victors to mean that this country is now 'socialist' in its thinking as is Britain. (Socialism is the first major step toward totalitarianism. Totalitarianism knows no state or national boundaries, denies the right of individuals to have religious conviction, to engage in an 'service' that isn't dedicated by, and the first revenue garnered by, the clique in power.)
>
> First among the American Institutions to be attacked are 'medical care' and 'disposal of the dead,' and if these fall, so may everything else that stands between rights of the individual and the power of political and military authority.[95]

By the end of the outburst, the author declares that patriots within the industry will do whatever it takes to defend the "American Way."

Of course the Cold War era only intensified the patriotic language emanating from the funeral industry. After *Collier's* published Bill Davidson's devastating attack on the business of death in 1955, the *American Funeral Director* published their response in an article entitled, "Truth vs. Fiction." It begins, "A well-informed news commentator once described Russian Communist propaganda as a 'skyscraper of lies and distortion built upon a pinpoint of truth.' This same definition might well be applied to Bill Davidson's article."[96] An organized conspiracy by socialist forces to destroy the American free enterprise system is articulated by H. M. Messenger, president of the Messenger Corporation in Auburn, Indiana. The industry journal quotes from his letter: "The 'Socialistic Planners' are laying siege to your business. The aim is to place all burial business in the hands of the State. . . . Your business is a natural for the Socialists to take over. . . . Because there are a few unscrupulous operators who charge more for caskets and funerals than the traffic should bear, the socialistic planners have a 'cause' and a sympathetic audience. . . . So, Funeral Directors, awaken! An enlightening, revealing public relations program is the need of the hour."[97] The message was clear: Outside political forces threatened to explode onto American shores, and when the government gets involved with the people's funeral, the end of individual rights is not far behind.

One of the most popular quotations among funeral directors is from British prime minister William Gladstone, who purportedly said, "Show me the manner in which a nation cares for its dead, and I will measure with mathematical exactness the tender sympathies of the people, their respect for the law of the land and their loyalties to high morals."[98] The treatment of the dead, and more important in the image-conscious world of public relations, the services for the living, were expressions of the highest American ideals. The fact that funeral directors were relying on the words of a British statesman to appeal to both religious and political sensibilities did not upset the seamless nationalistic rhetoric flowing out of the industry. In a 1960 editorial dedicated to Gladstone's quote, the political events of East Germany, "Communist-dominated Cuba," and Soviet Russia are read through the prism of denied funeral rights. By the end of the editorial, the author stresses the important lesson critics of American practices should learn: "The doctrine so eloquently expressed by Gladstone is a humane, civilized one; the dogma enforced by Kruschchev, Castro and their ilk are completely evil."[99] Unfortunately for the funeral directors of America, a more menacing force was about to burst into the public arena than evil dictators. Ironically, she too was a Brit, and her words, more than Gladstone's, shaped the public perception of the American way of death.

GOOD GRIEF! JESSICA MITFORD MAKES
THE *NEW YORK TIMES* BESTSELLER LIST

Then the door was open and the wind appeared,
The candle blew then disappeared,
The curtains flew then he appeared. . . .
Don't fear the Reaper. . . .
"Don't Fear the Reaper," Blue Oyster Cult, 1974

An Easy Target

The year 1963 was not good for the public image of funeral directors in America. A half-century of public scrutiny, skewering, and scepticism did not prepare undertakers for the fallout of Jessica Mitford's *The American Way of Death*. This book, contained just the right mixture of social criticism, witty satire, and scandalous exposure to make it a bona fide cultural sensation. Funeral directors had believed the ceremonies for President Kennedy would drown out the charges of corruption and abuse swirling in the media in the final months of 1963, but *The American Way of Death* did not disappear from public consciousness. Instead, it continued to serve as a lightening rod for public denouncements of the entire industry in the weeks, indeed the decades, after its release.

Her arguments resonated with a significant segment of the American population who had become quite familiar with the figure of the funeral director—as both a real person operating a local funeral home and, perhaps more importantly for public perceptions, as an entertaining stereotype haunting the American imagination. Mitford's book exploited popular American obsessions with death, money, and scandal, and reinforced clear cultural trends in the evolution of a funeral director stereotype. Despite desperate attempts to sway the public with heartfelt national campaigns, the funeral industry never would be able to alter the national image of the undertaker. For Mitford and many others, the undertaker turned funeral director turned mortician was easily cast in the role of heartless profiteer, confidence man, and social pariah. In the face of this stinging popular indictment, funeral directors fought to maintain their innocence and project themselves as noble public servants performing an indispensable community service.

They persevered in their futile attempt to shape popular perceptions, mounting numerous public relations campaigns to convince the nation of the gravity of their work. But try as they might, undertakers could not control the fate of their public image. As an artifact of the collective imagination, the stereotyped figure of the funeral director represented something completely different from the image crafted by media-savvy spokespersons, hired consultants, and civic-minded undertakers themselves. His presence on the stage, in novels, over the airwaves, on the silver screen speaks to the complicated set of relations between the living and the dead that were overtaking Americans in the early decades of the twentieth century, as well as to the familiar ambivalence toward corpse handlers found across global cultures.

As Mitford's book became a springboard for public attacks on the industry, funeral directors themselves had to respond to these denunciations and the cruel cultural depictions in popular media, and find a fitting public relations strategy that demonstrated the true social and personal value of their work to the people who really mattered: neighbors, acquaintances, and other local community members living in the vicinity of their funeral homes. To make the funeral a healing ceremony for the living and humanize the role of the funeral director in the face of such scandalous charges and damaging stereotypes, many in the industry began to embrace an additional role in their ever-expanding repertoire, a role originally avoided by early pioneers—that of grief specialist. In effect, funeral directors became integrally involved in an under-developed, though soon-to-be flourishing, field of professional expertise: the psychology of death. Despite Mitford's incredulous ravings about the legitimacy of the new "mythologies" surrounding the American funeral industry, grief therapy provided survivors with a new language in which to express themselves. It also gave funeral specialists a meaningful rationale that supported the logic of American funerals in general, and, not surprisingly, embalming in particular.[1]

Mitford portrays individuals within the industry as greedy buffoons whose inflated rhetoric about their own importance is the linguistic edifice supporting a deluded "dreamworld" completely disconnected from the true reality of American consumers.[2] In addition to textual evidence produced within the industry, Mitford draws on a wealth of anecdotal evidence, including her own undercover investigations into funeral homes in San Francisco, material evidence covering a range of outrageous funeral products, and statistical evidence provided by governmental and funeral-related agencies. It is a damning portrayal, characterizing the business, and especially the funeral director, as driven by profit and dependent on the fine art of deceit. The sweeping accusations were not based on a few cases of outright illegal activity, but instead on the general "outlook" of America's undertakers. In the foreword, Mitford clarifies: "The vast majority of ethical undertakers is precisely the subject of this book. To be 'ethical' merely means to adhere to a prevailing code of morality, in this case one devised over the years by the undertakers themselves for their own purposes. The outlook of the average undertaker, who does adhere to the code of his calling, is to me more significant than that of his shadier colleagues."[3] While individual cases provided Mitford with the most incriminating evidence, she is really writing about a pervasive, industry-wide ethic she found to be depraved, duplicitous, and deceiving.

Public reflection on the "average undertaker" has been a preoccupation from before the turn of the twentieth century, and continues to perpetuate the often humorous stereotypes about the disturbing work associated with disposal of the dead. Stereotypes do not emerge ex nihilo, of course, but arise in specific contexts and historical moments. At first glance, they appear to be rather straightforward and uncomplicated habits of thought, but with more sustained attention to their social evolution they lose their translucency. Rather than offering a clear-cut picture of Jews, or blacks, or the poor, stereotypes simultaneously reveal and mask changing social conditions and emerging attitudes within dominant cultures toward members of troubling, usually marginalized communities. They are often the product of real-life experiences, to be sure, but they also take hold in the popular imagination because of shifting power structures in society and unexpressed rage about outsiders who are felt not to deserve a place within "normal" society. Mitford undoubtedly recognized that, before the 1960s, Americans were already well-acquainted with a popular figure that automatically brought to mind the behaviors, motivations, and tactics of modern funeral directors. Even though these stereotypes made little impact on the daily lives of undertakers, they captured the public imagination and obliterated all the public relations efforts by the industry to humanize their work.

The stereotype of the undertaker has deep roots in Western culture, as Mitford points out in the opening chapter of her book: "[T]he Dismal

Traders . . . have traditionally been cast in a comic role in literature, a universally recognized symbol of humor from Shakespeare to Dickens."[4] Whether laboring in the trenches like the comical gravedigger of Hamlet, or exploiting mourning family members in the big city like Mr. Sowerberry in *Oliver Twist*, those involved in the "dismal trade"—a term that goes back to the eighteenth century—have been depicted in broad strokes as objects of ridicule, subjects for satire, and generally as cardboard characters who are both predictable and despicable. Americans were aware of these and other English and European variations, and some immediately saw the comic possibilities of deriding and capitalizing on the rapidly developing industry and, in particular, the master of ceremonies at the center of it. Not surprisingly, on the American scene a pivotal characterization that shaped popular perceptions for the entire twentieth century came from the pen of Mark Twain. In *Life on the Mississippi*, Twain describes a hilarious encounter with an old acquaintance whose life takes a happy turn after finding his "true" vocation as an undertaker.

Twain writes about this chance encounter after offering readers some saturnine reflections on New Orleans cemeteries ("It is all grotesque, ghastly, horrible"), the utility of cremation ("The adoption of cremation would relieve us of a muck of threadbare burial-witticisms; but, on the other hand, it would resurrect a lot of mildewed old cremation-jokes that have had a rest for two thousand years"), and the financial drain on a poor black family purchasing a coffin for their deceased child ("It cost [the father] twenty-six dollars. It would have cost less than four, probably, if it had been built to put something useful into"). Twain then describes his old friend J. B., whose appearance has changed dramatically since the last time they saw each other. No longer "sad and oldish," he is now full of "youth and bubbling cheerfulness" for one specific reason—he is making a financial killing as an undertaker.[5]

For the rest of the conversation, J. B. exuberantly describes his newfound profession as an extremely lucrative racket that has one crucial built-in assurance of success: Consumers will not attempt to bargain when it comes to the disposition of the dead. When Twain innocently asks about the market value of a coffin, J. B. sets him straight:

> There's one thing in this world which a person don't ever try to jew you
> down on. That's a coffin. There's one thing in this world which a per-
> son don't say,—'I'll look around a little, and if I find I can't do better

I'll come back and take it.' That's a coffin. There's one thing in this world which a person won't take in pine if he can go walnut; and won't take in walnut if he can go mahogany; and won't take in mahogany if he can go an iron casket with silver door-plate and bronze handles. That's a coffin. And there's one thing in this world which you don't have to worry around after a person to get him to pay for. And that's a coffin. Undertaking?—why it's the dead-surest business in Christendom, and the nobbiest.[6]

Consumers refrain from negotiating over the costs of goods and services in this unusual market, but J. B. suggests they are driven by a rather fundamental principle in a capitalist economy: competition with their neighbors. Contrary to the budding sense of national pride exhibited by early funeral pioneers, for Twain and many others in the "Gilded Age," the funeral was a particularly poignant display of crass materialism, class consciousness, and misplaced sentiment—a social embarrassment rather than an evolutionary triumph.

This undertaker also reveals a variety of trade secrets, such as why epidemics are bad for business rather than a boon. When an epidemic strikes, bodies are immediately interred in the ground—no funeral and no chance to preserve the body. J. B. then explains that consumers will pay outrageous charges for preservation and preparation of a corpse. Although the common method of preserving a body was to place it on ice, J. B. notes that a new method is on the scene: "embamming." Like many of Twain's characters, J. B. is a shifty, ambitious, callous, deceitful, and arrogant schemer. But he recognizes that the promise of embalming as a moneymaking enterprise is related to a basic irrational human wish: "You can mention sixteen different ways to do [embalming]—though there ain't only one or two ways, . . . and they'll take the highest-priced way, every time. It's human nature—human nature in grief. It don't reason, you see. 'Time being it don't care a dam. All it wants is physical immortality for the deceased, and they're willing to pay for it. . . . There ain't anything equal to it but trading rats for di'monds in time of famine." Although at the end of the encounter Twain insists, "I have not enlarged on him," J. B. is both realistic and larger-than-life, a figment of the imagination and an increasingly common fixture in towns and cities throughout the country.[7] Twain understood the social implications of the fledgling industry, and playfully satirized both the entrepreneurial spirit eager to capitalize on death and the popular desires making consumers vulnerable.

By the early decades of the twentieth century, the national image of the funeral director assumed very specific, even formulaic features that mirrored many of Twain's characterizations. The cultural dissemination of this public image, and its continuing resonance in the popular imagination, was shaped by a variety of factors, including social changes affecting the space of dying and death, the numerous journalistic exposés about the costs of burial, and the creation of a thoroughly modern diagnosis about death in modern America that was integrally linked to the undertaker: American denial of the reality of death at the time of the funeral. While these stereotypes, like all stereotypes, appear one-dimensional, they embody complex social, emotional, and religious systems of meaning Americans drew on to wrestle with the experience of death. In the first half of the century, the static image of the funeral director appeared in an incredible variety of media, signaling both the utility of the stereotype in provoking a response from audiences as well as the symbolic power of portraying his role as a mediator between the dead and the living.

In Thomas Wolfe's compelling first novel, *Look Homeward, Angel: A Story of the Buried Life* (1929), one of the most famous death scenes in American literature is followed by a pivotal encounter with the local mortician, Horse Hines. The book recounts the experiences of Eugene Gant, a lonely, alienated Southern youth on a journey of self-discovery. According to one critic, the novel is representative of Southern Gothic, a literary genre that includes writers such as William Faulkner, Tennessee Williams, and Flannery O'Conner: "It shares with other Southern Gothic works the significant elements of both Southern and Gothic setting (bells, darkness, wind, a decaying mansion, labyrinths, an abyss, and eerie music), a quest, imprisonment, a ghost, and themes of isolation and fear of annihilation."[8] The awareness of death, indeed the ever-present reality of death in Gant's life—early experiences in the boarding house where he lived, morbid obsessions about his own death and burial, his father's employment carving tombstones, and the cancer that is slowing killing him—contributes to the overwhelming sense of separation Gant feels in relation to others, but also ultimately becomes a condition for meaningful, even mystical self-knowledge and triumph over death.[9]

In this fictional setting, the figure of the undertaker assumes significance as both a conventional agent of comic relief and a surprising source for profound self-realization. Following the heart-wrenching death from pneumonia of Eugene's beloved brother, Ben, the action shifts to the local beanery, where gallows humor dramatically changes the tone and texture of the story. Here Eugene and his other brother, Luke, encounter the undertaker Hines while they are eating breakfast at the counter with other customers. As soon as Hines enters the scene he is immediately perceived as an opportunist looking to make a buck, even in the most tragic situation. "Horse Hines came in briskly, but checked himself when he saw the two young men. 'Look out!' whispered the sailor to Eugene, with a crazy grin. 'You're next! He's got his fishy eye glued on you. He's already getting you measured up for one.'" Everyone in the beanery ridicules the undertaker, who carries on his conversation with the two brothers without responding to anyone else. After promising Eugene and Luke that they will not recognize the body of their dead brother when they see it, one patron exclaims, "God! An improvement over nature, . . . His mother will appreciate it." Another one asks, "Is this an undertaking shop you're running, Horse, . . . or a beauty parlor?"[10] The undertaker inspires sarcasm, anger, and resentment in the beanery, but when the brothers do visit the mortuary later that day, he unwittingly sets the stage for what one literary critic identified as a crucial "epiphany" in Eugene's life.[11]

By the time he wrote *Look Homeward, Angel* in his 20s, Wolfe, who grew up in Asheville, North Carolina, had experienced many deaths, including that of his own father in 1922.[12] Like Americans throughout the country at the time, Wolfe also witnessed firsthand the emergence of funeral homes as the new institutional setting for managing the body between the last breath and final disposition, and the appearance of self-proclaimed experts who made a living organizing and overseeing the rituals of death. Wolfe's familiarity with these new institutions is apparent not only in his depiction of the crafty Hines, but in Eugene's reaction to the entire scene in the mortuary. As soon as Eugene enters the mortician's office, with its peculiar, funereal odors of flowers and incense, he is impressed with the changed demeanor of the man they had met earlier in the morning. His mind is also immediately filled with a range of images and thoughts that capture both the dread of having to interact with this man and the desire to leave everything in his hands:

How like Death this man is (thought Eugene). He thought of the awful mysteries of burial—the dark ghoul-ritual, the obscene communion with the dead, touched with some black and foul witch-magic. Where is the can in which they throw the parts? There is a restaurant near here. Then he took the cold phthisic hand, freckled on its back, that the man extended, with a sense of having touched something embalmed. The undertaker's manner had changed since the morning; it had become official, professional. He was the alert marshal of their grief, the efficient master-of-ceremonies. Subtly he made them feel there was an order and decorum in death: a ritual of mourning that must be observed. They were impressed.[13]

When the stuttering Luke asks Hines to help them pick out an "appropriate" coffin, what appears to be the mortician's true calling—salesman extraordinaire—determines his behavior with the brothers. In the showroom, Wolfe depicts Hines as fiercely trying to prove his sincerity ("I take a personal interest in this funeral . . . I have had business dealings with your father for nigh on to twenty years.") and as relentlessly manipulative with the grieving boys (after showing them the most expensive casket in the place, Hines tenderly advises: "There's no need for you to take that one, either. What you're after, Luke, is dignity and simplicity.") After giving the boys a break on a suitable casket ($375 instead of $450), Hines takes the brothers to the back room to see their deceased brother, Ben. What they see laid out on the table—a nicely-dressed, freshly-groomed body with a fake, artificial smile—is not Ben, according to Eugene, but only a shell that has been "tailored" for an empty funeral service by the sly mortician who, in the end, is "hungry for their praise."[14]

Indeed, Hines is shown as quite pleased with his work when his "fish-eye" lovingly rests upon the body—a pleasure not simply reducible to the promise of profits. When Luke stammers about the face being a bit pale, Hines springs into action, applying his technical know-how with cosmetics to bring "a ghastly rose-hued mockery of life and health" to the cheeks of the deceased. Hines is even more impressed with himself after this final touch-up, not because it will yield even more profit, or because of its potential to provide healing relief to the mourners, but because it represents the work of an artist: "'There are artists, boys, in every profession'. . . . 'Look at it!' said Horse Hines again in slow wonder. 'I'll never beat that again! Not if I live to be a million! That's art, boys!'" Instead of supportive exclamations acknowledging the artistic genius of transforming a cold, lifeless body into a natural-looking simulation of life and personality, Eugene bursts into a fit of both laughter and tears listening to the words of the "horse-faced" mortician. Although feeling a combination of pity and tenderness for the man,

Eugene is literally floored after he can no longer restrain the "dogs of laughter" that explode from his throat.

> Eugene staggered across the floor and collapsed upon a chair, roaring with laughter while his long arms flapped helplessly at his sides.
>
> 'Scuse!' he gasped. 'Don't mean to—A-r-rrt! Yes! Yes! That's it!' he screamed, and he beat his knuckles in a crazy tattoo upon the polished floor. He slid gently off the chair, slowly unbuttoning his vest, and with a languid hand loosening his necktie. A faint gurgle came from his weary throat, his head lolled around on the floor languidly, tears coursed down his swollen features.[15]

Wolfe blends comedy and tragedy in this morbid scene, especially as an immediate follow-up to the excruciatingly difficult treatment of Ben's final passage. Whether or not he ever read Twain's depiction of the happy undertaker, Wolfe masterfully brings Horse Hines to life as a self-absorbed, self-aggrandizing, obsequious funeral director worthy of both laughter and pity (Twain would certainly enjoy Wolfe's play on "jackass"). On the other hand, the encounter with Hines, and everything he represents at this confused, painful moment in Eugene's life, contributes to the profound self-realizations that come at the end of the novel. Literary critic John Hagan argues that this encounter "is a masterpiece of macabre comedy. . . . But it also makes a serious point, which can easily be missed, in relation to Eugene's discovery of his vocation. For when Hines attempts to give the appearance of 'life and health' to Ben's corpse, he is only trying to perform, in however bizarre and parodic a way, that very function of triumphing over time and death which belongs to genuine art itself, and Eugene, in crying out hysterically as he does, seems to recognize this fact."[16] Hagan contends that this episode, in relation to epiphanies that occurred earlier in the book when Eugene contemplated his father's stonecutting and reflected on Homer's poetry, leads to the climactic resolution of the protagonist's quest in the final chapter, after conversing with the ghost of his dead brother: Eugene's realization of his true calling as an artist.[17]

Eugene's initial thoughts upon entering the mortuary—how the undertaker embodies death, his knowledge of the unspeakable mysteries of death and burial, his repulsive intimacy with the dead, the contaminating effects of embalming, and his impressive professional management skills—hint at the emerging complex and contradictory attitudes of many Americans toward their local funeral experts. But in the end, Hines the mortician simply presides over a meaningless, misplaced ceremony that is portrayed by Wolfe as a farce. Eugene's thoughts during the funeral indicate the depth of his disgust for the whole scene: "To Eugene came again the old ghoul fantasy of a corpse and cold pork, the smell of the dead and hamburger steak, the glozed corruption of Christian burial, the obscene pomps, the perfumed carrion. Slightly nauseated, he took his seat with Eliza in the carriage, and tried to think of supper." Despite the integral role Hines plays in Eugene's search for meaning, and Hines's own estimation of his miraculous artistry with the corpse, Wolfe delivers a well-crafted and revealing lampoon of the new American death specialist. The final image of Horse Hines in the novel is at the graveside, before the casket is lowered into the earth: "Horse Hines bent ceremoniously, with a starched crackle of shirt, to throw his handful of dirt into the grave. 'Ashes to ashes'—He reeled and would have fallen in if Gilbert Gant had not helped him. He had been drinking."[18]

With few exceptions, from the 1930s to the 1950s, fictionalizations of the funeral director simply recapitulated familiar themes, and aroused the same range of emotions that included rage, humor, resentment, and ridicule.[19] The caricature also served as a vehicle for a thoroughly modern set of criticisms of the American response to death: too materialistic, too secular and too unrealistic. The undertaker embodied all the critique's of the industry, personifying everything that was wrong with American's perceptions of death and their choices about corpse disposal.

But even with the significant modern innovations in the symbolism associated with undertakers, in a very short time the stereotyped treatment of the funeral business had become old-hat for many. Before the English writer Evelyn Waugh published *The Loved One* (1948), his uproariously vicious satire of Forest Lawn in Los Angeles, California, he chose to submit the story to magazines in England and the United States. The London-based *Horizon* printed Waugh's piece, but it had already been turned down by *The New Yorker, Town & Country, Good Housekeeping*, and *Atlantic Monthly*. According to biographer Selina Hastings, Waugh was somewhat surprised by the reasons given by editors at *The New Yorker* for turning down his submission: "Far from being shocked by his sending up of Hollywood and of Californian burial customs, they felt this was stale stuff, had already been done before."[20] Roughly a decade after the release of the book, Hollywood brought Waugh's story to cinematic life. But the 1957 black comedy about Whispering Glades, a Hollywood funeral home, and Happier Hunting Ground, a Hollywood pet cemetery, was a bit too lugubrious for most Americans. Even with an inspired cast that included Rod Steiger, Jonathan Winters, and Liberace, the film never achieved much popular or critical success.

From the regional inflections of William Faulkner to the brutal cynicism of J. D. Salinger, the image of the funeral director in American culture became a cliché by the 1960s, familiar to audiences that clearly had mixed feelings about the growing communal presence of friendly, neighborhood undertakers. Americans had gotten to know the public face of the industry even better in the wake of the great communications revolution in the early decades of the twentieth century. Film, radio, and television brought new life to the image of the funeral director in ways that bent, but did not break, the mold established in literature. As mortality rates made death a less frequent occurrence in American households, and thereby reduced the number of family visits to the local funeral home, new forms of media ensured an ongoing intimacy with a figure most Americans wanted to avoid in real life. In many entertaining situations, the undertaker enters the scene to promote either laughs or gasps, sometimes a mixture of the two, but rarely to rally the audience in support of his morbid vocation. An exception to this general tendency is one of the most beloved and popular undertaker characters in show business, who originally appeared on the radio program, *The Life of Riley*. Digby "Digger" O'Dell—"the friennnnnnndly undertaker"—bent the stereotype in some positive ways for the funeral industry, but never really broke it.

The Life of Riley, a pioneer family sitcom on radio and television in the 1940s and 1950s, followed the antics of factory worker Chester Riley and his friend, Gillis. In each episode, Riley had to find his way out of a difficult, though hilarious, set of circumstances, while his family—wife, Peg, and children, Junior and Babs—egg him on, put up with his frequent gaffes, and generally save him from himself. Riley's loyal undertaker friend often shows up in the middle of an episode's zany predicament, dispensing advice and delivering some of the funniest, most memorable lines of the program, such as: "You're looking fine, very natural"; "In my profession, we have a saying: Never give up, though things look black, 'till a case is closed a man can bounce back"; and "Cheerio. I better be shoveling off." Riley affectionately calls Digby, "Digger," and indeed everything about the character—his name, his words, his purpose—is a macabre parody on the flourishing funeral industry.

But even though Digger provokes the audience's laughter, he still comes across as something of a comic villain. In one 1949 television episode, Riley finds out he has to have a tonsillectomy and enters the hospital trembling with fear—after all, the hospital has replaced the home as the place for dying, and is assuming symbolic weight in public reflections on death. Digger visits Riley, and with a sly smile and somewhat troubling manner, attempts to comfort his hysterical friend just before he is to "go under" and have surgery. After presenting Riley with a couple of gifts—a bouquet of lilies and the book, *The Good Earth* (accompanied by the line, "You haven't lived until you've buried yourself in a good book")—the friendly undertaker informs Riley, "When you're ready to leave this place, I'll be waiting for you." Soon the nurse has trouble getting Riley to move onto the stretcher, so Digger assists her and proclaims, "If anyone can help him to lie down, I can."[21] These lines are played for laughs, no doubt, and contain enough double entendre to distract the audience from the dark reality underneath Digger's occupation.

While many within the funeral industry managed to tolerate Digger, this character and other popular stereotypes betray serious public suspicions about the motives of men in the business of death and a strong discomfort with their presence in life. The underlying motivations of undertakers are made painfully clear when juxtaposed with those of another group of professionals who also face death on a daily basis, but whose actions are more apparently based on goodwill and benevolence: medical doctors. Despite their best efforts, morticians have never attained the same social standing and prestige as physicians, and the professional antagonism between the two death-driven occupations were often depicted in popular TV programs. An episode of the series *Dr. Kildare* aired in 1963 with the title "The Exploiters." In this story, a humorless undertaker named Mr. Brown is depicted as a resentful, indecent predator who uses every trick in the book to get the business of, and profit from, a helpless widow in dire financial straits.

From the moment the audience sees him on-screen taking names of recently deceased or soon-to-be dead patients over the phone from an accomplice in the hospital, Mr. Brown has the look of a corrupt politician and the disposition of a heartless swindler. The characterization is greatly informed by the well-known cultural stereotype as well as the portrait offered by Mitford in her publication of the same year. Indeed, the dialogue suggests that the writers had knowledge of her work. Mr. Brown's slimy tactics include taking control of the widow's insurance settlement (depleting funds that could have been used for her son's college education), suggesting that any attempt to economize would be an indignity to her dead husband (though he does offer to provide her with a funeral with no flowers, which she quickly refuses), and paying a visit Dr. Kildare's superior at the hospital to try to force the good doctor to desist from meddling in the widow's affairs. The chief doctor has a strong dislike for undertakers and chastises Mr. Brown for the rampant corruption in the funeral business, lecturing him about the lack of dignity in American funerals today in a harangue reminiscent of Mitford's polemic. In a stern, admonishing tone, he informs Mr. Brown that the funeral is "a time for reverence. I said reverence, Mr. Brown! Not a production with make up, men in mink-lined coffins, and recorded birdsong."

When Dr. Kildare later speaks with his boss about the incident, he laments the fact that, in spite of his genuine effort to dissuade the grieving widow from buying an expensive funeral, the disingenuous undertaker won the day. "You're up against something that's hard to change," the boss informs young Kildare. "It's a national habit. The average American family spends more on funerals than anything other than a car or a house." "The high cost of dying," Kildare sighs. "Yeah," the elder doctor concedes, "every year we spend over two billion dollars on funerals." When the young doctor asks if all funeral directors are like Mr. Brown, his more experienced superior assures him that every profession has its "hucksters" who exploit the poor and defenseless.[22] The ultimate moral of the story? It is only human to be vulnerable and irrational in a crisis, so friends and loved ones should not hold people in grief responsible for their actions. Mr. Brown, like Digger O'Dell, Horse Hines, and an assortment of other fictional portrayals of American funeral directors, is a one-dimensional stereotype who brings the high cost of death, and heartless exploitation in the business of death, into sharp relief. The "typical" funeral director—sometimes portrayed as laughable and buffoon-like, sometimes as malevolent and crafty as the devil—provided Americans with a convenient scapegoat for a number of dramatic changes in everyday life, including the increasing commodification of every rite of passage, such as birth and marriage. He also could be blamed for disturbing, though common, responses to death, such as the ambivalence and fear associated with the corpse itself, and the conflicted desire to see a pleasing image of the deceased before burial.

Like many before her, Mitford condemned the industry for making a business of selling services for the final passage out of this life. The impact of her condemnation, and the extent of its penetration into popular consciousness, depended in part on the power and accessibility of the preexisting undertaker stereotype. The CBS documentary, "The Great American Funeral," reiterated many of the charges contained in the book and further reinforced the notion that the stereotypes were in fact accurate depictions of reality. In his introduction to the now infamous funeral director's skit by Elaine May and Mike Nichols, Jack Paar said, "I saw Mike and Elaine perform a sketch based on their indignation at a particularly outrageous American custom, a custom which Jessica Mitford has since called the 'high cost of dying.'"[23] Once again, Mitford's serious and entertaining exposé struck a chord in the popular imagination and became the source for entertaining, though serious, characterizations in the media.

Working Against Type

Before Mitford's appearance on the *New York Times* bestseller list, funeral directors and others in the industry lived comfortably with the dissonance between their own personal experiences and the popular caricature of a mortician's life circulating in entertainment culture. Depictions in literature and on television may have reinforced popularly-held suspicions and ambiguities about the figure of the undertaker in general, but most community members throughout the country continued to support their local funeral directors, interacting with them in a variety of social settings, and even joking with them about the stereotypes being circulated. Georgia funeral director Jimmy Fletcher remembers fondly the Digger O'Dell character and how he never minded laughing with others about his chosen vocation: "I didn't mind somebody calling me Digger O'Dell. I thought it was a compliment."[24] Asked if he or his father experiences much social isolation as a result of the way funeral work is depicted in the popular imagination, New York funeral director Tom Kearns responds: "I don't think so. People tell jokes about us. I think a lot of the laughter is that people are uncomfortable. I think people who get to know a funeral director know that he is a decent guy like anybody else. Their friends are grateful that they can come to somebody they know well."[25]

Undertakers increasingly worked against "type" in the services they offered to grieving family members. In the face of mounting attacks and governmental investigations, the industry made adjustments at the local level and, as a result, continued to survive economically (so much so, that large corporations soon realized the potential value of controlling the disposition of corpses and began to buy into the business). Still, the public face of undertaking could not be touched up by image-conscious industry insiders, even though various funeral-related organizations attempted to address these public relations problems. While many pro-industry figures attacked Mitford as a subversive communist out to destroy both the free market and the Christian religion, many others tried simply to ignore the furor created by Mitford's book and denied that any actions taken to improve public perceptions of the American funeral had been inspired by it. So, for example, when two national funeral directors' associations announced the creation of a new code of ethics that specifically required full disclosure of funeral costs to grieving families in advance, spokesmen for both organizations refused to give Mitford's critique any credit.[26]

By mid-century, many funeral directors began to see the advantage of playing against the stereotype and tried to introduce themselves and their homes to local residents when they were not in the midst of grief. Real-life funeral directors were generally well-liked, even though the point of reference for most Americans was a heartless, often ghoulish figure preying upon vulnerable mourners. Many were quite active in the community and local civic organizations. Wayne Baxter remembers that, for his father, and before the rise of home entertainment, "clubs were important. He was a member of all these clubs—you were more social and knew the community more."[27] New Jersey funeral director Bill Monday recalls his father's involvement in community affairs, communal appreciation for his work, and the response to his unexpected death:

> He was a fireman. He was a charter member of the Elks Club, . . . made up of businessmen and professionals in the 1920s and 1930s. [Later, he was] in the Masonic order. . . . The nicest thing and the thing that keeps us in business is the fact that a family keeps coming back. If a family has a doctor or dentist, they also have a funeral director. One expression [of gratitude] that stands out in my mind is that my dad died suddenly in 1961 of a heart attack and there was a wonderful outpouring of love by people within the community and families that he served. He had been here his whole life. People don't stay in one place anymore.[28]

Popular stereotypes entertained the public, but day-to-day interactions with local undertakers and their families ensured that these images did not deter neighbors, friends, associates, or less familiar clients from entering the funeral home for assistance when someone close died. Despite the national attention on corruption in the business, most undertakers were confident that, given the chance, they would exceed consumer expectations shaped by popular stereotypes and provide family members with a meaningful funeral ceremony. In 1971, *Casket & Sunnyside* carried the essay, "Does the Funeral Director do the 'Devil's Work?'" by Donna Pelzel, who wrote about her eye-opening visit to a local funeral home in Clovis, New Mexico. Inspired by a child's question regarding the size of the casket for a classmate killed by a car, Pelzel drove around her neighborhood to find the funeral home that "looked the least forbidding" to tour. Her encounter with the proprietor was a great surprise: "Meeting the funeral director, Dexter Todd, who began work in the Steed-Todd Home in 1942, and bought an interest in it in 1965, was the first of many surprises in store for me. Mr. Todd was a far cry from the Boris Karloff type of person I had expected. He was tall, handsome, soft spoken, and, as I later discovered, a very religious man who spoke of God in the highest manner." Thanks to the child's question, Pelzel informs the reader, she is no longer under the sway of the conventional restrictions inhibiting open conversation about the truth of funerals: "I lived with the concept that the funeral director is an abnormal man who does the work of the devil, and most people in my area take the position that death is a very taboo subject—rarely to be discussed by anyone. I would probably still be living under these concepts if it weren't for a small eight-year-old boy I know who has a knack for asking questions." What truth does she report learning from this liberating visit? That funeral directors are not interested in the choice of casket made by bereaved family members (children's caskets are housed in a separate room from the main display area), and that cosmetics and lighting play a key role in the lifelike appearance of the deceased (in some states, she is informed, cosmetics are not used at all).[29] Unfortunately for the industry, Pelzel's genuine awakening to the chasm between popular depictions in the media and real life was not echoed in media storylines about the American funeral.

A disjuncture between public perceptions of the funeral director and personal experiences with him characterizes American views for most of the century. Robert Fulton, a sociologist who wrote frequently on death and funerals, explores the contradictory nature of American attitudes toward the funeral director in his 1960 study, "The Sacred and Secular: Attitudes of the American Public toward Death, Funerals, and Funeral Directors." In this sociological investigation, Fulton reports on responses to a questionnaire mailed to over 10,000 Americans. When it comes to undertakers, Fulton claims, a majority of Americans had a favorable impression of theirs. Additionally, speaking to the persuasive power of the media, Fulton discovered that "more people think the funeral director exploits or takes advantage of a family's grief than say they have personal knowledge of such incidents."[30] Fulton argues that the public's ambivalence about the entire experience of death produces the social and cultural conditions to transform the figure of the undertaker into a scapegoat.

> The public may feel hostile toward the funeral director because of the role he plays. The guilt generated by desire on the part of the bereaved to rid themselves quickly of the body, and by the death itself, the possible confusion and anxiety in the selection of the "right" casket, and the attitude toward the funeral director as the constant reminder and associate of death, prompt the public to lash out at him.[31]

In the battle over their public image, however, funeral directors were simply no match for Jessica Mitford. The success of her book marked a new era in the history of American funerals, and significantly altered the everyday, real-life world of funeral homes, allowing the stereotype to infringe on reality as never before. While many reformers and critics had made very similar accusations in the past, often using the same combination of shock, sarcasm, and sensationalism, Mitford convincingly incorporated the deeply-rooted stereotype into her journalistic exposé and, in turn, brought new life to the cultural vitality of the popular representation. Funeral directors were consoled by reading about the eye-opening experience of Pelzel, as well as by their own personal encounters with neighbors and customers. In one fell swoop, however, Mitford had persuaded the public that the stereotype was indeed the reality. The case she presented, and the dominant storyline of media reports supporting the familiar charges, led to massive changes in the rules and regulations governing disposition of the dead, as well as the range of choices available to consumers.

Rather than exert too much energy fighting the deeply entrenched (and now culturally vital), stereotype, funeral directors focused their attention on a new, emerging area of expertise that would solidify, at least in their own minds, their total control over the experience of death, and bolster their sense of value for the services they offered. Grief therapy, lambasted by Mitford as a term "conveniently elastic enough to provide justification for all of their dealings and procedures,"[32] had begun to acquire a great deal of social currency within the industry by the early 1960s. After the publication of her book, it gradually became a central and highly touted professional service that could soften the hard edges of the popular image, and greatly strengthen the logic for turning to the local funeral director at a time of disorienting psychological trauma. In an era of virtual silence on the subject of grief, undertakers increasingly relied on psychological theories to justify their traditional funerals. These theories, invented and propounded by funeral men and women who had no training in psychology (until mortuary colleges began including psychology courses in the curriculum in the early 1950s), were completely new perspectives on the status and meaning of grief in American lives.

Face-to-Face with the Truth: A Psychology of Death, Memory, and the Body

During the middle decades of the century, funeral directors began to understand the ceremonies they arranged for their clientele in a new way. Funerals served the public good because they were sanitary, civilized, and religiously sanctified, according to industry commentators and national organizations. But in time, morticians realized that in addition to the purely social benefits of embalming, dressing, and presenting a corpse in a home away from home, modern funeral traditions offered distinctly individual rewards as well. Drawing from the increasingly dominant therapeutic language taking hold in popular psychology, theology, and other arenas in American culture, funeral directors and funeral industry supporters from the 1930s to the 1950s articulated a new way to speak about grief that shaped American sensibilities about living with death. This idiom framed the funeral as an instrument of psychological as well as spiritual healing for survivors, and the viewable body was defined as the active agent in the eventual triumph over the pain of losing a loved one. It was a moment to confront the reality of death, by looking in the face of the deceased without seeing the unsettling signs of decomposition, and thus begin the process of working through personal grief by creating a living memory. Many began to believe that the skills of the embalmer, and especially his "artistic" cosmetic touches, could minister to the bereaved and rescue them from a lifetime of psychic damage. According to the industry, failure to gaze upon the remains of the deceased leaves those in grief susceptible to a range of debilitating psychological effects.

At the very time funeral directors were propagating this logic—to themselves in industry literature, and to the customers who entered their homes—outspoken critics blamed them for producing a psychological and cultural environment that was, in fact, detrimental to healthy grieving. Critics commonly referred to the undertakers' own words, and particularly their growing reliance on euphemisms to identify the ways in which people in the undertaking business were distorting the reality of death and preventing people from taking a more stoic, realistic, and rational approach to their grief. Elmer Davis pointed out as early as 1927 in *The American Mercury* that the recently invented label, "mortician," indicates the perverse cultural influences resulting from changes in language: "Death grins out from the very word, but it seems to be bad form for a bearer of that title to mention death in any other way. This ritual reticence, this indirection, this avoidance of words of ill omen suggests the Neolithic savage; it seems a deliberate revival of primitive tabus."[33] Beyond the evidence of shifting linguistic terminology—from "coffin" to "casket," "hearse" to "coach," and so on—numerous commentators focused on the embalmed body to convince the public that any healthy response to the loss of a close relation was being thwarted by an industry built on concealing the true realities of death and awakening irrational superstitions in the poorest segments of society. Rather than encouraging healthy grieving, selfish funeral directors really were promoting pagan forms of religion and keeping the reality of death hidden behind a grotesque mockery of cheap surgery and cosmetic artifice. What could be more unhealthy for the mourners?

Mitford correctly identified the prominent role "grief therapy" played in the ongoing efforts to legitimate the form and function of the American funeral by people within the industry. She also presents a devastating critique of the "patently fraudulent claims of undertakers" that psychological healing will follow a well-executed, traditional funeral ceremony that includes viewing the embalmed and carefully presented body of the deceased. Although Mitford disregards the "specious claims of those who peddle grief therapy to the grieving,"[34] many inside and outside the industry contended that funerals could provide psychological relief to mourners, and that as modern ritual specialists who control the final disposition of the body, funeral directors were particularly well-positioned to play an integral role in this relief. At the very least, her analysis revealed the rather peculiar state of grief in American culture at the time, and the confusion around its value in the lives of busy, hard-working Americans.

In *American Cool: Constructing a Twentieth-Century Emotional Style,* historian Peter Stearns offers a brief cultural history of grief in the first half of the twentieth century. He argues that near the end of the nineteenth century modern sensibilities overtook Victorian preoccupations with grief and transformed the way Americans mourned their dead. No longer an emotional time to wallow in suffering and sorrow, the moment of death, according to modernists, should be a time of certitude, self-control, and objective rationality. By the First World War, science had authorized new perspectives on death and dying that gradually displaced dominant Christian fears and attitudes. Scientists advanced a straightforward, realistic view of aging, dying, and decomposition, and promoted the argument that the moment of death, regardless of the individual's condition, was actually pleasurable rather than painful. With this enlightened knowledge and a growing faith in the wonders of medical science to unravel all of life's mysteries, including death, Americans were encouraged to let go of grief and get on with life when death strikes a friend or family member.[35]

According to Stearns, the First World War produced a short-lived flurry of popular commentary reaffirming these modernist views: "This event, which might have prompted a return to older notions of the comfort and bonding qualities of grief . . . in fact served in most public commentary as yet another sign of grief's misplaced, even offensive qualities."[36] The growing cultural tendency to interpret expressions of grief as unhealthy symptoms of psychic imbalance dominated most discussions of the topic into the 1920s, when it virtually disappeared from the public eye. From the 1920s until the 50s, Stearns writes, "discussions of death and emotional reactions to it seemed out of bounds, either not worth pen and ink or too risky to evoke. . . . The contrast between the 1890s–World War I decades, when active discussion was almost an essayist's staple, and the subsequent cessation of comment was genuinely striking."[37]

One exception to this silence was a pioneering empirical study of grief by psychiatrist Erich Lindemann in 1944. In "Symptomatology and Management of Acute Grief," Lindemann studied 101 bereaved people, including some who had lost a loved one in the Coconut Grove nightclub fire in Boston, which killed close to 500 people after a football game between Harvard and Yale in 1942.[38] While this was one of the first social-scientific studies of grief ever produced in the United States, the topic did not strike a chord in the field of psychology until the late 1960s and early 70s.[39]

Stearns identifies an "antigrief regime" operating in middle-class America during the middle decades of the century and sees its manifestation in a variety of social trends. Although an occasional article reinforcing modernist views appeared in print here and there, the overwhelming silence on the topic soon after the war demonstrated a prevalent aversion to displaying grief and a tendency to see it as a form of pathology. Additionally, the growing cultural dominance of the therapeutic model, based primarily on Sigmund Freud's psychoanalytic theories, championed emotional detachment and overcoming grief as soon as possible. In many ways, Freud instigated the pathologization of grief and popularized the theory that a mourner's ego must become free of its attachment to the deceased to restore psychic balance. And finally, in Stearn's analysis, the changing content of advice books written for parents advocated careful avoidance of the subject of death with their children. If it had to be broached at all, parents were advised to discuss it as dispassionately as possible.[40]

Stearns briefly mentions how funerals factored into the early arguments against grief, and that economic good sense, minimal ceremonial observance, and emotional restraint were espoused as modern values that could defeat the morbid, exploitative, and heartless maneuvering of funeral directors who profited off of excessive, uncivilized emotions.[41] Although Stearns is correct in pointing out the striking public silence about grief in popular magazines and journals after the war, a chorus of voices emanating from industry literature began to promote their own psychological theories about the funeral and grief, and the steps one can take to experience healthy grief when faced with the heartbreaking loss of a close friend or relation. These views did not make it into popular media, but internally trickled down and transformed the thinking, language, and posture of America's death specialists. In the early decades of the century, chemical companies began to rely on psychological rationales to promote their embalming fluids—advertisements produced by these companies linked the last look, the memorable image, full apprehension of the reality of death, and meaningful healing. Over time, funeral directors embraced grief as a perfectly natural area of expertise that further legitimated their authority over the final passage and enhanced the ritual value of modern American funeral traditions. If Stearns is correct, they were the only ones who were interested in talking about grief—among themselves and to those struggling with death—until Mitford finally brought the matter to the American public.

Funeral directors lived with grief, but many others working within the industry, and especially those involved in manufacturing embalming chemicals, were writing about the crucial importance of embalming and a pleasing last look at the deceased in both artistic and psychological terms early on in the century. Indeed, the cosmetic dimension of embalming, concentrated on bringing the facial features of the deceased to life, came to be called a "restorative art." This dimension did not lead to a denial of death based on fear, as critics charged, but rather to a safe, humane confrontation with death's undeniable reality. Embalming allowed survivors an opportunity to look death square in the face and, in its still silence, recognize life's finality without experiencing the destabilizing terror and dread typically associated with corpses and the processes of dying. One early writer casually made the connection between visual imagery of the deceased and consolation for survivors: "Humanity, being socially and sentimentally minded, derives a great deal of mental satisfaction from mental images. The last view of a departed one may bring consolation if evidences of disease and suffering have been eradicated."[42] Commenting on the artistic elements of embalming, and how embalmers aspire to what many artists strive to achieve—an idealized representation of a reality no longer present, in this case a living person now dead—a well-known educator in the field writes: "The rebuilding of features is really a work of art. It all is the work of an artist and requires the technic of an artist to fully perform this feat. . . . In every human face there are certain points that are essential and that we must bring out if we would produce a face that is in any degree natural. . . . We must not see the face before us, but the face we would have before us."[43]

Funeral directors lived and died by the face. Their livelihood depended on whether friends and relatives recognized the deceased, on whether mournful pilgrims were satisfied with their last encounter with the material frame. From the beginning of the century, research and development in embalming chemical companies, educational improvements in mortuary schools, and private experiments with surgical techniques, all looked for ways to improve the facial features of the dead so the living will have a satisfactory experience at the funeral and a pleasant last memory of the physical appearance of the deceased. The epitome of a successful funeral was one with an open casket and an embalmed body that appeared familiar and nonthreatening to visitors. Significant increases in accidental and work-related deaths, as well as the appearance of new forms of disease that decimated the body, led early embalmers to experiment with reconstructive surgery on the cadaver. Indeed, an entirely new form of surgery emerged in the first half of the century that relied on surgical interventions and innovative artificial manipulations, including most importantly the artistic cosmetic touch to restore the face of the dead individual and, many believe, save the living from painful morbid consequences.

In a trade article on the state of embalming in 1921, Thomas Hirst identifies this important development, as well as situations in which these kinds of efforts should definitely not be pursued: "Demi-surgery is a name given the art of restoring mutilated features in accident cases or in cases where a cancer has eaten part of the face away, or maybe a bullet or stab wound. . . . I have seen and done many wonderful things by resorting to demi-surgery, such as making a new upper lip, cutting out a cancer on the face and filling it in to match the other side, but if the head is crushed, nothing can be done and it is better that the body not be viewed." The principal aim of the artistic reconstruction? "Proficiency in this field of endeavor will enable the mortician to improve one of his greatest services to the public, and that is the alleviation of grief."[44] Funeral directors and embalmers understood their duties as a moral imperative with real therapeutic results: Laying hands on the body of the dead for the relief of the human community was not only the basis for an economic transaction, it was also an ethical, religious duty that eased the pain of those in mourning.

Embalming chemical companies were particularly invested in promoting a connection between successful embalming and successful psychological recuperation—increasingly confident that a natural-looking corpse would not only ease the suffering of the grieving family as a healing balm for memory, but also be a potential source of good public relations with the local community. In one advertisement from 1928, for example, an embalming fluid company asks what becomes the key question of any self-respecting funeral director: "Shall the last picture become a comforting memory?"[45] This is indeed the crux of the matter. From early on, the industry was built on rhetorical and ritual links between the last look at the body, the creation of a lifelong memory image, the realization that death really has happened, and meaningful healing through the funeral experience. The production of a memorable corpse, therefore, required a delicate balance of capturing both life and death in the features of the departed: The funeral director must present a body that simultaneously captures a living personality and forces the living to confront the fact of death.

One of the major fluid companies took a novel approach in expressing the supreme value of the embalmed body for funeral directors who depend on return business and for mourners who must now grapple with their feelings of grief. A bulletin entitled "The Man of the Hour," one of a series in the *Champion Expanding Encyclopedia of Mortuary Practice*, was published by the Department of Service and Research, a division of the Champion Company, and distributed to funeral homes throughout the country. It begins:

> He is the dead man. Although his tongue be silenced, this is his hour. He may have been a timorous soul while here, but now he has become a hero. . . . He may have been a liar, but the message he speaks in death is true. Regardless of his character, he will have an audience. His audience will be small or large in proportion to his few or many friends. They will be impressed by the truth of what he is saying and he is talking about you, to whom the duty of preparing his remains have been entrusted. . . . You cannot refute his message if its unfavorable to you. If he has praise for you, it is worth more than all the advertising space you can buy.[46]

The author goes on to imagine a scenario in which the customer is unsatisfied with the appearance of the body (with the body "speaking" to the audience, sending such messages as "Look at my swollen neck and cauliflower ears!"). Positive word-of-mouth about the corpse after the funeral is clearly a critical element in the success or failure of a funeral home, according to this bulletin. If the skills of the embalmer allow the body to communicate to the audience, "I present to you a picture of me that is a true resemblance of my healthy, vigorous condition when were so closely associated," the rewards will come both to the funeral director, who will have an increase in future business, and to the mourners, whose memories will be sufficiently comforted by their last look at the restored body. The author imagines the dead body saying to the living viewers, "Even though I have been dead for several days, there is no odor to remind you of unpleasant things. Such indeed, is the memory of my appearance that I would have you carry, and this you owe to the man who was responsible for preparing my body for burial. . . . He realized that his greatest obligation was to present my remains, for a last view, in such a condition that my appearance at the time would alleviate some of your sorrow, rather than increase it."[47] Although others claim the funeral director's greatest obligation is to the bottom line, the reality for many within the industry is that it refers to a more serious calling that is, for the living relations, psychologically a matter of life and death.

One of the earliest textbooks to focus exclusively on psychology and funerals was written by Edward Martin, a Colorado mortician. His book, *Psychology of Funeral Service*, published in 1947, boldly proclaimed in the preface that "Whether he realizes it or not, every successful mortician is successful in the application of psychological principles. The foundation of the funeral-service profession is embalming and the basis of financial profit is merchandising. But the entire public relations program upon which every funeral establishment depends for its continued existence rests upon the soundness of the psychological practices of the management and personnel of that mortuary."[48] Chapters cover a range of related topics, including "The Nervous System and Glands," "Learning and Memory," "Adjustment to Mental Conflict," and "Psychology in Action." Without any formal training in psychology, Martin and others in the funeral industry based their theories on personal and highly professional experiences with their grieving customers. These work-related experiences which are embedded in the very fabric of a morticians daily life, led Martin to unabashedly declare in an earlier article, "The new funeral director is a Doctor of Grief, or expert in returning abnormal minds to normal in the shortest possible time!"[49]

Not surprisingly, the appearance of the embalmed body is the cornerstone of Martin's pseudo psychology; the impression left by this vision—the "memory picture" promised by chemical companies—will determine whether those affected by the death of loved one eventually overcome their grief. "We know that people are generally emotionally upset when they call us for our service. It is our purpose as morticians to give to those we serve a memory picture of their tragic experience that will leave them with comforting thoughts in the years to come."[50] A comforting last look at the body was understood by Martin as psychologically healthy for the individual and, like so much in the funeral industry, ultimately an expression of religious sentiments that had evolved over time. Taking on critics of the traditional funeral and the central role of embalming, Martin explains:

> Our American burial customs were not devised by funeral directors or by anyone else. They grew up over thousands of years, stemming from many different religions, lands and ages. . . . They are deeply rooted and founded on tradition. . . . Even though some such customs may seem pagan or grotesque to an outsider, let him not forget that these customs afford comfort to those persons who are the most concerned directly with the funeral, the heartbroken family of the deceased.
>
> This sentiment as expressed in the reverence shown the dead is the spirit which has brought about present-day American funeral standards.[51]

For Martin and others, psychological comfort resulted from viewing the body and engaging in ceremonial activity in its presence, and these elements of the modern traditional funeral were securely founded in the religious history of the human species. Many instructional textbooks and articles for morticians aspiring for respectability in their communities, as well as financial success in the market, began to include sections on the psychology of grief and some form of "applied" psychology. These rehearsed the same basic arguments articulated by Martin, which blended religious language with perspectives on the emerging science of psychology. For example, Anne Franz's manual, *Funeral Direction and Management* (1947), informs the reader that "Psychology, a relatively new science, means the way an individual reacts mentally and emotionally to an outside stimulus." Funeral directors must learn the scientific "facts" of emotional stress because they must constantly "minister" to people in the grips of grief, which causes sever emotional imbalance. Franz describes the physiology of grief ("Grief and despair cause slow heartbeat, irregular breathing, and depression"), as well as the accompanying mental state ("Grief stricken people cannot reason"), and encourages morticians to work with clients on finding appropriate channels for emotional expression—even if that means giving in to their demands for an extravagant funeral when the undertaker knows full well it will create a severe financial burden.[52]

Once again, creating the right impression, through both arranging a suitable service and preparing a suitably presentable body, brings comfort to the living and responds to deep-rooted religious sentiments. For Franz, the mortician "must be a keen analyst of human nature, a psychologist" who can meet the needs of his diverse individual clients and respond accordingly.[53] He must recognize that grief-stricken family members require the body for a proper ceremony, and that these very individuals see the funeral director as a religious figure engaged in religious work. After quoting the industry's favorite English commentator, Sir William Gladstone, who supposedly could "measure with mathematical exactness" the moral worth of a people based on their treatment of the dead, Franz writes, "A dead body in itself is worthless; but to a family it is a sacred trust. It is surrounded by sentimental memories and has a value beyond price. This is exemplified by a family's insisting on the recovery of a drowned body or a charred mass of bones. To be selected by a family as one into whose hands the last remains of a loved one are placed is an act of the greatest confidence the living can bestow. Treat it as a sacred obligation."[54] Increasing efforts to sound even more scientific in the 1950s did not result in the suppression of these religious inflections in industry literature; instead, attending to the psychological dimensions of grief led naturally to the hallowed, universal, and at this stage of evolutionary development, highly refined religious sentiments about reverence for the dead. Successful grieving depended on understanding both the psychological value and the sacred character of mortuary work.

The Triumph of Grief Mythology

It is this kind of sanctimonious logic, which mixed religious sentiments with the science of psychology, that Mitford challenged in her investigation. In her assessment of the "new mythology," invented and perpetuated by crooks in the industry to ensure the ongoing routinization of embalming in American death rituals, Mitford identifies the increasingly popular assertion within "mortuary circles" about "the need for 'grief therapy.'" [55] These concocted "myths" about the supposed therapeutic value of viewing the body, and the deep reservoir of religious feeling which most funeral directors claim underpins their understanding of the psychology of grief, are based more on public relations strategies than on any scientific evidence. However, Mitford acknowledges the mythology struck a chord in the American public that "proved very effective" and, at least at the time of her investigation, has "been safe from authoritative contradiction."[56] According to Mitford, because no one in the industry could satisfactorily ground these theories about grief in any concrete scientific studies within the field of psychology, they were mythological—that is, simply false and made-up—justifications that served one purpose and one purpose only: profit.

Historians of religion will argue, however, that myths are effective not because they are true or false, but because they provide a sacred context for meaning and action in everyday life. The myth of origins undergirding the explicit psychological mythology Mitford was challenging had tremendous explanatory power for funeral directors who wanted to place their work in a larger human context that affirmed their calling. It does not matter whether ancient Egyptians were truly the first to embalm for the myth to take hold. Even though Mitford disregards grief mythology as "based on half-digested psychiatric theories" and concerted strategies by undertakers to legitimate further their claims to professional standing in American society, in the years following the publication of her popular book, the mythology played an increasingly powerful role in how many Americans made sense of their grief—Mitford may not have bought into it, but the mythology worked in American lives.[57] Charles McCabe, a correspondent for the *San Francisco Chronicle*, wrote a Mitford-esque column a few years after her book which recognized this very point: "The grief therapist is undoubtedly a bit ashamed of his job, despite the pay, because fondling stiffs is not a fashionable thing to do. But the customer . . . has his share in all this. The grief therapist conducts his biz along the time-honored custom of giving the customer what he wants. . . . In the death biz, what the customer/client wants is anything but death."[58] While McCabe argues that grief therapy simply reaffirms the larger cultural tendency to deny the reality of death, morticians, and many others outside the "biz," contend the American funeral offers profound psychological value for coming to grips with grief and facing the truth of death.

One of the most authoritative voices in American popular psychology, Dr. Joyce Brothers, wrote a column on funerals after seeing Mitford interviewed on the October 1963, CBS special report, "The Great American Funeral," in the weeks preceding Kennedy's assassination. In her article, entitled "Why They Behave That Way: Even Bizarre Funeral Serves Good Function," Brothers wastes no time turning the tables on the Englishwoman, and rips her countrymen for their "profoundly unsatisfactory" funeral customs, which, in her estimation, leads "presumably intelligent Englishmen" to believe in the existence of ghosts.

> Let me explain. When a loved one dies, grief spins a complicated web of emotion, which cannot be brushed aside, but which must be owned up to, endured, and gradually untangled skein by skein. If these

feelings are denied in their proper season, they will return to haunt the mourner later on. . . . [T]he British play down their agony. They try to resume an appearance of normalcy. Consequently, they may be left with the feeling that a lot of 'unfinished business' remains between themselves and the dead . . . as a countermeasure, they dream up ghosts.[59]

At a fairly early stage of her career, and in a time when clinicians and other researchers were only beginning to investigate the psychology of grief, Brothers spoke with professional confidence about the redeeming values upholding the modern American funeral. First, it gives the bereaved an opportunity to confront the reality of their loss. If no funeral is possible—the example she gives is death at sea—mourners may be indefinitely haunted by the dead in their dreams. Second, the funeral serves as a moment of clarity about the bereaved's future status; it becomes a moment in time that illuminates the social and emotional relations that will contribute to the mourners' speedy recovery and "the establishment of a new equilibrium." Third, despite the critics who ridicule the expense and forms of expression at funerals, Brothers argues that the funeral can be a statement about how much a life mattered and be a show of appreciation for the life lost. Fourth, the funeral can be a time of absolution—that is, an opportunity to allow "mourners to discharge some of the guilt they inevitably feel." Finally, Brothers writes about the tremendous religious value of funerals, which in her estimation can bring "reassurance and spiritual leadership." By the end of her short column, Brothers promises that a properly planned funeral can lead to the "fruitful and philosophical resolution" of grief.[60]

Unfortunately for an industry reeling from the impact of Mitford's book, when psychologists and psychiatrists began turning their attention to grief in the 1960s and 1970s, very few spoke about the connection between grief and funerals—and when they did, most had a much less favorable impression of contemporary funeral practices than Brothers. In contrast, they spoke about how these practices revealed the depth of the American denial of death. Elisabeth Kübler-Ross's groundbreaking book *On Death and Dying* (1969), lent medical and cultural weight to the growing arguments about the prevalence of a taboo on death, and that most Americans—including, she emphasized, many medical professionals—had unhealthy attitudes about mortality. Her work on stages of dying translated into popular discourse about responses to death in general, and reinforced the growing cultural observations about denial. She only briefly alludes to the state of American funerals, when reminiscing about her own experiences with death growing up in a small European village: "In that country today there is still no make-believe slumber room, no embalming, no false makeup to pretend sleep. . . . [In America we] use euphemisms, we make the dead look as if they were asleep."[61] In the wake of Kübler-Ross's profoundly important book, the vocabulary of denial became securely linked to the language of death in American culture; and the funeral industry, with all of its euphemisms and camouflage, was seen as a prime source of psychological difficulty with human mortality.

Even though the topic of grief was eventually taken over by the field of psychology, in the years after Mitford's book the funeral industry continued to promote their own arguments about the therapeutic value of their ceremonies. Next to the science of embalming, psychology soon emerged as a crucial dimension of the mortuary college curriculum. In 1970, the National Observer in, "The Key is 'Managed Grief': How Funeral Directors—and Students—View Their Careers," reported how integral psychology had become in the education of America's ritual specialists: "Today mortuary-science students concentrate on the mortician's two stocks in trade: funeral psychology and embalming."[62] Morticians generally failed to find many allies in the social sciences, but a few psychologists and psychiatrists came out publicly in support of the American funeral—and when they did, the industry made sure to publicize their views. For example, The Director published an article by Dr. Charles W. Wahl (a medical doctor, professor of psychiatry, and practicing psychoanalyst) in 1969 entitled "Human Mortality and Its Role in Human Affairs." It included sections on death in the unconscious, the fear of death among medical doctors, jokes about undertakers, and the fact that in many cultures death specialists are outcasts. He then turns to his own recent experience accompanying a friend to his mother's funeral. The friend, he writes, "experienced a deep and profound consolation seeing his mother with the lines of suffering erased from her face and lying at peace." Wahl then suggests that, contrary to Mitford's view, the memory image played an important role in his friend's psychological response to loss.[63]

For the most part, social scientists studying the dynamics of grief did not explore its religious dimensions, a significant though often implied dimension in many works championed by people in the industry. On the other hand, many religious leaders and theologians who spoke out in public media dismissed the psychological and religious rationales propounded by funeral supporters. Nevertheless, the industry did find some who had a different perspective, and came to the defense of traditional modern funerals. Two religious authorities who bridged theology and psychology in their writings on grief, Christianity, and the healing power of funerals in the 1950s and 1960s, were Edgar N. Jackson, a Methodist minister, psychotherapist, and popular lecturer on the subject, and Paul E. Irion, a Lutheran minister and professor of pastoral theology. Both provide some criticism of contemporary American funeral practices, but ultimately defend these practices by relying on a mixture of Christian teachings and psychological theories about grief.[64] Because of their educational backgrounds, ministerial training, social locations and, most important, their public statements about the integrity of funerals in the United States, the industry energetically publicized the views of Jackson and Irion in its effort to counter Mitford's charges.

At the National Funeral Directors Association (NFDA) convention in Dallas October, 1963, the public relations committee recommended that the NFDA purchase 100,000 copies of a soon-to-be-released book being written by Edgar Jackson.[65] The book, originally called *Death in America* (but eventually entitled the more funeral-friendly *For the Living*), came out by the end of the year and immediately served as an authoritative source of information about the psychological and religious values of current funeral practices. The introduction, written by James Knight, professor of psychiatry and director of the program in psychiatry and religion at Union Theological Seminary, notes the blossoming interest in pathological grief on the part of many medical professionals, and warns about the "hazards of unwisely managed grief." He calls for a "reorientation toward the funeral as a therapeutic ceremony," which can be understood as linking "the sacred, the bereaved, and the community"—in other words, harkening back to the title of the book, the funeral may be a rite for the dead, but it must also be a social and emotional exercise "for the living." By the end of this short introduction, Knight arrives at the matter at hand, the value of looking upon the physically transformed appearance of the deceased. Although Knight applauds "Dr. Jackson for providing a stable and experience-based approach to one of the most searching psycho-theological problems of our time," the real voice of authority informing Jackson's work is not a theologian or a funeral director, but a psychiatrist.

> For the purpose of illustrating the importance of the funeral, let us look closely at one part of it—the viewing of the body in the open casket—to show the healthiness of such a rite in meeting conscious and

unconscious needs. Dr. Jackson discusses Erich Lindemann's psychiatric research, which has revealed that one of the common denomina-
tors in individuals with unresolved grief reactions is their inability to
recall a clear picture of the deceased. The viewing of the body at the
funeral would greatly aid in this recall.

Another common denominator Lindemann identified is the individual's unwillingness to face the pain of his bereavement. The funeral helps enforce reality, and the communal nature of the ceremony
incorporates the community to share the pain with the bereaved.[66]

The book is organized as a series of simple questions, which are
answered by Jackson in a straightforward and erudite manner. Jackson discusses a variety of topics, from the controversy surrounding Mitford's
book, the American culture of denial, and cross-cultural practices treating
the dead body with respect, to contemporary psychiatric theories about
grief (primarily Lindemann's theories), the religious dimensions of grief
and funerals, and the costs associated with funerals. Of course, much of
the time Jackson is answering questions about the embalmed, visible body,
and the role of the funeral director, who is compared to psychologists, psychiatrists, and clergymen in "managing" grief. So, when the questioner
wonders, "Should a dead body be looked at?" Jackson responds that,
except for the case of an abnormal interest aroused by "morbid curiosity,"
viewing the body begins the process of recognizing a hard reality to accept:
"A sorrowing look into the fact of death confirms the truth of what has
happened—truth that our minds and hearts desperately wish not to
accept. Indeed, this moment often starts the process we call 'wise grief
management.'"[67] For Jackson, "normal" grief depends in large measure on
the work of undertakers, who provide the culturally-appropriate rituals
that have transformative powers in individual lives.

In Paul Irion's book, *The Funeral: Vestige or Value?* (1966), similar themes
are discussed, though often within a more specific religious context. The
funeral service is understood as a moment to realistically confront death, an
essential component in the movement from grieving to healing, and an occasion that can lead to true insight about the human condition.[68] Turning to
the theological value of funerals, Irion begins by claiming that ceremonial
practices surrounding the dead have always been religious. In contemporary
America, he writes, the funeral "represents a theological understanding of
the body of the deceased."[69] Although he expresses caution about placing too
much emphasis on the body, Irion argues that it should not be ignored or
despised. Indeed, much of the book focuses on the necessity of keeping the

body present at Christian funerals. He relies on the New Testament to explain to fellow Christians that the body must be seen as part of God's created order, and therefore as part of the whole person—even at death.[70] It also becomes, for Irion, a symbol of the resurrection: "But in spite of its transient nature, even its temporary presence after death can symbolize the conviction that somatic identity is reestablished and that there is a sense in which the continuity of personhood pertains to the resurrection."[71] For Irion, Jackson, and others commenting on American funerals but receiving very little press, the visible body plays a crucial role in healthy psychological and religious reactions to death.

Many articles pertaining to the religious psychology of funerals that appeared in industry publications after Mitford were written by religious leaders standing up and supporting the American way of death as an antidote to a culture of denial and a way to reinvigorate the perceived decline of religious commitments in modern society. The Reverend James L. Kidd, pastor of the Wellington Avenue Congregational Church in Chicago, Illinois, wrote about the deaths of his son and father-in-law in his 1969 article, "An Ecumenical Funeral Service for the 'New' Church." He stated in unequivocal terms that the presence of the dead body was critical for mourners to face the fact of death, conquer their denial, and allow for "creative grief" to assist in the transcendence of the emotional pain associated with losing a loved one. Discussing the death of his son, Bruce, Kidd describes how he and his wife were present with him in the hospital at the time of death:

> His fragile, broken body was almost unclothed and we watched helplessly as he struggled and gasped for breath until no more breath would come. It was a pathetic and tragic scene and it burned itself into our minds and forced us to relive those moments time and time again. . . . It seemed to us, on a deep emotional level, that he continued to suffer that agony. It was not until we viewed his body after the embalming and preparation that we knew any peace in this regard. At that point he looked like the boy we had known and loved, and we saw for ourselves that he experienced that agony no more. He was, as the Scripture says, 'asleep.' Seeing him this way provided us with a positive, healing image we could substitute for the image of his agonizing death.[72]

At the end of the ecumenical service for his son, which included leaders from other churches in the community, Kidd describes the "most meaningful" ritual for everyone attending: the "Blessing of the Body," by a Roman Catholic priest who was a close friend and neighbor.[73]

The presence of the body at the funeral, and the opportunity to see the deceased one last time before final disposition, was front and center in many commentaries written by supportive clergymen. Most attempted to identify both the Christian and psychological benefits of funeral services—services that generally included viewing the remains—and therefore repudiate the continued popular attacks on the industry. The Reverend R. Earl Allen, a Baptist pastor in Fort Worth, Texas, explained in the *Baptist Standard* that "funeral functions have some very definite values, both therapeutic and theological." In addition to being a time to comfort mourners with praise for God, the promise of heaven, and the certainty of resurrection, funerals bring dignity to the deceased, and enable mourners to experience "normal grief release." Allen informs his readers that "when normal grief release is denied, delayed reaction problems may arise to cause unhappiness and despair."[74] In these and other commentaries, money was not the real issue consumers should consider when planning funeral ceremonies, because nothing less than their spiritual and mental stability was at stake. As far as the industry was concerned, keeping the body present and visible in modern ceremonies was tied to the maintenance of sacred religious traditions as well as the possibility for healthy psychological recovery.

One Baptist pastor writing about the need for cooperation between the minister and the mortician in a 1971 issue of *Casket & Sunnyside* argues that the dead body deserves proper care and admiration, irrespective of cost. After all, the pastor explains, "The ancient Egyptians placed emphasis on respect for the body at the time of death. There are several references in the Bible that let us know of the concern people, including Jesus, had for the body at death. Lazarus, as well as Jesus, had special preparation for burial."[75] More than maintaining sacred traditions that treat the body with respect and reverence, the funeral director is potentially the best-suited professional to assist the living in their time of sorrow. Why? "More than most other men [the funeral director] lives with grief. Therefore I feel that the funeral director who is truly a religious man and takes part in the activities of his church is better prepared to give the kind of help which is really needed when death comes."[76] As many funeral directors, clergymen, and other supporters of American practices began to emphasize into the 1970s, funerals are "for the living"—both the mental and spiritual stability of survivors were at risk if people continued to turn away from modern traditions.

Managing grief through some form of therapy, support group, or crisis counseling has become common practice both inside and outside of funeral homes. While many more empirical studies appeared in the decades after Mitford, and many more psychologists and clinicians became experts in this now legitimate and highly popular form of therapy, funeral directors continued to believe their work contributed to the healthy resolution of grief and produced healthier individuals who would cope better with the experience of death than those growing number of renegades choosing alternative, highly nontraditional plans for the disposal of the dead. One of many NFDA brochures created in the aftermath of Mitford's book to inform the public about the real value of American funerals posed the question, "Should the body be present at the funeral?" The brochure begins with the now-familiar assertion: Public viewing of dead bodies has been an historically common practice in a variety of cultures. It then explains that the body is a meaningful symbol, a testament to the life of the person who has died. Viewing it bestows a dose of reality on survivors, and they are emotionally better off having had this intimate encounter with the face of death. Cosmetics and other restorative techniques are not employed to make the dead look alive, but to "provide an acceptable image for recalling the deceased." In a word, viewing has therapeutic value for children as well as adults. Finally, the brochure concludes with the words of Lindemann, identified as "a Professor at Harvard Medical School, [who] did pioneering and significant work on wise ways of coping with grief."

> When asked, "What do you consider to be the most useful part of the whole funeral process?" he responded, "The moment of truth comes when living persons confront the fact of death by looking at the body."
>
> When questioned further why he thought this was true, he said, "People tend to deny painful reality. . . . But when they experience that moment of truth that comes when they stand before the dead body, their denials collapse. They are facing reality and that is the first important step toward managing their grief. . . . Grief is a feeling. If you deny it you have difficulty coping with it, but if you face it you start the process of healthful mourning. . . ."
>
> From all this, one inescapable conclusion can be drawn— the funeral with the body present for most people becomes an experience of value as they work through the sociological, psychological and, where desired, the religious needs that are a part of the grief experience.[77]

The slight hesitation over religious needs here signals the dawn of yet another sociological adaptation of modern funeral traditions to the dramatically changing landscape in the 1960s, 1970s, and 1980s: Funeral directors had to accommodate the increasingly public and pluralistic religious cultures in the United States while maintaining their authoritative position over the dead body. Even in cases where religion did not seem to play a role in the funeral, the visible body still had some value to the individual, according to the brochure. The emerging grief mythology emanating from the mouths of undertakers as well as certified psychologists certainly reinforced a widespread cultural notion that grief could be healthy or unhealthy, resolved or unresolved, transcended or forever present. As a mythology that provided viable forms of meaning linked to specific, fairly uniform rituals that produced order in the midst of chaos, it appealed to undeniable religious sensibilities that sought to make sense of death and the dead body. While grief authorities may or may not refer to specific religious traditions, the dominant language used to describe and dissect the psychological state resonated with the public rhetoric of funeral directors in the "sacred" business of death.

Although familiar and demeaning stereotypes continued to appear in popular culture, and a flurry of governmental investigations added to the growing public distrust with the industry, funeral directors continued to act as ritual specialists who managed every detail of disposition. They responded to a fairly stable base of consumers who turned to the local funeral home at the time of death and were pleased with the work provided by the owner and his employees. By the middle of the century, funeral directors had established a new and therapeutic language that transformed the cultural meanings associated with the experience of death and the confrontation with the physical remains. While their language changed to better serve the living, the fundamental truth of their professional existence remained the same: Funeral directors are the chosen ones to stay close to the corpse after death and before final disposition. In addition to the triumph of grief therapy, the industry ultimately benefitted from another post-Mitford development: The routinization of business and ritual practices that overtook the industry in the 1970s and 1980s in many ways solidified the social power of funeral directors at the time of death and reaffirmed the cultural force of a truly "American" way of death. During a period of increasing social diversification, and consequent diversifying interpretations of the meaning of death and funerals, the industry achieved an even greater degree of uniformity and structural consistency across ethnic, racial, and religious communities. Funeral directors simultaneously changed with the times and made sure time stood still.

First Lady Jacqueline Kennedy looks at the coffin of her slain husband during a memorial service in the U. S.Capitol rotunda. © Wally McNamee/CORBIS.

Renouard Training School for Embalmers, photographer unknown, 1920. Burns Archive.

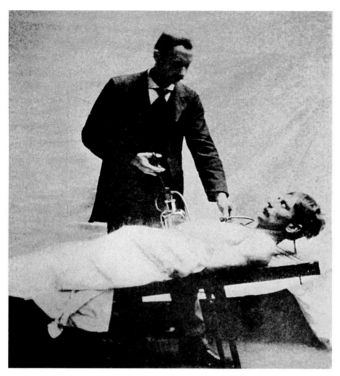

Photograph of early twentieth-century embalming process.
Burns Archive.

Advertisement for funeral home organ. *Southern Funeral Director,* July 1929.

Rudolph Valentino on display, New York City, 1929. Burns Archive.

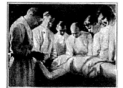

SIMMONS
School of Embalming

"The School of Practical Instruction"

A practical embalming demonstration under the supervision of Professor Baxter G. Simmons.

Laboratory practice in restorative art under A. McCallum Law, Sculptor.

Practice in embalming, derma-surgery and funeral work.

Instruction in anatomy, bacteriology, sanitary science and other subjects necessary for preparation for state examinations.

Special courses in plastic-surgery and restorative art, for licensed embalmers.

DAY and EVENING CLASSES

For catalog and further information address:

PROF. BAXTER G. SIMMONS

Office and School, 1901 S. Salina Street, Syracuse, N. Y.
Phone: 5-4568

Trade advertisement for the Simmons School of Embalming. *Casket & Sunnyside*, July 1, 1934.

Wartime trade advertisement, Galion Metallic Valult Company. *Southern Funeral Director*, March, 1944.

Scene from *The Trouble with Harry*, 1955.

Scene from *The Mummy*, 1959.

A last kiss, 1964.Burns Archive.

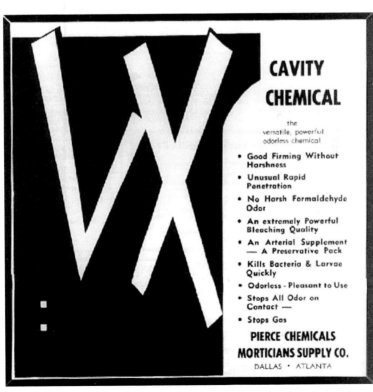

Cavity Chemical Advertisement,Pierce Chemicals Morticians Supply Company. *Southern Funeral Director*, February, 1967.

Preplanning card from Trevino and Sons Funeral Home, 1995.

KEEPING THE DEAD IN PLACE:
OLD AND NEW PATTERNS OF CONSUMPTION

Darkness falls across the land,
The midnight hour is close at hand
Creatures crawl in search of blood
To terrorize y'awls neighborhood
And whosoever shall be found
Without the soul for getting down
Must stand and face the hounds of hell
And rot inside a corpse's shell.

"Thriller," Rap by Vincent Price, Michael Jackson, 1984

The Trouble with Corpses

National funeral organizations and state associations worked hard to counter the negative press stemming from *The American Way of Death* and win the trust of the American people. In curricula reform and public relation campaigns the industry emphasized the therapeutic value of traditional funerals, and began to rely on grief relief as a crucial factor in legitimating the value of modern funerary customs. At the same time, basic structural elements of the rituals upholding American traditions were dramatically altered as a result of growing governmental concern about the vulnerability of consumers in this market. In addition, self-imposed changes in the 1960s, 1970s, and 1980s responded to an increasingly diverse clientele whose tastes simultaneously sustained and transformed these traditions. Without question, Mitford's book was a turning point in the history of American funerals, leading to heightened public awareness about the costs of disposal, the need for consumer protection, and the availability of alternatives to the traditional funeral.

In the face of this heightened awareness, and in the aftermath of dramatic changes in the way they interacted with clients, funeral directors strove to continue to provide the same basic ritual services they had before the publication of Mitford's book: removal of the body from home or hospital, embalming and preparing it in the funeral home, displaying the deceased in the casket before and/or during services in the chapel, and transportation to the grave. The trappings of the funeral ceremony varied according to the religious and cultural peculiarities of the deceased, but American funeral traditions across ethnic, racial, and religious communities solidified because of national industry efforts to streamline, standardize, and normalize the final exit. From last breath to final disposition, most bodies followed a well-trodden path out of sight, but never quite out of mind, of the living.

The persistence of ritual patterns established in the early decades of the twentieth century provided the industry with some degree of stability and legitimacy. But in the 1960s and 1970s, local funeral directors and national industry organizations confronted a variety of new, though now fairly standard, public challenges to their control over the dead. Vigorous charges that the industry was out of control and in need of regulation posed serious problems for funeral directors, who were dismayed by what they saw as misguided reform movements trying to put them out of business and by the incessant investigations digging up dirt on renegade undertakers in towns and cities throughout the country. The troubling evidence resurrected familiar accusations about corruption, exploitation, and disingenuous, if not outright illegal, business practices among modern death specialists. This evidence also contributed to the growing cultural currency of age-old fears and images of death—particularly the return of the menacing dead who wreak havoc in living society—in a variety of popular media.

Confronted with the grave, and widely-circulating public charges against the industry, funeral directors reiterated a now-familiar refrain: They were deeply patriotic Americans who adhered to a strict ethical code of conduct and who prided themselves on their passionate and professional commitment to the well-being of their customers, venerable funeral traditions, democratic forms of government, and the sacrosanct status of the free market. While they attempted to convince Americans that their loved ones were in good hands, they faced a variety of social, political, and cultural forces delivering a drastically different message about some dead who do not rest in peace and arousing obsessive fears about the contaminating, dangerous effects of their disconcerting presence in modern life.

No doubt the Kennedy funeral in November, 1963, momentarily provided the nation with an exemplary display of social solidarity, public order, and collective transcendence over death. For funeral directors across the country it was a source of pride, a demonstration of the "Great American Funeral" that millions of Americans cherish and return to, death after death. But the afterglow did not last long. With the escalation of fighting in Vietnam and domestic conflicts tearing at the fabric of civic life, the symbolism of death and the rituals surrounding the dead body became increasingly political in American public life. The prominent dead of the 1960s did not elicit expressions of social unity, collective commemorations of public grief, or unified displays of patriotic jubilation. The Vietnam war dead, as well as assassinated public figures like Malcolm X, Martin Luther King Jr., and Robert Kennedy, brought increasing attention to the serious divisions within the social body, and growing dissatisfaction with American myths that in earlier times of trouble had revitalized a broad-based sense of participation in a shared, public culture.

One of the most revealing cultural documents from the period morbidly captured popular suspicions about failed American myths and growing distrust of conventional patterns of meaning and transcendence to make sense of death. It was a small, independent film released in 1968 that went on to become an enormous commercial success and cult favorite: George Romero's *Night of the Living Dead*. The film has a remarkably simple plot line: The dead return to eat the living. The story begins on a Sunday evening, when a brother and sister visit the grave of their father, buried in an isolated rural cemetery. After some good-natured, if rather sacrilegious, taunting by the brother, Johnny, who clearly shows no respect for the dead, the first zombie appears and attacks Barbara. Johnny tries to save her, but is soon killed by the rigid, drunken-looking figure who throws him to the ground and cracks his head open on a tombstone. The sister escapes and runs to a farmhouse down the road. Inside, she meets up with a few other terror-stricken people—including the heroic but doomed young black man, Ben—who are trying to escape from the murderous hordes of undead. Eventually they learn that a bizarre epidemic of mass murder is overtaking the eastern United States, hearing in radio and television news reports that "the killers are eating the flesh of the people they murder," and that the "unburied dead are coming back to life and seeking human victims." The film then follows, often in disturbingly graphic detail, the monstrous zombies killing and devouring their human victims—sometimes their own "flesh and blood" relatives, in the case of one young girl shown munching on her recently-killed mother—as they attempt to break into the old country farmhouse to consume the living holed up inside.

The history of cinema, as suggested earlier, displays a curious obsession with the return of the uncontrollable dead. From exotic Egyptian mummies to familiar monsters like Frankenstein to unnerving mobs of cannibalistic zombies, watching the undead return to disturb the peace of the living was a popular, spine-tingling pastime for many Americans throughout the twentieth century. Even the master of Hollywood cinema, Alfred Hitchcock, toyed with this narrative trope in the 1955 release, *The Trouble with Harry*. The trouble with Harry, you see, is that he is a corpse that will not stay in the ground. In the film, which demonstrates Hitchcock's agility with suspense, high comedy, and romance, townsfolk in a small New England community are repeatedly dismayed by the reappearing dead body. Harry does not come back to life, zombie-like, and wreak havoc on living society. The return of his lifeless body to the sight of the living simply inspires some rather harmless high-jinx, and serves as a vehicle for carrying forward the romantic entanglements of the two main characters. *Night of the Living Dead* is a completely different exercise in the imaginative use of the dead to tell the story of living society, and it supplies some commentary on the turbulent times in which it was produced.

Romero's film is a pivotal moment in both the history of cinema and the history of the horror genre. As one film critic writes, "In earlier horror eras, the monster could be conquered with science, engineering, and a group guided by good men . . . [in *Night of the Living Dead*], however, science, technology, engineering, and community effort will not repel an attack of slow-moving, flesh-eating zombies even though a hard blow to the skull puts them out of action."[1] This film set the standard for subsequent horror films, which liberally borrowed from the unsettling conventions established by Romero, including situating the horrible in the mundane, everyday life of American society. After Romero's film, many critics pointed out that the possibility of maintaining human dignity and value in the face of menacing, unexplainable threats vanishes in the horror films of the 1970s and 1980s. The sacred integrity of the family, the optimistic possibilities after the monsters have been ultimately vanquished, the promise of moral action reestablishing moral order and the rule of law—all of these crucially important American myths evaporate in such films as *Halloween* (1978), the Friday the 13th series (beginning in 1980), and *Prom Night* (1983).[2]

Monstrous corpses coming back to life with a murderous vengeance captured the popular imagination during an historical era of social change and upheaval that included, among other developments, major protests against an increasingly unpopular war, the tragic killing of student protesters at Kent State University, the disgrace of an American president, and heightened fears associated with the escalating Cold War.[3] Some would argue that this theme also represents a more universal ambivalence experienced in the encounter with a dead body, and a common fear about the dead returning to haunt the living. Media studies historian Jonathan Lake Crane links the complex work on abjection by psychoanalyst Julia Kristeva to the powerful draw of horror films. For Kristeva, the human mind often seeks to discard those difficult, indeed horrifying images that betray corporeal wholeness and ego solidity, images usually tied to bodily fluids such as blood, excrement, urine, and other discharges reminding humans of the presence and inevitability of death in all bodies. Yet in spite of determined psychic efforts to remove these images from consciousness, they are too compelling to disappear for good. Horror films, Crane suggests, screen the return of the abject for popular entertainment, and give new life to these unpleasant reminders that death, and the dead, remain in both the psychic and physical landscape.

> The most menacing piece of waste, far more threatening than any mere bodily excretion, is the corpse. . . . The corpse must be packed away if we are to survive the psychic damage inflicted by the dead; however, even if the object must be removed, we simply cannot treat the flesh of our loved ones like just any disposable bit of waste. We must reconcile our desire to stow the dead with the equally powerful need not to forget the beloved soul that once animated the cold meat. . . . When we take account of our chary connection to the dead, we must also consider our relationship to the monster. What is a monster other than a reanimated corpse? We may turn our back on the dear departed and hurry home once the coffin lid is strewn with dirt, but the horror film returns us back to the dead and forces us to confront that which we had hoped to confine to the quiet grave.[4]

The monsters in Romero's film are the dark side of luminous angels. While angels are eternally alive though disembodied, these zombie cannibals are eternally dead yet fully embodied. The film troubled and entertained many Americans because it tapped into deep-rooted fears and phobias about the cadaver, and it provided an incisive commentary on the disintegration of contemporary social life. At a time when traditional patterns of meaning and authority were breaking down on numerous social fronts, *Night of the Living Dead* simultaneously captured and anticipated a growing sense of anxiety with how the living relate to their dead and with the question of whether the dead could really be kept in place at all.

People within the funeral industry were troubled by these signs of social unrest, and found numerous ways to demonstrate their own united allegiance to national security. They wanted to convey to the American people their fervent desire to uphold social order by ensuring ritual stability in the disposal of the dead. If Mitford posed a threat to the economics and integrity of American funerals, many in the industry felt discord in the streets during the Vietnam era represented a more diffuse, but equally sinister, threat to sacred American institutions like the funeral home, and sacred American values like respect for the dead. In this climate of rule breaking and explicit challenges to many of American traditions, concern about popular protests against the war, and particularly concern about the moral and mental state of America's youth, led many within the industry to speak out against the rebellious spirit sweeping across the land, and declare the nation's funerals safe from any possible infiltration by polluting social forces currently eating away at the body politic.

In August 1968, the *American Funeral Director* published an article comparing the "spirit of lawlessness" affecting college campuses around the nation with the patriotic, "professional" sensibilities of students in training to become practicing morticians. Asking whether or not this "spirit" had invaded the nation's mortuary schools, author Albert Kates summarizes the results of conversations with officials at seven of these institutions: "A spot check, . . . indicates that mortuary colleges are free from such disorders and the assortment of 'weirdies' and troublemakers who cause them." He then speculates on why the nation's future morticians have been immune to such dangers. First, students go to mortuary college for sound educational reasons related to career building and upholding the values of this career; second, these morticians-to-be want to promote the American way of life rather than tear it down; third, campuses have been safe from "ultra liberals, would-be social reformers, etc." who have strange ideas about personal freedom and civic life; fourth, the application process allows mortuary officials to screen out any "hippies" who would be a discredit to the profession; and finally, mortuary institutions will immediately remove any students or teachers who "foment disorder" through disruptive acts or political speeches.[5]

Implicit in this and other articles is the notion that mortuary colleges produce strong, patriotic American citizens who preserve social order because they have a very special commitment to living society: to keep the dead in place by disposing of them in an orderly, humane, and meaningful way. The disordered presence of death, however, commonly appeared on television and in newsprint in unprecedented ways during this period, ranging from the familiar scenes of body bags containing dead American soldiers on TV to graphic published accounts of massacres occurring, for example, at My Lai. Never before had Americans been confronted with such accessible, pervasive, and disturbing portraits of death, and never before had Americans disagreed so strongly about the meaning, value, and power of the dead. Rather than providing living society with a profound source of unity and determination, the war dead raised questions for many Americans about national priorities and political purpose. Funeral families, on the other hand, would not countenance the political exploitation of the dead as a lever to critique federal authority. While morticians maintained a fortified position on the home-front—not only in schools but also in their day-to-day interactions with grieving customers and fellow citizens—funeral magazines reported on mortuary work in the killing fields of Southeast Asia to display the industry's commitment to preserving the body politic by preserving the bodies of dead soldiers and getting them home for final disposition.

In 1969, *Mortuary Management* published a series of articles by William T. Grafe, a lieutenant in the United States Army. In May, the magazine carried Grafe's overview of his three-years' experience with the army's Mortuary Affairs Program. He begins by explaining that the United States Army does not have a special unit for embalmers or funeral directors, but that men with this background can enter the army's Memorial Activities Program. Grafe then describes his participation in the army's Memorial Activities Course at Fort Lee, Virginia, which covered six academic subject areas: information about the Mortuary Affairs Program itself; identification of the dead; map reading; battlefield collection and evacuation; temporary cemetery operation; and finally, returning bodies to the States.[6]

Grafe covers his arrival in Vietnam in 1967, his work at the Graves Registration Collecting Point, his request to be transferred to one of two army mortuaries operating in Vietnam (one in Saigon, the other at Da Nang, where Grafe was sent), and the details of running a mortuary. He informs the reader that "Preservation of remains is accomplished according to the most modern techniques in embalming, and the latest embalming supplies and equipment available are used. This is the first time in history that a 'civilian type' Mortuary has operated in the field in a combat zone."[7] According to this account, bodies are "dressed, cosmeticized, and [em]balmed" before being shipped to one of the two ports of entry in the U.S. Travis Air Force Base in California, and Dover Air Force Base in Delaware. When they arrive at the port of entry, they are dressed and cosmeticized again, and then casketed before they are shipped to the next of kin. Grafe then reveals to his readers that the army is considering a new program that would incorporate the embalmer into America's armed services, suggesting that the army will "some day recognize the professional background of the Mortician as they do that for Nurses, Veterinarians, Doctors, Dentists, etc." He ends by encouraging his readers to enlist and enroll in the existing program so that "the minds of [American soldiers'] families can be at peace knowing their sons have been properly cared for and are finally home."[8] It is clear that Grafe understands his work as providing a soothing balm for the nation's broken families, whose peace of mind can be secured by ensuring the safe passage of a well-preserved and presentable corpse.

In a later article, published in September 1969, entitled "1968 Tet Offensive—A Tough Job," Grafe describes mortuary work during the infamous Tet Offensive in which the Viet Cong unleashed a massive, nationwide assault that crippled the South Vietnamese and destroyed crucial political support for the war in the States. In the article, Grafe provides funeral industry readers with an insider's view of the messy, often unsettling work of identifying dead American soldiers and preparing them for transportation home. From the mortician's perspective, the Tet Offensive was the most challenging episode of the Vietnam War. The challenge of course, what made it such a "tough job," was the dramatic increase in the number of bodies needing attention at American mortuaries. The Da Nang Mortuary had the personnel and resources to process not more than 350 remains per month. According to Grafe, soon after the start of the offensive in February, more than 100 remains per day were being brought into the quarters. Although there were fluctuations in these numbers, Grafe reports that "high figures were to continue for the next three months, averaging over 1000 per month. Under these circumstances, which caused "some monumental problems as well as some humorous and some tragic moments,"[9] creative thinking and purposeful actions were required to make sure the proper, orderly care of the dead did not stop.

One of the most urgent problems faced by a mortuary staff already over-taxed by the sheer volume of bodies was the rapid decay of corpses in the hot, humid climate of the region. The refrigeration units at the mortuary could only hold 100 bodies, which created a particularly distressing problem for Grafe: "Now we were in deep trouble! If we didn't receive more refrigeration, all our efforts to ship viewable remains home would be lost to decomposition." Trouble continued to mount with the body count. According to Grafe, a plea to General Westmoreland's office for more embalmers brought a tremendous outpouring of "'misplaced' embalmers from the 101st Airborne, 1st, 9th, and 25th Infantry Divisions," as well as other units throughout the armed forces. With more personnel, increased refrigeration capacity, and relocation of some bodies to nearby Clark Air Force Base in the Phillippines, the mortuary could continue to operate with a minimal degree of efficiency.[10]

Grafe describes a whole series of additional problems created during the offensive, including dwindling levels of embalming fluid, equipment malfunctions with such essential items as electric aspirators, lack of adequate space for mortuary personnel to do their work, and increasing difficulties associated with identification of remains. At the end of the article, he shares three anecdotes, one pathetic (keeping the embalmed remains of a young, red-headed, freckled-faced soldier for over two months, only to learn that his wife back home never thought to inquire about her missing husband), one humorous (realizing that one of five charred remains from a helicopter crash was not a human as the morticians initially assumed, but actually a dog, the mascot for the crew), and one uplifting (after two days of inquiries from numerous officers concerned that the body of President Johnson's son-in-law would make its way into the Da Nang Mortuary, the staff learns that Captain Robb is in fact safe and sound).[11]

Embalming the dead and shipping them home proved to be an essential service sanctioned by the federal government and appreciated by

living relations in the United States during the Vietnam War. While
images of human carnage, tales of horrific slaughters, and reports of young
lives wasted in an unwinnable war contributed to social outrage and public protests throughout the country, men and women associated with the
task of delivering bodies to family members imagined their work in terms
of patriotic duty and civic responsibility. As suggested by Grafe, having a
viewable body to bury made a substantial difference in how families experienced the sacrifice they had made for the good of the country. Despite
the chaos and disorder of the Vietnam era—in the dangerous jungles
of Southeast Asia and the wild streets and college campuses around the
United States—for funeral directors the embalmed body securely
anchored in a traditional funeral setting represented a kind of permanence
and equilibrium sorely lacking in contemporary America. Responses to
death, and especially the war dead, during these troubled times no longer
produced the social solidarity, unanimity of meaning, and cultural con-
sensus that usually arose in periods of social crisis—an aberration that signaled a tremendous cultural shift in how Americans imagined death, and
their relations to the dead, in everyday life.

If the politics of death grew increasingly disruptive and divisive during
the Vietnam era, the growing popularity of the "death awareness movement" encouraged Americans to speak with one voice about the biological, psychological, social, and religious facts of mortality. This movement
is generally traced back to the 1959 publication of Herman Feifel's book,
The Meaning of Death. The publication of other popular books, such as
Kübler-Ross's *Death and Dying* ten years later, contributed to a new,
expanding field of inquiry soon to be labeled "thanatology," which
revolved around death education in various curricular settings, determined efforts to change the way Americans think about and care for the
dying, and a shared language about the experience of death and its place
in American society. Thanatology brought with it a new repertoire of
images, meanings, and practices which could be used to make sense of, if
not completely demystify, the human experience with death. In many
ways, the popular movement brought legitimacy to a wide range of death
professionals—such as academics studying and teaching on the topic,
nurses caring for the dying, psychologists treating the grieving survivors,
and ethicists providing normative commentaries on the way Americans
die—who frequently challenged the traditional authorities on death in
modern society: medical doctors and funeral directors.

Despite the enormous variety of subjects covered in this literature, all writers agreed on one crucial thesis: Modern Americans fear death and deny its reality in their lives.[12] Indeed, the movement defined itself as an antidote to this serious social disease which, according to the popular diagnosis, had been affecting American life for much of the twentieth century. From this perspective, death no longer had substantial meaning in social life, it had disappeared from public view, and it had lost its utility as a source for moral order. Many argued that Americans simply ran away from death rather than look it squarely in the face, and that this flight, particularly in relation to the two primary institutions that control the dying and the dead, was a distressing symptom of deeper psychological and cultural fears. The popular resonance of these criticisms, and the success with which they evoked a potent nostalgia for the pastoral, familiar, even intimate knowledge of death that had been lost shaped conventional wisdom on this matter and, indeed, created an uncontested historical fact about the denial of death.

The historical evidence suggests a much more complex reality in the period between the First World War and the Vietnam War, and a confounding, but culturally entrenched, tendency in American public life to keep death firmly in mind. Death, and the presence of the dead, troubled the sensibilities of modern Americans increasingly enamored with scientific and technological advancements, youth culture, consumer convenience, and good hygiene. But this did not bring about an absolute cultural silence on the matter of death. In the first few decades of the century, critics of the emerging industry were already publicly charging that funerals obscured the true reality of death, and that embalming was an especially pernicious, death-denying practice. Funeral representatives, on the other hand, responded by extolling the realism produced by gazing upon a prepared body in an open casket and the undeniable psychological healing they witnessed in their clients. By the end of the 1960s, funeral directors—already quite familiar with the terms of this debate—were arguing forcefully against charges that their mediation between the living and the dead translated into a social obstruction that barred the stricken from facing death with maturity, realism, and honesty. Instead of challenging the validity of the denial thesis in toto, they reacted by transforming this popularly accepted social fact about American culture into a professional advantage.

Funeral magazines and journals published numerous articles claiming that modern American mortuary traditions provide a remedy to the rampant forms of denial afflicting contemporary society. Most were written by industry insiders, but some came from individuals in separate, though allied, fields, such as ministry and insurance. *Mortuary Management* published a speech by Presbyterian minister M. Dudley Rose at the National Funeral Directors Association annual meeting in November 1969. In "DEATH—Denying It Or Defying It," Rose tries to bridge the generation gap that exists between most practicing morticians and young adults, and encourages a more humane, sympathetic attitude toward the under-thirty crowd. Like the aging clergy population, funeral directors must appreciate the passions of the younger generation and understand their suspicions of institutional authority. In addition to learning how to listen and empathize with young people, undertakers and clergy have a common educational goal in their efforts to reach out to youth, an ethical responsibility to teach the value of facing up to the reality of death. Rose suggests that funeral directors take their local church leader to lunch and "let him know that you too hope that the people he serves as a pastor learn to defy death as Christians, not deny it." He then quotes from the "well-known writing" of Dr. Edgar N. Jackson, by this time a wise, convincing voice for many interested in the psychology of death:

> The funeral is a time of facing reality rather than for denying it. Death is a part of man's experience. It cannot be ignored or avoided without disrupting moral practice and social responsibility. Even though it is a natural inclination for man to seek the comfortable and avoid the unpleasant, it is not a good enough basis from which to meet life. . . . The viewing of the body prior to the religious service and the presence of the closed casket at the service are the quiet evidence of death and man's willingness to stand in the presence of it in faith, not fear, in fact, not in fancy.[13]

Funeral directors saw themselves as liberators, not conspirators, when it came to ensuring a proper place for death in American awareness. Their work opened the eyes of people to the hard fact of death in a soft, unthreatening way, and regardless of the amount they charged for their services, funeral directors believed that the presence of the corpse had incalculable positive effects in the lives of survivors.

Ralph A. Head, president of Pierce National Life Insurance, wrote about the consequences of ignoring the reality of death in an issue of *Casket & Sunnyside* in 1971. Taking on the disconcerting public desire to privatize, minimize, or, even more outrageous, forego altogether funeral services with the body present, Head relies on theological, psychological, and anthropological evidence to uphold American traditions. First, Head notes that Christians have believed in the resurrection of the body and life after death for 2,000 years, and that the funeral is an affirmation of the biblical view of "total embodiment" that encompasses both flesh and spirit. He then claims that the funeral provides a "true group experience" that is psychologically therapeutic for participants.[14] Finally, he looks to archaeological studies to identify the powerful symbolic meanings of earth burial as a valuable act of closure or, in his words, the "natural denouement for the funeral," and how these meanings reinforce a critical value animating the entire ritual: "An affirmation and an awareness that death has taken place, a willingness of family and community to accept the pain of mourning, and the acknowledgment that the relationship with the deceased has ended."[15] For Head and many others, the funeral industry is an institution particularly well-positioned to bring the realities of death not only to those in grief, but also to a larger public audience through various funeral industry–sponsored informational texts and open houses at local funeral homes.

Federal Investigations and Interventions

Unfortunately, many Americans were not willing to acknowledge an end to their relationships with the dead after handing them over to the industry. Indeed, the return of the dead—that is, as evidence in the ongoing public battles to reform American ritual traditions—signaled a much stronger attachment to the dead than industry-leaders had imagined. Their efforts to persuade the public of the sociological and psychological value of the traditional services offered at local funeral homes were spoiled by yet another embarrassing public scolding, but this time it came from a much more distressing source than the English-born muckraker Mitford. The federal government entered into the debate over the high cost of funerals when the Federal Trade Commission's Bureau of Consumer Protection began a survey of funeral prices in Washington, D.C. in the early 1970s. Although the funeral industry wanted to participate in bringing death "back" into American consciousness, this action, as well as subsequent public investigations into the 1990s, raised serious questions as to whether funeral directors were reliable, trustworthy, and sympathetic voices in the cacophony of the larger cultural awakening to the truth of

death. The investigations eventually led to a funeral trade rule, mandat-
ing certain changes in the way funeral directors do business, and sending
a clear message to future clients who must enter into this unfortunate
market: Buyer beware, and do not lose sight of your God-given rights, as
well as your obligations as a consumer, to shop for the best deal when
deciding about ritual choices in the inevitable confrontation with
the death of a loved one. Even though the investigations acknowledged
the extremely difficult economic position of grieving relations making
one of the most expensive purchases they will ever have to face, the trade
rule reinforced, perhaps even reinvigorated, the industry's relevance to
the marketplace.

The Federal Trade Commission (FTC) was created in 1914 in
response to the economic turmoil at the end of the nineteenth century
and to the "corporatization of America" at the turn of the twentieth
century.[16] Its primary duty was to ensure fair, open business practices and
prevent monopolies from manipulating free market competition with
deceitful advertising and marketing. Like other governmental commissions, the FTC was understood in the early twentieth century as a champion of consumer interests and the enemy of corrupt businessmen,
though at different moments since that time it has had increased or
diminished power depending on the ideological leanings of the acting
administration. As one of the federal government's chief independent
regulatory commissions, the FTC has made an impact in certain areas of
trade by changing the rules governing certain business practices. The
passage of a new "trade rule" for funeral industry practices, first proposed
in the 1970s and subsequently revisited in the following two decades,
was experienced within the industry as a disturbing (if not outright
undemocratic and subversive) act of government interference in the
consecrated work of funeral directors.

One of the first actions against the funeral industry occurred in 1939,
when the FTC served the infamous Washington, D.C., undertaker,
William Chambers, with orders to "cease and desist from misleading representations in the sales of caskets, vaults or undertaking facilities."[17]
While governmental agencies and civic groups held various investigations
into the industry in the middle decades of the century, the FTC began a
more serious examination of business practices in the early 1970s, near the
very beginnings of America's death-awareness movement. It is important
to note, however, that the commission itself reported that between 1922

and 1963 it carried out roughly 80 investigations of the funeral industry, primarily focused on casket and vault manufacturers.[18] In fact, according to communications from consumer organizations not associated with the FTC, complaints against funeral directors were relatively rare before the release of Mitford's book. For example, in 1952, the New York–based Consumers Research, Inc., responded to a consumer query about the costs of funerals with the following statement: "We don't think we will come back to the question [of funeral costs] because it has been a subject of almost negligible interest to our readers, as evidenced by their lack of correspondence concerning it."[19] Even in 1963, representatives of the consumer group responded to another letter: "In our locality, some of them [funeral directors] are fine men and would be happy to cooperate with anyone who wishes to discuss his own funeral."[20]

Even the published 1978 report from the FTC stated that the federal probe into industry practices was not the result of a large number of consumer complaints, but instead arose from a staff-initiated recommendation. A footnote to the section describing the genesis of the federal proceedings explains: "The inquiry into funeral practices was not based upon the number of complaints on the subject in the funeral files (in fact very few had been received) and for this reason has been criticized by members of the industry and some members of Congress."[21] What motivated the investigation? On the one hand, the report asserts that an inquiry was necessary because so many consumers do business with funeral homes each year; funerals can be one of the most costly transactions in a consumer's lifetime, and there was growing public concern that the bereaved were particularly vulnerable to consumer abuse. The 1960s witnessed the awakening of a powerful movement of citizens into political action on behalf of the consumer, led primarily by Ralph Nader who entered the public spotlight with the 1965 release of his book, Unsafe at Any Speed, which demanded greater regulation of the automobile industry. The FTC undertook their investigations in the same spirit of activism.

On the other hand, the report states that questions circulating more generally in the public arena—questions raised in antitrust hearings, magazine articles, and books—compelled the agency to engage in a close, careful, and thorough examination of industry business practices. In addition to data collected from industry publications, visits to funeral homes, and interviews with a variety of relevant figures including lawyers, members of memorial societies, state officials, funeral directors, and consumers themselves, the report relied on material compiled from a survey of funeral prices in the nation's capital.[22] According to the initial report, enough variation and irregularities existed to raise serious questions about unfair and deceptive practices.[23] The *New York Times* covered the release of the commission's findings in March, 1974, with the last paragraph informing readers where to obtain a free copy of the final report.

As might be expected, funeral directors responded with outrage and fear to the government proceedings, especially to what they perceived to be the ultimate goal of the inquiry. In 1975, at the ninety-fourth annual convention of the National Funeral Directors Association, executive director Raether charged that "people in positions of power" wanted to displace the ritual services provided by morticians, replace traditional funerals with the body present with immediate disposition and no body, and put in place a "funeral-less society."[24] For Raether and others in the business, whose livelihoods depended on the integral placement of the dead body at the center of the funeral service, this unprecedented public examination by the United States government threatened the industry at its very core. In their minds this was not simply reform in the interest of protecting consumers, but rather an act representing a deeply disturbing, if not outright menacing, development that could destroy the moral order of America and, therefore, the entire cosmos—imagine what Gladstone might say about a society without any funerals! One of the key countermeasures proposed at the meeting was to enhance the knowledge and psychological sophistication of funeral directors; caring for the dead clearly meant ministering to the emotional needs of the living, a particularly difficult service to factor into the price of a funeral.[25]

Things only got worse for funeral families in the next few years when the FTC decided to propose a "trade rule" regulating the business of death and carry out even more extensive investigations. An FTC news bulletin released in the summer of 1975 succinctly communicated the rationale behind the far-reaching proposal for the $2 billion dollar industry: "The Commission declared that it has reason to believe that bereaved buyers are in an especially vulnerable position and that their vulnerability has been exploited by undertakers through a variety of misrepresentations, improper sales techniques, nondisclosures of vital information and interferences with the market. Such practices have, the Commission believes, inflicted substantial economic and emotional injuries on large numbers of consumers." The bulletin compares the commission's actions with its recent prescription drug rule—both are directed at anticompetitive restraints that hurt consumers. In this case, funeral directors would be prohibited from, among other things, embalming without permission, bait-and-switch tactics, impugning consumers who expressed concern about price, misrepresenting public health requirements and state and federal laws bearing on the dead, and refusing to furnish less expensive, alternative forms of disposal, like immediate disposition and cremation. Additionally, the proposed rules would require morticians to provide grieving family members with the following: a fact sheet covering legal aspects of disposal; a casket price list; an itemized list of prices for all services and funeral accoutrements, with "conspicuous disclosure" of the consumer's right to choose which services are desired for the upcoming funeral; and a written record of all the financial details once arrangements have been finalized.[26]

As noted in the title of an article from the October 1975, issue of *Business Week*, the FTC's decision would surely give "Undertakers Something to Cry About." This article discussed the commission's goals (including securing a consent order from the nation's biggest funeral chain, Houston-based Service Corporation International, to return $150,000 in improper charges to customers), and more pervasive government intervention in the funeral transaction between the consumer in grief and the ritual expert for hire. Some news reports tried to present both sides of the story and allow supporters of the industry to defend themselves. For example, the *Business Week* article includes the following quotations from the owner of one small funeral chain in McKeesport, Pennsylvania: "I welcome anything that will take the bad apple out of the bushel." On the accusation of overcharging, NFDA executive director Raether states "If funeral directors are overcharging, it would show up in their profits. And they just aren't making a lot of money." On unit pricing, or collapsing all charges onto the price of the casket, NFDA president Edward J. Fitzgerald explains, "It became popular because it allows the rich to subsidize the funerals of the poor." On matters that transcend price, particularly the incalculable value of facing the reality of death by seeing the body, associate professor of sociology, former funeral director, and industry-consultant Vanderlyn R. Pine warns, "A service that is psychologically distressing but therapeutically beneficial might now be eliminated for price reasons. But the $50 saving that might result could cause hours on a psychiatrist's couch."[27]

Most of the press coverage, however, kept the industry's defense from public awareness and featured horror stories of funereal proportions, stories that have continued to shadow undertakers to this day. Articles highlighted the persuasive stories of abuse, greed, and lawbreaking running unchecked in the death market. In one anonymous opinion piece, "The Distrusted Undertaking," that ran in the *San Francisco Chronicle* in 1975, the author relies on the testimony of various FTC witnesses to shame the out-of-control industry. After the publicity from the earlier pilot study in Washington, D.C., the article reports, hundreds of letters poured into the FTC offices, all with examples of dubious practices and outrageous treatment by American undertakers. "If men can abuse, cheat, and demean the grieving survivors of the dead, they will do anything," one woman wrote. Another recounts her terrible experiences with a Eugene, Oregon, funeral home: "There may be a few who are honorable but for the most part they are vultures!. . . . When my husband died, a local funeral director tried to sell me a more expensive casket than I wanted by belittling me. He said, 'If you want a less expensive casket, I can show you what people on welfare get.'" Finally, an Episcopal priest from Santa Monica, California, criticized "the most objectionable practice" of embalming the dead," and criticized for promoting deception and denial in the way Americans process the realities of death. Instead of seeing the funeral home as a place of business providing a service, the priest explains, the bereaved are hoodwinked into accepting the funeral director as someone who can legitimately supervise the last rites.[28]

At the next national convention, in 1976, NFDA president R. Jay Kraeer stated in his Presidential Address that the country was in the midst of what could only be labeled a "revolution." Kraeer begins with a brief history of the "evolution" of Christian funerals to establish the centrality of the dead body—present, viewable, with a community around it—in modern American ritual traditions. The meddling of the federal government in funereal affairs, according to Kraeer, constituted a mortal danger to both industry mythology and everyday practice.

There are those in opinion-making positions, including some of the FTC staff, who apparently feel that following death the body should be placed in a pouch and if there are to be any services conducted, such services are to be without the body present. . . . Those who would like people to revolt against the idea of viewing, label it as

cruel, as barbaric, as repulsive. . . . Having looked at the evolution
of the American funeral, we get to what some feel is a revolution
. . . . Some things are so important today, they could to an extent,
determine what will happen to us as funeral directors tomorrow.
. . . To me the hearings themselves are part of that revolution.[29]

After discussing "evolution" and "revolution," Kraeer arrives at the
final piece of his presentation: "Resolution." The industry is unlikely to
receive a fair hearing in the media Kraeer admits, so the efforts of individual funeral directors should, in part, be devoted to educating the public about their profession, and clarifying the emotional costs to the
bereaved of opting not to give the body a prominent place during the
funeral.[30]

Industry representatives remained deeply skeptical about the possibility of a fair hearing in the media reports of the hearings. In the months
preceding the public release of the FTC report, in 1978, however,
the *New York Times* published a series on the funeral industry, and in the
last of three articles journalist Richard Severo allowed industry representatives to air their side of the story and rebut the damaging charges
swirling around the government investigations. The article includes a
drawing of ancient Egyptian embalmers at work on a body, with the caption: "Mortuary workers were ritually pelted with stones so mourners
could vent their grief."[31] This caption captures a shift in the mythology
driving and sustaining the industry, a shift that hinges on convincing the
public that, contrary to the image being carved by the federal proceedings,
funeral directors are ritual specialists who play an integral role in the ven-
tilation and resolution of grief in their local communities.

Severo notes that many funeral directors, who confidently describe
themselves as grief specialists, say that they have the training and indeed
a social duty to help bereaved relations understand the profound emotional and psychological consequences of their choices when planning a
funeral. The article quotes NFDA executive director Raether, who by now
had written extensively on the value of traditional funeral rituals and
become the primary public spokesperson for the industry, as boldly stating,
"We not only have a right, but the time has arrived when we can say we
have a responsibility" to challenge anyone, even clergy, relatives, and
close friends, about decisions being made in the planning and execution
of the funeral. Others quoted in the piece including a New York rabbi,

disagreed, arguing that a mortician cannot be both salesman and counselor. Severo identifies the cross cultural and historically-familiar stigma associated with that class of individuals in every society charged with disposing of the dead. He alludes to the work of Sigmund Freud and Sir James Frazer, relevant fields on the common cultural phenomenon of "shunning" corpse handlers in many preliterate societies.[32] The article ends with the observation that Americans are talking more about death—indeed, are more aware of death—than ever before. One salient probable consequence of this development, writes Severo, is that Mitford's long-standing critique will not remain unchallenged. Along with Pine, psychologist Robert Kastenbaum, one of the leading scholarly authorities to emerge in "thanatology" circles during the death awareness movement, is quoted as dismissing Mitford's analysis and championing the healthy benefits of modern American traditional funeral rituals.[33]

Despite the arrival of new voices of authority in the public arena—credible voices emanating from the academic community beyond mortuary college doors—that were sympathetic to the functions and plight of America's underappreciated funeral directors, the FTC finally imposed its will on the nation's undertakers. After the release of the 1978 report, oversight hearings by the Consumer Committee of the Senate Committee on Commerce, Science, and Transportation, congressional approval of modifications to the original language of the rule, various legal maneuvers by the funeral industry, and negotiations between the industry and the FTC, the "Trade Regulation Rule on Funeral Industry Practices" was enacted in September 1982, and became fully effective in April 1984.[34] The rule prohibits misrepresenting any facet of the funeral service to potential customers, disallows the common practice of loading various fees onto the price of a casket, provides consumers with a right to choose which elements of the funeral they desire instead of having to take entire packages, orders funeral directors to disclose information about legal and cemetery requirements in their state, especially as they concern embalming, and perhaps most important, requires directors to furnish clear and unambiguous details about the costs of the funeral in the form of itemized price lists.[35]

It also stated the will of the consumer must be honored, even if that meant providing the antithesis of a traditional funeral—immediate disposition with no viewing, cremating the remains rather than preserving them, and memorializing the deceased without a final, intimate, personal farewell with the casketed body present in the funeral home. Finally, it encouraged a rather unusual activity that only slowly began to gain support throughout the industry: planning ahead. This novel idea encompassed a range of possibilities for wary consumers, such as comparison shopping, preplanning and even prepayment for your final ceremonies, and leaving your friends and relatives out of the funeral loop so they do not have to face questions they have never considered.

In 1994, after persistent lobbying by the industry and ongoing review by the FTC, the rule was amended to respond to a surprising fact: The rule had made no impact on the overall costs of a funeral. Given this consideration, and the reality of a changing funeral marketplace propelled by greater consumer choices, the FTC backpedaled on some of its original regulations. For example, the rule now lets "funeral directors . . . recover overhead costs through the non-declinable professional service fee, by means of a mark-up on caskets, or by mark-ups on other goods and services."[36] Many would agree with Mitford's pessimistic reading of the amendment, as expressed in the revised edition of her book, that it resulted from FTC "capitulations" to the pressures of the industry, that abuses of the rule are rampant, and that the "agency has abandoned any pretense of consumer protection . . . [clearing] the way for an era of unprecedented profitabilty."[37] Others see federal intervention in this market in more optimistic terms. One textbook on death and dying, for example, concludes that as a result of the final rule, "mortuary businesses are now offering greater flexibility in the kinds and costs of funeral services."[38] Although the cost of an average funeral still has not decreased as a result of the rule, consumer-driven modifications in the specifics of disposal have led to increasing customization of ceremonies to suit the individual traits of the deceased and the tastes of the family.

When asked about the ultimate impact of the rule, many contemporary funeral directors agree on at least one point: consumers are in fact paying more now than they did before federal involvement. As for the impact of itemizing funeral expenses, Houston funeral director Trevino Morales claims that "you have to comply with [FTC rules], but in my files and in my father's files we got a better price on the service by the funeral directors just charging a price for everything. Itemized they have to pay a lot more money. Better service, better price the old way."[39] Thomas Lynch states the case even more forcefully, and humorously: "[The new FTC rules] raised prices. Because funeral directors said, 'We have to itemize?

Well, what do we do?' [Laughing] Cha-ching, cha-ching."[40] Commenting on how these investigations and interventions have affected personal relations with community members, New York funeral director Wayne Baxter states, "The FTC was a major change. When my father entered the business you priced the funeral as you saw fit. He did unit pricing. [After FTC began their investigations] the state of New York demanded functional pricing. It made us become more of a bookkeeper and a businessman. . . . It was different when your buddy came in—we'd never talk about money. Now you say, 'I love you dearly but I'm going to ask you to sign this paper.'" [41]

Federal efforts to regulate the cost of funerals, and ensure the reliability and trustworthiness of practicing undertakers, may not have succeeded in altering the industry in ways originally intended, but they did accomplish one thing: The dead remained firmly under the control of America's modern death specialists. In many ways the FTC, at first quite antagonistic in its investigations and hearings, ultimately provided a certain degree of legitimation to the industry. In effect, the government offered its seal of approval for keeping the spirit of capitalism alive in the death industry and making sure the dead stay in the funeral home. According to the language of a recent FTC consumer's guide on funerals, the long-standing confusion over the occupational status of undertakers is now clarified: "Most funeral providers are professionals who strive to serve their clients' needs and best interests."[42] Rather than being disgraced and displaced, funeral directors continue to be proudly at the center of one of the most disruptive, disorienting, and disheartening events in the journey of life.

Another important development that led to greater federal regulation of the industry, and in turn, a greater degree of legitimacy for those involved in disposal of the dead, was the AIDS epidemic that exploded into American consciousness in the mid-1980s. Although the biological mechanisms of this disease are complex, AIDS (acquired immunodeficiency syndrome) results from the breakdown of a person's immune system caused by infection with the human immunodeficiency virus (HIV). The death of Hollywood screen idol Rock Hudson and the subsequent hysteria and confusion surrounding the transmission of AIDS captured the public imagination and inflamed popular fears about sexuality, drug use, and modern plagues. In addition to its rapid rise to prominence as one of the leading causes of death in the United States, AIDS also shaped new perspectives on how communities care for the dying, offered a fuller appreciation for the politics of death and the common reliance on scape-goats during troubling times, and provided Americans with yet another reminder of the exorbitant costs associated with dying and the limitations of the current health care system.

The American funeral industry, like many institutions affected by this epidemic, moved from initial homophobic fears to a more reasoned recognition that AIDS can strike anyone in any community. A number of funeral directors speak directly to this progression and admit that many in the industry responded inappropriately when news of the disease first spread through the nation. For Atlanta funeral director Ralph Turner, "AIDS was a shocker. When it first came out everybody was afraid they were going to get [it] because they thought if you look at it you caught it. The information that was going around about that time was not specific, not related to touching the body."[43] New Jersey funeral director Bill Monday remembers, "When it first came to our knowledge, we were concerned about the risks. Like everything else there [was] an overreaction and I think what has come to be is that the funeral director is the professional person and handles those things. You take the same precautions [now] for everybody."[44]

During the AIDS era, funeral homes began to be required to follow certain federal guidelines promulgated by the Occupational Safety and Health Administration (OSHA), requirements that reinforced, at least in the minds of many funeral directors, the delicate, dangerous, technologically-sophisticated nature of embalming. In May 1988, OSHA began to enforce the Hazard Communication Standard, which compels all employers to identify any dangerous chemicals in the workplace that could harm their employees. Now companies that deal with hazardous materials, such as formaldehyde and phenol, two chemical products routinely used in funeral homes, had to establish a communication program that includes employee training about these materials, clear procedures to follow in case of an emergency, protective measures to prevent harmful exposure, and the maintenance of material-safety data sheets. Noncompliance with the regulation, many recent funeral industry textbooks note, could lead to severe penalties and costly workers' compensation claims.[45]

More relevant to AIDS contamination fears is OSHA's *Bloodborne Pathogen Standard*, published in December 1991, and applicable to all occupations that expose individuals to blood, products that might contain human blood, bodily fluids, and other materials that might carry infectious diseases. In addition to establishing an Exposure Control Plan, a training program for employees, the use of warning labels for potential biohazards, and careful record keeping, the regulation also requires that all workers who may come into contact with human blood wear personal protective equipment to prevent exposure to potentially deadly infectious materials. Embalming textbook author Robert Mayer explains further:

> To understand the pathogen rule, it is important that we understand universal precautions, a term originated by the Centers for Disease Control and Prevention (CDC). In brief, it is a method of infection control in which all human blood and certain human body fluids are treated as if known to be infectious for human immunodeficiency virus (HIV), hepatitis B virus (HBV), and other bloodborne pathogens. The practice makes particularly good sense for embalmers, as embalming is often done before the cause of death is known. Even when the cause of death is known to be something other than blood-borne disease, that is not necessarily positive proof that a bloodborne disease was not also present. If all bodies are treated as though the person had died of a bloodborne infection, there will be no need for second guessing.[46]

Concern about AIDS and other infectious diseases has changed the way funeral homes operate in significant ways, such as modifying the traditional garb worn by embalmers, and instituting the use of masks, gowns, and gloves. When asked about the impact of this form of federal intervention, Wayne Baxter states that "OSHA has put the fear of God in us. When they realized that formaldehyde was a carcinogen they came around and we had to hang a sign on the prep room door that says 'entering these premises may be hazardous to your health.' We have formaldehyde tests done yearly. . . . They started to say you had to work with universal precautions. Every time I enter the prep room I have to be suited up."[47] Even though many funeral directors will mention these kinds of changes, and sound quite informed about the health risks associated with the dead body and embalming, when it comes to understanding the dead AIDS victim, at least one recent study suggests that the industry remains under a cloud of misunderstanding about means of transmission and ways to reduce professional risk.[48]

In addition to initiating these operational changes, many funeral directors began to exhibit an entirely new attitude toward the dead and community responsibility in the early years of the epidemic. Perhaps for the first time in the history of American funeral directing, some morticians refused to work on bodies—often young, horribly disfigured bodies that spoke of inexpressible human suffering. Individuals suspected or known to have died of AIDS were singled out by many within the industry as a potentially harmful source of the deadly contagion and, coupled with common associations between the disease and homosexuality, social contamination. One brief news item from 1985 reported that the Maryland Board of Morticians voted to allow funeral directors to turn away AIDS cases or, even more surprising, refuse to embalm the body and arrange for a more immediate form of disposition without any viewing.[49] In the words of George Cabot, a third-generation funeral director in Southern California, "we were telling families, 'no viewing, no embalming,' which was sad. That was a mistake but [we thought] it's not worth giving up your life for a job. The panic eased about 1987."[50] Howard Raether remembers this period particularly well, and his personal and official position on the matter:

> There was the question: "Do I as a funeral director refuse to take AIDS cases?" My statements were strong against refusal. In 1982 I had four bypasses. I believe I had more than five transfusions. I didn't know where the blood had come from. What scared me is that a couple of years later, the hospital called and said I should come in and leave a blood sample because they are not sure if I did or didn't get AIDS because of the transfusions. Fortunately I did not get AIDS. When I talked with funeral directors they said they wouldn't [care for the dead body of an AIDS victim]. I'd tell them this story [and say,] "My forty-five years of funeral service and when I die you refuse to take care of me?"[51]

AIDS also opened the door for greater industry acceptance of cremation as a viable—indeed, in many AIDS cases, actively encouraged—form of disposal. Up until this historical moment, the vast majority of America's funeral directors would rarely under any circumstances recommend cremation. The advent of AIDS, however, led to greater interaction between funeral homes and crematoria facilities in most metropolitan areas by the late 1980s. Atlanta funeral director Bill Head remembers, "When it [AIDS] first came out there were funeral homes that would not touch them. They promoted cremation or direct disposition."[52] Cremation became the method of choice for both friends and family members who no longer recognized the earthly shell that once contained the spirit of the deceased, and for funeral directors who assumed that the risk of contact with blood-borne pathogens during the process of embalming could be entirely avoided by immediate disposition. Cremation, however, could still produce a sacred object—the ashes—that easily fit into the ceremonial desires of family and community. Ritual would not die in the gay community, even if America's fearless ritual specialists reached their professional limits in the face of AIDS.[53]

The Times They Are A-Changin': Preserving Traditions by Being Progressive

Through regulation, the federal government took actions on behalf of defenseless consumers, who no longer have to accept the traditions so vigorously upheld by funeral homes throughout the country. Instead, each individual is now able to craft the funeral of her or his choice, with full disclosure of the price of every item and service, and complete knowledge of all relevant information about the transaction. Because of the disabilities associated with grief, consumers are also encouraged to plan for their funerals in advance, so rational thinking and sound judgment can guide the funeral director's actions when the time comes. The federal investigation of the industry beginning in the 1970s, coupled with the growth and popularity of the death awareness movement during the same period, actively encouraged patrons to take control of the funeral and create ceremonies that suit their own tastes rather than simply conform to the modern traditions established over the first half of the twentieth century.

Yet funeral directors continued to make the claim that they have the best interests of the unprotected consumer in mind when defending the sacrosanct traditions that undergird modern funeral institutions, such as a last look at the deceased, a ceremony with the body present, and interment in a cemetery— the basic ingredients that served undertakers and the public so well in the past. But after Mitford's book, and certainly over the course of the FTC investigations, funeral directors sensed a shift in American funerary sensibilities and an increased willingness to defy the institutionalized prescriptions that ritually removed the dead from the living community. While governmental investigations, outspoken critics, and generally bad press contributed to the shift, many within the industry identified a variety of social factors working against the preservation of hallowed customs, including declining rates in church attendance, escalating generational tensions between young and old, and, in larger metropolitan areas, diversifying tastes among customers from a host of new immigrant communities.

In a 1970 industry article entitled, "Let's Change the Changers," author Jack G. Ebner contends that the move away from traditional funeral ceremonies is related to a growing trend away from traditional values in American society. Particularly disturbing to many was the decreasing number of people who regularly attended church services on Sunday—a sure sign of rebellion in Christian America. Ebner, however, reassured his readers that Americans are not less religious, or less likely to believe in a supreme being, than before, but instead have become suspicious of institutions "too steeped in tradition to help man in this world where the need is immediate . . . not the next." He goes on to predict that, within the lifetime of students currently enrolled in mortuary school, funeral traditions will likely be completely eroded, and ceremonies in the future will probably take place without the sacred remains present. The answer for Ebner, as for many working within the industry, was to fight individually to preserve traditions at the local level, and to understand these traditions in religious terms, as a "legacy of faith" passed on by the founding funeral fathers throughout the generations.[54]

Charles Kates, editor of *Casket & Sunnyside*, looks at generational factors to explain current trends. Kates responds to the widely-read 1970 article about attitudes toward death in *Psychology Today*. He questions the demographic bias of the magazine's pool of respondents and challenges the validity of statistical evidence that a majority of people downplay the significance of funerals. In brief, Kates argues that readers should not put much credence in the views of people who filled out the questionnaire, who were mostly young women. Young people tend to become more conservative as they get older and, Kates explains, "more inclined to value the stability and reassurance that time-honored customs represent." Because death is so removed from the everyday worlds of young women and men, they think about it in "practical" and "unsentimental" ways. Kates encourages readers to be cautious about these transient, innocent views of death. Only with time and growing maturity will "the callous insouciance of youth" be replaced by a deeper understanding of the meaning of life and by more venerable attitudes toward important traditions— in other words, death will one day enter the lives of these youngsters and change their views forever.[55]

Modern American funeral traditions, shaped by innovative ritual specialists and safeguarded in the nation's funeral homes, were threatened at every turn in the post-1960's cultural environment. Nothing jeopardized these sacred traditions more than two increasingly popular options for reform-minded people: immediate disposition and cremation. A *San Francisco Chronicle* article in the early 1970s reported on the unprecedented national efforts by the industry to publicize the benefits of traditional funerals at a time when these alternative forms of disposal were growing in popularity, especially among those with higher levels of education and income. The piece puts this development in the context of a larger erosion in formal ceremonial decorum around the dead and offers yet another example of changing American deathways: "Also making inroads into the once-inviolate realm of ceremony are progressive cemetery authorities who are allowing everything from bicycle paths to hiking trails to picnics on their property."[56]

Without a doubt, Californians were exposed to "progressive" alterations in funeral traditions earlier than most of the country; alterations that, according to one industry trade article in 1974 on the "unconventional funerals" growing in popularity in the state, jeopardize industry traditions but allow for personally meaningful ritual expression. "Those who choose these do-it-yourself ceremonies seek what they consider a more personal approach, one, they believe, that gives greater meaning to funerals." Surprisingly, this "spirit of change" among Californians, the article reports, is not limited to young people, but includes older, even more conservative individuals. Funeral men and women did not know if this regional trend anticipated larger national fashions, but clearly understood that pervasive changes were afoot, and that their livelihood, indeed their very homes, could be in mortal danger.[57]

But not everyone in the industry felt this way. Indeed, the industry was of two minds about the status, stability, and saving power of tradition in the pivotal era between the publication of Mitford's book and the promulgation of the Funeral Trade Rule. At the same time as a chorus of industry voices were defending the central role of the body in traditional funeral services, increasing numbers saw the writing on the wall, and began cautiously to embrace the cultural and social shifts taking place as professional and economic opportunities rather than signs of moral decay. As early as 1972, NFDA President Amos Dunn opened his presidential address at the annual convention in Boston with a sobering realization: "The time has come for us in funeral service to talk about change not as though it is something in the future. It is here." He continues with a realistic assessment of the current social realities in the marketplace: "Do we not find it difficult to admit the fact that needs are different now? That the services for an octogenarian with few living contemporaries is not the kind that will be meaningful to those who survive the sudden death of a husband and father or those grieved by the suicide of a teenage drug addict?"[58] In the span of roughly ten years, and in the midst of tremendous social and cultural change touching all areas of national life, including sexuality, race relations, politics, religion, and economics, funeral industry leaders and public relations experts began to demonstrate a new attitude toward their role as America's ritual specialists: Change with the times.

This strategic position quickly gained momentum among funeral directors and emerged as an industry crusade embraced by leaders, mavericks, and local undertakers not beholden to the "legacy of faith" associated with embalming. Instead of upholding, and indeed urging, customary forms of ritual that had become standardized in most communities by the 1960s, many directors saw the value—economic, for sure, but also social insofar as it had a bearing on community relations—of loosening up conventions handed down from one generation to the next, and adopting a more progressive posture. The new watchword on the lips of many within the industry was "adapt," and the subsequent rise of unconventional, stylized funerals represented a democratization of the consumer marketplace, where individuals can, in the words of the ubiquitous contemporary fast-food slogan, "Have it your way."

At the 1973 NFDA convention, Raoul L. Pinette noted in his presidential address some of the demographic changes that he expected to lead to a dramatic increase in deaths of people over 65, and discussed some of the structural social changes occurring because of even greater social mobility and the pervasive fragmentation of the American family. "Times are changing fast and we must adapt to them. . . . Funerals must not be justifiably termed sterile or stereotyped. They must be adaptive and meaningful."[59] Of course it should be noted "adapting" for Pinette and others did not mean abandoning tradition completely—especially the tradition of hiring the local undertaker to care for the dead. Instead, it referred to a complicated set of occupational adjustments for funeral directors that included expanding the range of goods and services available at the local funeral home, and inserting themselves with greater care into the decision-making process when a customer calls or walks in to arrange the final disposition of the deceased.

At the Centennial Convention in 1981, a prominent theme of the presidential address was "Tradition in Transition." NFDA president Richard Myers covered the revolutionary changes in the one-hundred-year history of the association from its founding in Michigan in 1881, when "modern embalming was still in its infancy," to the present, when funeral directors provide an extensive array of services "dealing with all phases of the funeral ceremony and even post-funeral counseling and support services." Proudly glorifying the accomplishments of the old "pioneers" who established modern funerary traditions, Myers extols his listeners to seize the present moment, with its "golden opportunities," and become the new pioneers for the next one hundred years.[60] In other words, venerate traditions, but do not be held back by them when working with clients who have unconventional ideas about disposal.

The call to change came from all quarters of the industry. In their 1971 centennial issue, the editors at *Casket and Sunnyside* asked a variety of funeral men to publicly reflect on the most important contributions to funeral services over the past one hundred years. While many chose to write about such things as the development of modern embalming, the shift in job title from undertaker to funeral director, the growing academic legitimacy of research in death and dying, and new, diverse color schemes associated with funerals—for example, funeral coaches no longer had to be draped in black—others pondered the challenges of the present and prognosticated about the future. Charles H. Nichols, director of the National Foundation of Funeral Service in Evanston, Illinois, wrote that as more and more demanding, individualistic, frugal, and unsentimental clients seek assistance, funeral directors had to be better prepared to adapt to the often foreign value systems these clients bring with them. Nichols is quite clear about occupational commitments: "We had better keep . . . service personalized and tailored to the individual client." But this is not to suggest, Nichols reminds his readers, that funeral directors should neglect their duties as cultural authorities on the meaning and texture of America's last rites. Indeed, the very opposite is true: in these troubled times, undertakers must be actively engaged in determining the changes overtaking the market, and continue to be discriminating, well-armed, and controlling specialists as the bereaved exert more and more consumer power in this market.

What we say and, more importantly, what we do, will play an important role in shaping and modifying [attitudes toward the funeral]. But we must be well-fortified with cogent, valid and defensible reasons for what we say and do. Mere assertion will not suffice, and anything smacking solely of self-interest will be fatal. We must scrutinize each change, actual or potential; we must evaluate that change in the interest of those we serve; we must then try to decide what we can do about it—by way of fostering, modifying, or impeding; and then we had better do it![61]

In the same issue, Richard H. LaVigne, executive vice president of sales for the National Casket Company in Boston drew on biblical language to persuade readers that they will, eventually, have to change with the changing times: "Hosea told the children of Israel 'old men shall dream dreams—young men shall see visions.' Dreams and visions are aspects of the same vista, thus we can readily achieve our purpose of serving the people of our nation, by making the funeral service field an endeavor attuned to their needs and wants."[62]

Whether framed in the colorful language of religious mythology or in the prosaic forecast of economic indicators, the reality of a changing marketplace could not be denied by funeral directors in the 1970s who did not yet know what impact higher rates of cremation and immediate disposition, as well as increasing numbers of low-budget funerals, would have on their chosen profession. Even people outside of the industry encouraged funeral directors to adapt responsibly to the changing cultural climate. In 1972, *The Director* published a supportive article by Dr. Jeannette R. Folta, Professor of Psychiatry at the University of Vermont, who had conducted a survey of more than 60 college students, male and female, ages 18 to 30, and over 100 attendees at a death and dying workshop sponsored by the NFDA and the Vermont State Nurses Association. Folta begins her piece by naming Mitford as a catalyst in transforming American views of the funeral, and in identifying the ambivalent perceptions surrounding the funeral director—someone charged with doing society's "dirty" work, but also in charge of the "sacred aspect of providing burial ceremony according to the religious and moral mandates of society."[63]

In spite of this undeniable ambivalence and contrary to numerous commentaries predicting the end of funerals in America, Folta's study revealed that "the funeral is not ending, merely changing." According to her numbers, 59 of the 202 respondents (almost 30 percent) would like to have a "simple" funeral; 48 would have "minimal traditional" services; 35 would be cremated; 29 would have no services at all; and 9 would have a fully "traditional" ceremony. Based on this and other survey evidence, Folta suggests that funeral directors adopt yet another occupational duty and serve as "teachers" engaged in the education of the general public, arrange even more open houses to diminish the "mystique" surrounding local funeral homes, and bring clients into the planning and execution of funerals in a responsible manner that ensures, whatever the ultimate decisions, dignity remains. Folta concludes by recognizing the inevitability of change in the future:

> This middle class sample clearly shows that the funeral is no longer a mere reflection of one's station in life. Like other ceremonies in our culture the funeral must be adapted with social responsibility a prime factor. Human dignity, individual personality and cultural satisfaction must be highly regarded if the funeral is to remain as a viable relevant part of life and living.[64]

A variety of surveys charting American views on death and funerals emerged at this time, emanating from research in the field of thanatology and from studies within the funeral industry. Yet despite the availability of this information, many funeral directors remained unclear about how to read the signs of the times and respond in a way that preserved their role as professional mediators between the living and their dead. As Bill Bates wrote in a 1975 *Mortuary Management* article, "The Adaptive Funeral," funeral directors like himself are kept awake at night wondering about the future of the business, especially with "prophets of doom" predicting the American funeral will soon disappear completely, and with it, the funeral home as an institution. Bates identifies the dilemma of contemporary funeral directors who are told to defend funeral traditions until consumers come back to their senses and "true American values," while, Bates continues, "we are told to make funerals adaptive and personalized to the needs of individual clients—to offer to the funeral buyer more funeral alternatives and new funeral forms." Bates soberly concludes that, in fact, it is not a matter of whether the funeral industry accepts these changes, but how it plans to live with them.

In his dissection of the contemporary scene, and his evaluation of how the funeral industry must adapt to it, Bates is unequivocal about one thing: the individual rules. Indeed, Bates's assessment of the times leads him to believe that standardized funerals are on the way out and adaptive funerals based on individual tastes, beliefs, and memories are here to stay. "Like the individualized clothing styles of today, a funeral service should conform exactly to the contours of those who choose to clothe themselves in it."[65] Bates and many others with intimate knowledge of changing funeral desires recognized something about Americans that would soon be echoed in many scholarly studies—they are fiercely, if not religiously, committed to the cult of individualism.

In this cultural atmosphere, funeral directors like Bates encouraged colleagues to let the living control the ceremonial aspects of disposition, but to make sure that, in the end, they kept control of the dead body— even if this meant a funeral stripped of "antiquated ideas and useless death-centered tinsel and trappings." For Bates, one of the crucial skills a progressive undertaker will have to learn is how to conduct a "controlled interview." During the interview, family members tap into meaningful memories of the life lost. This data then should be used to plan a funeral suited to the personality and lifestyle of the deceased. As undertakers become more adept at "new funeral and grief interview techniques," Bates argues, they will be able to cut down the number of people who choose a mode of disposal harmful to the industry and, according to death specialists, to the well-being of survivors themselves—immediate disposition. At the end of the essay, Bates takes a surprising turn and offers up a quotation from the Danish theologian, Soren Kierkegaard: "To venture causes anxiety, but not to venture is to lose one's self—and to venture in the highest sense is precisely to become conscious of one's self." Accepting the present challenge, and daring to change, Bates also suggests, can lead to a profound transformation in self-awareness.[66] The only answer for the industry is to add the adaptive funeral to its repertoire and do what it has always striven to do: Stay close to the dead, and make sure the physical remains do not disturb the peace of the living—something about which Kierkegaard would no doubt have a considerable amount to say.

Encountering Diversity: Historical and Contemporary Perspectives

Over the course of its seventy-year history, the funeral business had in fact shown remarkable signs of adaptation, even as funeral homes instituted a set of uniform practices centered on embalming that helped shape and define modern funeral traditions. Although a majority of white male Protestants with ethnic roots in the British Isles and Northern Europe

imagined, invented, and ignited the funereal revolutions of the late nineteenth and early twentieth centuries, in time many American communities would either operate their own funeral homes or modify ritual practices under the watchful eye of the local funeral director. Historically, the
ease with which funeral homes entered the social landscape of diverse
communities in all regions of the country suggests that the modern traditions forged in dominant Protestant culture could be adapted to fit different cultural settings—so long as the dead body continued to play a central
role in the funeral. Regardless of the particularities of social identity and
the dynamics of cultural negotiation, however, in the end most Americans
who stepped into a funeral parlor became consumers, a unifying characteristic at the heart of the modern American funeral.

From the very beginning of the twentieth century, people throughout
the funeral industry were exposed to death rituals from around the world.
Even if the mythological narrative predictably placed America at the top
of the mortuary evolutionary ladder, this exposure broadened the horizons
of many funeral directors and may even have led to greater appreciation
for, if not outright toleration of, variation in ritual patterns. Indeed,
displaying the best qualities of American ingenuity and the spirit of capitalism, some U.S.-born undertakers operated profitable businesses outside
of the States precisely because they took so much interest in learning the
cultural intricacies of foreign death rites, and because they saw
the value—moral as well as financial—of adapting their services to satis-
fy the customer.

In a 1940 funeral trade profile of William Borthwick, a Kentucky-
born funeral director who owned and operated the Borthwick
Undertaking Company, Ltd., of Honolulu, Hawaii, readers are given a
glimpse into the strange customs of Chinese, Japanese, and "natives,"
along with a lesson on how to succeed in the business of death.
"Traditions and customs surrounding funeral services are sacred to most
people, even though they are vastly different in race and nationality.
This fact is fully recognized by every member of the funeral profession.
Generally speaking, all funerals are 'tailor-made,' to fit the individual
needs of a bereaved family, depending on their social and financial
position, personal preferences, and the station of the deceased in life."[67]
The reader then learns a bit more about the ins and outs of this funeral
director's life with the dead in a strange, ethnically and religiously
diverse, land.

Success for this Kentuckian depends on a few key business practices. First, Borthwick claims, he does not try to persuade people to adopt American traditions; he only acts as any funeral director should and provides services desired by the grieving family. He does this by remaining partially color-blind—the only time color or nationality should enter the equation is when knowledge of an individual's cultural background would help in planning a pleasing funeral. After noting that the "Chinese people buy good funerals," Borthwick describes various elements of Chinese custom. The anonymous author of the profile then reveals a particularly significant secret of Borthwick's success: "By having a deep insight into all nationalities and by trying to know just what each requires, Mr. Borthwick has succeeded in establishing a demand for many of the better type of funerals." "Better" does not necessarily mean more expensive. In his description of native funerals, Borthwick notes that when families have money or get insurance, they tend to get overzealous and spend too much, often over his own protests.[68]

At the end of the piece, the celebration of cultural diversity is slightly modified to conform to industry mythology and Borthwick's testimony based on his wide-ranging cultural experience: "People of all classes know that the last tribute to a loved one is a mark of progress in the family life of any nationality."[69] In the United States, where much more was at stake in preserving modern traditions, funeral directors understood what the ultimate "mark of progress" should be: a visible body. Embalming was the key modern innovation that signaled Americans had achieved the highest form of ritual practice, and so long as that practice and everything it entailed (hiring a specialist to embalm the body, display of the casketed body in a funeral establishment, etc.) had a place in the funeral preparations, the industry could be quite open-minded about ceremonial details.

Early trade articles from the 1920s, 1930s, and 1940s, made strange funeral customs from other times and places quite familiar. In addition to a few profiles of American funeral directors in foreign lands, some articles reported on the strange permutations taking place on American shores, particularly in highly diversified urban landscapes like New York and Chicago, where people lived in close proximity to others quite different from themselves, economic and labor markets heightened class divisions, and multiple religious sensibilities made a mark in the public arena. Funeral homes that catered to specific ethnic and religious communities sprang up in these urban areas during the early decades of the century and merged modern funerary traditions with local customs in the neighborhood of the deceased.

For example, *Casket & Sunnyside* published an article in 1930 with the following informative heading: "Charley Boston's Funeral a Blend of Old and New; Presbyterian Rites at Funeral Chapel First, Then Confucian Ceremonies at Grave—Massed Band and Escort of Fifty Police Lead Procession Through New York's Chinatown." The author reports that Lai Quong Young, known to his friends and associates in Chinatown as Charley Boston, "was reputed to be the first of his countrymen to adopt American clothes."[70] A Presbyterian and purported leader of Chinese settlements throughout the country, Boston eventually came to be known as the "Mayor" of New York's Chinatown. His funeral, the article mentions more than once, contained a "strange mingling" of eastern and western customs. Indeed, the description of activities surrounding his funeral and final disposition tells an increasingly familiar story of ritual confusion, negotiation, and reinvention in early twentieth-century urban America.

When Boston died, Chinese leaders did not know what to do about his funeral, and where to ultimately dispose of his remains. According to the report, Boston's body stayed for ten days in America's first and (at the time) only Chinese-owned and operated funeral establishment, the Chinese Cheung Sang Funeral Corporation, on Mulberry Street. During this time, "members of the tong he helped found and of the Three Brothers Society—Lai Gong Ho Association—were gathering as far as San Francisco. Until almost the last minute, they were undecided whether to bury him with the Confucian or a Christian service, whether to inter his body in Cypress Hill or ship it to China."[71] Their compromise displays yet another example of American ingenuity: They chose all four options.

At the funeral chapel, American custom—and Christianity—prevailed, for the most part. A Chinese Presbyterian minister led the service in front of a gathering without any trace of "Oriental costume." Boston's body, dressed in a dinner jacket, was placed in a metallic casket with glass and a copper inner sealer. Mourners took one last look at Boston as they ritually walked around the bier. According to the author, at this point the Christian services ended and "the Confucian touch . . . mysteriously crept into the soundless ceremonial." During the procession to the cemetery, a lone individual followed the hearse and "slowly dropped torn pieces of paper to frustrate the demons who might wish to follow [him] to his resting place." Boston was then placed in the Chinese section of the cemetery, where the proceedings were dominated by other Confucian rituals, including the burning of white paper as an offering to spirits to ensure they "carry the Chinese Presbyterian to heaven," and the leaving of a chicken at the grave "for the Presbyterian soul to feast itself on."[72] After a few years, we are told Boston's remains will be transported to China for a final interment next to his ancestors.

Charley Boston's funeral illustrates the dilemma faced by many early-twentieth-century immigrants who sought to preserve old-world traditions in the new world of urban America. The arrangements made to mark his passing (both physical and spiritual) from this world to the next, required spontaneity, innovation, creativity, and a hallmark of American democracy, which drew people from all over the world to religious freedom. The Chinese were free to craft their own unique ceremony, drawing on an amalgamation of diverse symbol systems, modern and traditional institutional resources, and complicated local sensibilities. While Chinese immigrants had to find a way to bridge the chasm between "east" and "west," immigrant communities from Southern and Eastern Europe and parts of Russia had to contend with cultural reorientations that could be equally confusing. In addition to the discomfiture associated with relocating to another part of the world, immigrants often confronted a curious new reality in the United States: extreme cultural differentiation within their own community. Some new immigrants strove to maintain old world traditions at all costs, others abandoned tradition completely to live unfettered in the new land, and still others struggled to find a middle ground.

American Jews provide a case in point, especially when it came to planning their funerals. Eastern European Jewish immigrants began arriving in droves during the first few decades of the twentieth century, a movement identified by historians as a "third wave" of Jewish immigration after Northern Europeans in the colonial era, and German Jews in the antebellum period. By the time these immigrants arrived, Reform Judaism had become the dominant form of religious expression and practice for most American Jews. This brand of Judaism, in effect a denomination within the tradition, embraced modernity and liberalized religious practices in an effort to assimilate with greater ease into Protestant America. They stood in sharp contrast to the recent émigrés, who were primarily Orthodox Jews or, in many cases, non-practicing Jews heavily involved in labor and socialist movements.

In this context—in the new world of urban America and the fragmenting world of Judaism—when a Jewish immigrant died, her or his family had to make a decision about how to dispose of the body, a social reality that rarely emerged in European communities. Many Orthodox Jews
relied on a hallowed, deep-rooted European tradition, turning to the
hevra kadisha, or "holy burial society," to make all the arrangements and
attend to the corpse. This society, made up of pious and established community members, was held in the highest regard by traditional Jews who
lived according to Jewish law and appreciated the selfless work of those
who volunteer their time for such an unpleasant task. Members not only
arrange details of the funeral, they constantly watch over the body and ritually wash and prepare it for its final disposition. No embalming, no viewing, no flowers, no funeral home—for these and other reasons, the
Orthodox funeral stands starkly opposed to modern American traditions.[73]

First generation Jewish immigrants, however, did not have to follow traditional patterns of thought and action when death struck a member of the
community; early twentieth-century urban America offered alternatives
that trampled on these patterns in the effort to redefine the identity of the
deceased according to a completely different set of values, commitments,
and sacred symbols. In the first few decades of the century, it would not be
uncommon to witness on the streets of New York City another custom carried over from Eastern Europe, the public funeral pageant for certain local
community leaders. According to historian Arthur A. Goren, these pageants only survived for one generation in the United States. Although they
were enacted for key Orthodox and Zionist leaders, they were particularly
popular for those associated with the labor movement. In contrast to the
generally traditional funeral details upheld in the pageants for the former,
public funerals arranged for leaders of the Jewish labor movement displayed
a distinctly untraditional, indeed modern, sensibility.[74]

In his historical analysis of politics and public culture in Jewish
America, Goren describes the funeral pageant of socialist Meyer London,
who died in 1926 in an automobile accident. Instead of visiting the home
of the deceased before the funeral, the organizers of the event—the
Forward Association, the Workmen's Circle, the Socialist Party, the
Jewish Socialist Farband, and the United Hebrew Trades—elected to
place the physical remains in the hall of the Forward Building. Handled
by a local Jewish undertaker, here the body stayed, though not shut away
in a plain pine box. It was embalmed and put on display for all to see.

According to local reports, twenty-five thousand people came to pass by the open casket and smell the red and white roses in the floral tributes. Goren writes, "Among the mourners were old Jews who needed help climbing the stairs, mothers who raised their children to view the corpse, and high school youth sent by their teachers." A memorial service with a closed casket followed, a time for people to speak about London's passion for social justice and concern for the working class. Then a procession, numbering as high as fifty thousand, walked the streets of the Lower East Side, stopping first at London's home, and finally ending at the Workmen's Circle Mount Carmel Cemetery, where an American flag and socialist banners flew from a platform above the grave.[75]

European Jewish immigrants could bypass tradition at the time of death, or blend traditional and modern ceremonies—a choice that usually meant working closely with a funeral director in addition to, if not as a substitute for, the hevra kadisha. By the late nineteenth century, Jewish undertakers began to establish themselves in the business of death and adopt the traditions of their Christian colleagues. After the death of famous Yiddish political activist and dramatist Jacob Gordin in 1909, New York funeral director Sigmund Schwartz arrived at Gordin's home with specialists to help embalm the body before its public display at the Thalia Theater.[76] Jewish funeral directors were available for new arrivals to urban America, and although they generally did not play a role in Orthodox ceremonies, they got most of their business from nonpracticing Jews involved in the labor movement, and in the Reform Jewish community who found ways to preserve their faith and adopt American values at the same time.

In *The Wonders of America: Reinventing Jewish Culture, 1880–1950*, American religious historian Jenna Weissman Joselit explores the emergent Jewish funeral industry, which took control of the "Last Farewell" early in the twentieth century. Employing familiar language, rationales, and practices to support modern American traditions, Jewish undertakers completely shaped the ritual lives of their communities and gave friends and neighbors the mental, spiritual, and material tools to overcome their losses. Contrary to the imagery surrounding the hevra kadisha, indeed in direct opposition to the conventional imagery associated with Orthodox Jewish practices in industry mythology, enterprising Jewish funeral directors opened their homes as places of business, worship, and residence to customers who desired funerals that had more in common with the formalities taking shape among their Christian neighbors than with the traditions of the old country. Joselit writes, "With the exception of Orthodox funerals, which, by and large, remained scrupulous in their fidelity to tradition, the American Jewish funeral gradually lost much of its distinctiveness."[77]

Many American Jews adopted the "funeral aesthetic" driving industrial expansion, incorporating expensive caskets, elaborate floral displays, and spectacular monuments. The face of the dead, in addition to the well-dressed body, became a point of fixation in the short time before final disposition. Embalming made the body's presence at the final ceremonies possible, fulfilling the needs of the participants, and providing a living for the hardworking owner of the local funeral home. Joselit argues that embalming became routine in many early twentieth-century American Jewish funerals and quotes one Minneapolis funeral director from the 1940s to make the point: "In the early days all people objected to having any cosmetics used on the body or having it fixed up in any way. Today they no longer object. In fact they would, I am sure, remark if I didn't do these things as a matter of course."[78]

In the case of another Jewish funeral director in Columbus, Ohio, a discussion with the dean of the Cleveland mortuary school in the 1930s convinced him to open the first Jewish funeral chapel in the city. None of the Columbus funeral directors would apprentice the young man, so he had to work at a Catholic funeral home in Mansfield, a nearby town, to acquire the vocational skills and educational experiences to enter the burial market. "The fact that we learned how to embalm and how to direct a funeral—that came along with everything else. We had to do night ambulance work as well as removals of the deceased from the hospitals." After initial difficulties getting business, the funeral home became a success in the community, thanks to the work of his wife and brother, and the changing tastes of the Jews they welcomed into their homes.

> When I started out, all the families seemed to want was burial—burial by a Jewish funeral director. And after that, as things went on, the families came to realize that they could have a choice—whatever casket they wanted, whatever type of service they wanted, how many limousines they wanted and all of this was additional cost. And they came to want things nice. They, themselves, selected what they wanted in a casket and the type of services and how many limousines and police officers—and they were willing to pay for it as long as they had it.[79]

While many in the Jewish community joined with other religious lead-ers in publicly condemning the rise of the industry generally in the 1920s, 1930s, and 1940s, the rapid expansion of Jewish funeral homes during these decades may have at least two explanations. First as a significant number of Jews wanted to make sure Jews buried their own dead, many elected to leave the body in the hands of a specially trained mortician who could find ways to adapt his specialized funeral service training to meet the special needs of the family, regardless of their particular social or religious identity. Second, as funeral homes gained greater economic stability, Jewish funeral directors, on occasion, would even work closely with members of the hevra kadisha and establish a mutually respectful relationship.

The funeral industry made inroads into many other communities in the first half of the century as well, including Catholic and African-American neighborhoods in urban and more rural settings. Funeral homes gained a foothold in these areas because of one simple fact that applied throughout the country: Enough customers were willing to pay funeral directors to care for and dispose of their dead. But the success of these homes depended on a complicated set of historical circumstances, cultural negotiations, and changing religious sensibilities that gave death new meaning, and the dead a new role, in the everyday lives of Americans.

Like America's Jews, Catholics and Blacks embraced funeral directors as legitimate authorities who had the resources, knowledge, and community trust to establish order and meaning for the bereaved at the time of death. While many outspoken priests railed against the barbarism and extrava-gance of the American funeral, funeral homes spreading the industry gospel took root in a variety of Catholic settings. Some brought life to foreign tra-ditions by adapting them to more deeply rooted cultural and ethnic pat-terns of thought and behavior. Others completely wiped out any trace of these traditional patterns. The presence of the funeral director, either as a local insider doing business or an outsider with a local facility, did not auto-matically signal the death of distinctive customs from other parts of the world. Instead, it opened the door for profound social and religious read-justments that indicated a genuine willingness among community members to entrust their dead to the local funeral specialist who shaped new ritual patterns that blended the modern with the traditional.

For first-generation Catholic immigrants from southern Italy and their children, the local community undertaker, trained in the art of embalming at the closest mortuary school and licensed to practice by state governing boards, stepped into the cultural breach when death struck. According to Phyllis H. Williams, who wrote a handbook for doctors, nurses, social workers, and others frequently exposed to unusual customs and superstitious behavior among urban Italian immigrants in the 1930s, undertakers operated in these communities as they did almost everywhere in America, "as master of ceremonies of the whole proceedings, from immediately after death to the final scene in the graveyard." In this cross-cultural exploration of folkways in Southern Italy and New York City, Williams discusses the retention of certain cultural behaviors from the old country, such as loud "ritualistic wailing" in the house immediately after death to ward off evil spirits, and a belief that ghosts return home after death, which should not be understood by culturally ill-informed social workers or doctors as a sign of mental breakdown.[80]

Even though continuities with the old country remained, Williams explains that rising standards of living and the availability of mortuary facilities "changed decidedly" the experience with death in urban Italian-American communities. The local undertaker, or becca-morto, allows certain customs from the old country to persist, especially those connected with dressing the corpse and decorating the casket, but also authorizes the institution of new traditions for mourners to adopt in their new homeland. She identifies areas the funeral director manages more closely, like keeping track of the life insurance policy of the deceased, determining the number of cars in the funeral procession, and monitoring what gets buried with the body, that bring the experience of these Catholics in line with the rest of the country.[81]

In a more recent historical analysis of Italian Catholics in South Philadelphia, Elizabeth Mathias explores how funerals reflect "persistence through change." According to Mathias, by the 1940s, Catholics in this city had come to live with embalming and, in time, felt at ease in the funeral home. "The padded luxury of the funeral parlor has become the scene for the drama of the last hours with the body of the deceased, the funeral director has taken over the duties which had once been performed in the peasant culture by the family alone."[82] Changes in ritual choices for the funeral are tied to the diminishing interest in the life of the soul among first-generation immigrants, who gradually placed more "emphasis on the body and display" even though they and their descendants retained, though in a more covert form, folk religious sensibilities about the power of the dead.[83]

By the time Mitford's book came out, American Catholics were heavily engaged with the funeral industry at all levels, including but not limited to the establishment of the National Catholic Cemetery Conference in 1949 to protect and preserve the huge amount of cemetery land held by the Catholic Church. Despite the vocal, public support of Catholic leaders throughout the country for the anti-ritual crusade of the English Protestant woman, Catholic funeral directors did not disappear from the scene, but became even more established members of the local community. In the wake of the Second Vatican Council in Rome, between 1962 and 1965, funeral homes acquired even more prestige as legitimate institutions. The reforms taking place in most areas of worship and morality—changes that ultimately brought American Catholics closer to Protestant forms of religious expression—bolstered funeral industry strategies to make the service a psychologically and spiritually healing event for the living, rather than a dark, depressing affair morbidly focused on sin and the reality of death.

For young Catholic priests from Columbus, Ohio, in the early 1970s, the new liturgy for the mass was optimistic and hopeful, with more emphasis on resurrection and overcoming sorrow. One enthusiastic supporter of the changes stated, "The old Black mass music and prayers were very depressing, but recently, with the new liturgy, I've had several funerals with no tears at all."[84] Along with alterations in the details and tone of the funeral mass, the presence of flowers, and the change to white vestments, from black, other funeral innovations reinforced the necessary involvement of the funeral director, who could adapt his learned traditions to the creativity bubbling up in local Catholic communities. This involvement became even greater once leaders in the Catholic Church allowed mass to take place in funeral chapels—according to one report, a modification that led 90 percent of Catholic community members in one city to hold religious services in funeral homes.[85]

The rise of funeral homes in African-American communities in the early decades of the twentieth century provides even more historical evidence for the incredible expansion of the funeral industry across racial, ethnic, and religious boundaries. On the other hand, the social status of the Black undertaker in these communities was radically different from that of his white counterpart, though both were doing much of the same work. In the autobiographical account of a Black funeral director in Richmond, Virginia, Robert C. Scott reminiscences about his father's move from the shoemaking trade to undertaking at the turn of the century, "largely for my benefit, to inspire me and give me the opportunity I said I wanted."[86] The son quickly followed the father into the business. In 1906, Scott received his embalming license from the Virginia State Board of Embalmers and entered one of the few avenues of entrepreneurship open to Blacks in early twentieth-century America.

After the Civil War and through Jim Crow and the Civil Rights Era, professional opportunities were generally limited to certain integral social institutions that took root in African-American communities, such as the church, insurance companies, and funeral homes. In the case of funeral homes, like similar businesses in other ethnic and religious communities, the emergent industry supplied ideas, technologies, and products without discrimination. Writing about Scott, and African-American entrepreneurship in Richmond, author Michael Plater notes, "The funeral industry provides a rare example of an industry that successfully operated under the separate but equal doctrine, and had the absolute consent of most ethnic groups. Funeral service was a profitable industry that African-Americans engaged in without white competition. Yet, while the industry segregated clients, new technology and services flowed across racial boundaries, limited only by economic constraints."[87] So when African Americans were excluded from joining the National Funeral Directors Association, they organized their own organization in 1925, the Independent National Negro Funeral Directors Association.

At 18, Scott was probably one of the youngest licensed embalmers in his state, and his enthusiasm and enterprising spirit led him to encourage his "conservative" father to give up the cooling board and adopt a more "progressive approach" to preserving corpses. Claiming that old ways were "unreliable, unsanitary, and generally unpleasant," Scott looked to modern ideas by "reading everything I could get my hands on relating to the very latest methods and techniques known at that time." He not only tried to persuade his dad, he did what every forward-looking funeral director would do: "I also lost no opportunity to educate the people in the community to the virtues of embalming."[88] By the time the infamous flu epidemic struck the United States in 1919, Scott remembers, the community had been won over. While other local African American-owned funeral homes came and went in the first half of the century, Scott's aggressive business tactics and public investments in modern technologies—for example, he was the first funeral director in town to purchase one of many automobiles designed exclusively for the industry, the Packard Floral Funeral Coach—made him a respected, powerful, and successful member of the Richmond community.

Plater examines the cultural transformations taking place in African American funeral homes in this period, when modern death specialists were inventing stylized ritual traditions that combined religious and cultural perspectives about death from various parts of Africa, contemporary desires within the black community to ensure a proper and responsible disposal of loved ones, and industry-backed practices and knowledge that served as the foundation for the local mortician's authority to keep the body in his control. For example, he claims that African American funerals maintained certain African traditions, but also expressed modern American sensibilities and values: "[African-American] rituals and the symbolism attached to them are transplants of African death rituals. They are extensions of the elaborate funeral rites used by the Bakongo to secure a pledge of ancestral goodwill. The Bakongo honored the dead and practiced ostentatious funeral rituals as important survival techniques for the living. The African-American community held ostentatious funeral rituals to establish the status of the living."[89]

Like other early twentieth-century communities across the nation, African Americans welcomed funeral directors into their lives because they accepted their authority over the dead, and because they trusted them to adeptly steer the lifeless body to its final resting place with the appropriate mixture of respect for old religious traditions, modern American values, and changing local desires. Black funeral directors took control of the dead, adapting industry-supported myths and rituals to fit comfortably in the diverse social worlds of African Americans across the country. In many tragic, uncomfortable circumstances, they gave the Black community the same final moment white America desired with key public figures, an intimate look at the face of death that speaks the truth and shapes collective memory.

Funeral directors of all stripes shared these myths and rituals with Americans when they opened the doors of their funeral homes; accompanying structural changes in the movement of the dead out of sight of the living guaranteed a long institutional life for the undertaking industry.

The presence of funeral homes in nearly every sector of American society normalized relations between the living and the dead according to a moral code embedded in the industry myths and rituals. Despite local adaptations, modern funeral traditions established unity in diversity at the time of death. Regardless of social identity when alive, all dead bodies follow the same directions home. In the words of anthropologists Peter Metcalf and Richard Huntington, who included a chapter on American deathways in their 1979 cross-cultural study of mortuary rituals: "Given . . . the cultural heterogeneity of American society, the expectation is that funeral practices will vary widely from one region, or social class, or ethnic group, to another. The odd fact is that they do not. The overall form of funerals is remarkably uniform from coast to coast. Its general features include: rapid removal of the corpse to a funeral parlor, embalming, institutionalized 'viewing,' and disposal by burial."[90] By the time the FTC investigations came to a close, deep structural consistencies ruled American experiences with disposal of the dead.

For this reason, public calls for abandoning, or at least loosening, industry traditions seemed quite radical. With a notable history of establishing funeral homes in local communities, adapting new traditions to fit comfortably and sometimes not so comfortably with older customs, and gaining the trust of friends, neighbors, and associates, many funeral directors faced the challenges of the 1970s and 1980s without fear and without any doubt that they would continue to remain America's choice to ritually handle and remove their dead. Even if the rest of the country began to follow California's lead and request alternative ceremonies crafted to suit individual tastes, funeral directors could make the proper adjustments and stay alive economically, and the entire industry could continue to thrive, perhaps even be reinvigorated according to those willing to change with the times.

In addition to the changing personal appetites of local consumers, who began to feel a degree of freedom in crafting their own ceremonies, increasing numbers of recent newcomers required specialized services that strayed dramatically from the traditions of previous generations. In the aftermath of major changes in immigration law in the 1960s, undertakers in numerous metropolitan areas encountered new waves of immigrants from the Middle East, Asia, Central and South America, Africa, and other parts of the world. These communities do not yet have their own ritual specialists to take care of the dead, so they rely on local funeral directors who are even more flexible than their fathers about crossing lines of ethnicity, religion, and race, and who now want to make sure the customers get exactly what they want—as long as the corpse remains in their control after death and before final disposition.

New York City funeral director Thomas Kearns has a deep appreciation for the strong familial and communal emphasis many immigrant communities place on the funeral and the services around the body: "The immigrants we're serving now have some of the strongest funeral cultures that we see. The more the community is involved and the more the family is involved in this event, the more importance the funeral takes on, the more meaningful [it becomes]."[91] Kearns's grandfather, a mail carrier before a parish priest talked him into becoming the community undertaker in 1900, buried local Irish Catholics for much of his career. Now the four Kearns funeral establishments in the area serve Guyanese, Spanish, Middle Eastern, and other diverse populations.[92] In the new era of multiculturalism, Kearns's family even allows Hindus to come in and ceremonially wash and dress the embalmed bodies of their loved one, as long as they do it with the help of trained professionals from the staff.

But sometimes America's ritual death specialists must mediate between old world traditions and New World regulations. Ned Phillips, a banker for twenty-three years before entering the funeral business in Las Vegas in the 1980s, recalls his early encounter with members of the flourishing Hmong community. Catching a glimpse of a flame in a visitation room, Phillips walked over and opened the door to find mourners burning what he thought was money. He had to intervene: "I explained to them that our fire laws would not permit them to do that inside. . . . Instead of just emphatically pounding the table and saying 'we don't do this here,' I wanted to find out a little bit more about their needs and their tradition. And so I made arrangements for them to go out there and burn it in the parking lot in the back." Phillips describes how later that month, mortuary yard workers reported finding three dead chickens in the cemetery. "My initial reaction was 'Damn those vandals, why don't they leave us alone.' You know, occasionally people steal flowers, turn over a gravestone, whatever it may be. . . . And then I thought I better check this out. Well, it turned out that these had been some form of sacrifice . . . I went to the grave space and there it was and it was the Hmong that we had buried. So I called the family and again, we need to as human beings and as funeral directors, and certainly in our business, we need to listen and inquire and learn."

Commenting on the cultural shift from traditional, more uniform funerals to a wider array of ceremonies, Phillips remarks on the limits of adaptation:

> Most of us have discovered that we had to change our paradigms a little bit. And we will do whatever a family may request so long as it is legal, so long as it doesn't infringe on the rights of others, so long as it will not be damaging to our property and so long as it will not be considered undignified because we want to preserve our reputation.[93]

Funeral directors embraced multiculturalism as an unavoidable social and business reality in late twentieth-century America, although the transformation from a monocultural institution to a multicultural one took some time. In Oklahoma City, one funeral director had never seen a Buddhist monk burn incense and chant prayers until arranging his first Vietnamese Buddhist funeral. He grew accustomed to these and other unfamiliar Buddhist practices in subsequent visits. The Vietnamese accepted the funeral home as a viable location to carry out distinctive and important traditions from their home country, and the ritual specialists they hired assisted them in acculturating to American ways and values. Handing over control to funeral directors, allowing their dead to be routed through the funeral home, seeing them embalmed and on display did not pose any problems for Vietnamese community members who drew from religious reservoirs of meaning—Christian as well as Buddhist—to make sense of death in their lives.[94]

The diversity of views and practices surrounding the dead have been the subject of numerous media stories, trade articles, and scholarly studies since the 1970s. One newspaper article from Fremont, California, highlighted the profound changes taking place in a neighborhood funeral home, and the fact that mortuary colleges and national organizations had to find ways formally to educate funeral directors who were navigating the multicultural waters on their own: "Just as immigrants bring their native food and language to their new Bay Area homes, so, too, do they bring their funeral customs. And, local mortuaries, . . . eager to win their trade, will now separate mourners by sex, close coffins on food and extra clothes, . . . and keep extra incense on hand in case a Buddhist or Hindu family forgets to bring theirs."[95] A *New York Times* story about Cypress Hills cemetery reported on the intermingling of practices, the multiplicity of cultural values, and the combination of religious traditions taking place within the cemetery gates, resulting in a curious range of distinctly American customs that blended old and new ritual patterns. In one of many illustrations of this phenomenon, the author describes the visit of two Chinese brothers to their father's grave. Instead of pouring the traditional wine on the site, the brothers substituted beer because they were pressed for time. "It's a rush, rush thing," one of the brothers explains. When the author asks them about the incense and candles they have, he laughs and says, "I don't know. I'm Yankeeized almost."[96]

Funeral directors increasingly wrote about these experiences in trade publications from the 1970s on, and described the erosion of tradition with less and less scepticism. For example, *The Director* published a piece in 1997 by LaVone Hazell, a funeral director, instructor at the American Academy McAllister Institute of Funeral Service and St. Joseph's College, and executive director of the A. L. L. Bereavement Center in New York. Beginning with a recognition of the transitional state of traditional funerals, she immediately calls the reader's attention to a thanatological truth to reassure funeral directors about their necessary involvement in disposal no matter what the families request: "There are cultural universals that have remained consistent in funeral service: announcing the death; care of the deceased; a method of disposition; a possible ceremony or ritual; and some form of memorialization."[97] American funerals may be diversifying, but at bottom they share certain key, fundamental elements, for Hazell and many other funeral directors, "Cultural universals," that inevitably require trained experts to carry out the final details at the end of life.

She then reminds her colleagues that America is a "nation of immigrants" and that, even within various cultural groups, there is tremendous internal diversity. In her experiences as a professional undertaker, Hazell observes that all of America's ethnic, religious, and cultural communities, regardless of class, share at least one conviction that is strongly reinforced by the American society as a whole: respect for the dead. The continuity across Caribbean communities, African-American groups in the South, various urban Muslim neighborhoods, Latin American populations, and Asian-American Buddhist communities, "suggests . . . funerals are not only to provide closure for the deceased, but to assure ritual, attention and honor are respectfully, ethically, and appropriately given to the deceased." Even in multicultural America, funeral directors see themselves as safeguarding, at the very least, these universal desires for proper care of the dead. But individuals within various cultural communities also must recognize, as Hazell reports, that the "traditional American funeral still ranks highest in use among the cultural groups for whom I have directed services for more than a decade."[98] Embalming and preparing the corpse for display, conventional religious services in the funeral chapel, graveside ceremonies—these and other foundations of the traditional funeral demand the continued expertise of the funeral director.

Despite the best efforts of funeral directors to ensure the corpse did not return to haunt them or the industry, and to provide services that would bring satisfactory "closure" to those in grief, the dead continued to return to living society in many American communities—a social phenomenon common to cultures throughout human history, and an especially salient feature of American cultural history. One of the most familiar and popular examples of this interaction from the contemporary, multicultural present is "Dia de Los Muertos," the Mexican Day of the Dead. Around the time of Halloween, a holiday that only hints at the concern with otherworldly visitors deeply submerged in its roots, Mexican Americans construct altars, clean and decorate graves, and celebrate the presence of ancestors in culturally distinct, family-centered activities. This fiesta, tied to indigenous Mexican folk traditions and Catholic rituals associated with All Soul's Day, offers the living a chance, once a year, to intermingle with the dead in a joyous, macabre celebration. The popular media generally cover the event in ways that encourage the excitement and thrills associated with this momentary bridge between the world of the dead and the world of the living.

Today, Americans are exposed to the real presence of the dead in a variety of forms, such as channeled spirits who communicate with talented mediums or malevolent forces disrupting the health and well-being of the living. The phenomenal success of the John Edwards television show, *Crossing Over*, is only one of many examples from popular culture. In the reality-based show, currently advertised with the catchy plug, "The afterlife will be televised," host Edwards communicates with the dead relations of audience members, who are genuinely shocked and generally comforted by the intimate details that come up for public discussion.

The maltreated dead, and those who have died unjustly in American history, however, can also reappear to disturb the peace of the living; controversies surrounding the repatriation of Native American bones from museums and universities, and the exhibition of lynching photographs once popular in the

South are only two recent signs of the distressing return of the dead. While their presence may be experienced by one individual, witnessed by an entire family, or apprehended by a specific ethnic, racial, or religious community, the return of certain dead figures can also ignite popular religious movements that cut across diverse American communities.

Elvis Presley, who died in the summer of 1977, is a case in point. His death was a powerful moment that shocked the nation. The subsequent traditional funeral brought hundreds of thousands to view the embalmed body, and featured a Cadillac-filled procession to the grave and temporary burial in a local cemetery. (Later the body would be entombed on the grounds of Graceland.) These rituals provided throngs of fans with a communal service that signaled the loss of a cherished American personality. But Presley continues to live in the American imagination, for some as a spirit representing heartfelt, deeply personal hopes, dreams, and fears, for others as a physical being who cannot be contained by the grave. As one popular song states, even after death, "Elvis is everywhere," resurrected in consumer society for fans who desire to keep his presence firmly in their lives, rather than restricted to the soil of Graceland.

Perhaps if he had been cremated like John Lennon, another revolutionary popular music figure who transformed American culture, and whose shocking death in 1980 united millions of fans across the nation, Elvis would not be having such an active, and for many quite disturbing, afterlife. The immediate incineration of his body, rather than its prominent display for all to see, would surely have tempered the wild enthusiasm for his corporeal presence in the minds, hearts, and material lives of many Americans. While funeral directors were initially opposed to cremation as a viable alternative to the traditional funeral because they perceived it as a threat to the financial life of their funeral homes, by the late 1970s and early 1980s they began to realize that more and more people desired to have their loved ones consumed by fire. In the face of increasing demographic diversity, industry calls to adapt modern funeral traditions to meet the disparate needs of customers, and cultural interest in new forms of memorialization that did not rely on the visible body, funeral directors gradually incorporated cremation into their ritual practices and found ways to make this method of disposal both profitable and a source of healing. But before turning to the disappearing body in American funeral traditions at the end of the twentieth-century, it is necessary to explore other culturally relevant phenomena that have recently shaped the public presence of the dead.

5

FINAL FRONTIERS: INTO THE TWENTY-FIRST CENTURY

Eat, drink and be merry,
For tomorrow we die.
"Tripping Billies," Dave Matthews Band, 1993

The Dance Continues

"How will it change you?" This question is posed to the viewing audience at the end of a recent television commercial for Jeep Cherokee—an innocuous query, given the seemingly obvious referent of the pronoun, "it." But the commercial contains much more than a simple visual homage to the beauty and utility of the automobile. It begins with a baby sparrow that has fallen out of its nest, and the ominous approach of a skeletal hand that immediately brings to mind the image of the Grim Reaper. When the camera pulls back, the television audience sees that, indeed, their worst fears are realized and that the sweet bird is about to meet an early demise at the hands of a hooded, robed skeleton carrying a scythe. In a surprising turn of events, however, the dreaded figure exhibits some rather uncharacteristic behaviors.

After picking up the bird, the Lord of Death places the innocent back in the nest. In the background, an old, familiar Lovin' Spoonful song begins to play, awakening pleasant memories for all the baby boomers who are potential consumers: "What a day for a daydream, what a day for a daydreaming boy . . ." At this point, the Grim Reaper gets really silly and starts skipping rocks in a picturesque meadow, coasts down a hill on a bike (with his feet off the pedals), flies a paper airplane, sits atop a brand new Jeep Cherokee working on his tan, and finally uses his scythe as a golf club to whack a ball near the Jeep. The viewer sees how radically a Jeep Cherokee changed the personality of Death, who comes across as a fun-loving, pleasant companion. Many Americans cannot afford to buy a Jeep, so they will never know how owning one will change them. Every American can answer the initial question, however, if the referent shifts to the other, more sobering reality submerged beneath the consumer message of life transformation through Jeep ownership: How will a visit from the Grim Reaper change you?

This particular image of death—farcical yet undeniably serious, simultaneously harmless and bone-chilling—is all the rage in advertising these days. Commercials for cars, gum, insurance companies, computer games, gas and electric companies, and a host of other products and services rely on the figure of the Grim Reaper to grab people's attention, and prepare them to spend money for the comfort of body and spirit. One of the most easily recognizable characters in American consciousness—a tribute to his deep-rooted presence in the Christian imagination—is being resurrected not by leaders in the church but by ad agencies on Madison Avenue. Occasionally, the Grim Reaper plays a more conventional role in public culture than serving as a pitchman in consumer fantasies about new cars, violence, bad breath, and evading the touch of death. Instead of playful images confined to a thirty-second television commercial, the personification of death can be employed for more serious and conventional purposes, like instilling fear and reminding people that mortality is intimately linked to morality.

Before Halloween, 1999, for example, the Uptown Coalition for Tobacco Control and Public Health placed a series of anti-tobacco ads on billboards in African-American and Puerto Rican communities in Philadelphia. These billboards, originally a project for Black and Latina/Latino students at an alternative high school in the area, were designed to keep children from smoking by making crystal clear the connection between cigarettes and death.

The Grim Reaper, wearing white robes reminiscent of the Ku Klux Klan, brought the anti-smoking message home to these predominantly poor neighborhoods because it was such an obvious symbol of death and had enough cultural validity to grab and keep the attention of other children. The tableaux in these billboards, one with Death standing next to "Mr. Cigarette" and looking into the open casket of a young man, another with Death vacationing at the beach "'cause cigarettes are doin' my job," conveyed moral authority, collective urgency, and personal responsibility in the salvation of bodies.[1] Even though the primary audience for these dire admonitions were young people, Americans from all walks of life and all ages are quite familiar with the ominous form.

By the end of the twentieth century, the "messages" associated with the Grim Reaper multiplied dramatically and could no longer be restricted to banal theological perspectives on the end of time, death in life, and keeping life after death in mind. The figure of the Grim Reaper is a pervasive iconic fixture in American popular culture today, found not only in advertisements, but in comic strips, films, music, professional wrestling, books, cyberspace, and other settings that entertain, as well as educate, the masses. Though his presence immediately conjures up thoughts of death, in many cases the meanings have more to do with material matters for the living than spiritual visions of the life to come. Although the form has remained fairly stable over the centuries, the peculiar historical and cultural circumstances of the time shape the message Death brings to the often death-obsessed societies that keep him in view.

In the Christian imagination, the figure of Death is most commonly associated with one of the four horsemen of the Apocalypse, as described in the last book of the New Testament, the Revelation of John. Along with Pestilence, Famine, and War, Death enters the eschatological scene on horseback, cutting a swath of destruction and carnage at the end of time, and signifying mass, collective death before the final judgment. While the Grim Reaper has iconographic roots in this scenario, most historians turn to the waning of the Middle Ages and the beginnings of the Renaissance, roughly the fourteenth through the sixteenth centuries, to flesh out his historical appearance in Western culture.[2] In particular, the life of the Grim Reaper is tied to a specific cultural form that appeared in Italy, Spain, France, Germany, England and other parts of Europe at a pivotal moment in Western history—a time of numerous wars and revolts, severe economic hardship and inequality, terribly poor living conditions for most, and, perhaps more importantly, a series of deadly epidemics commonly identified as the Black Plague.

The "danse macabre," or dance of death, displayed a cultural fascination with rotting corpses at various stages of decomposition interacting with the living in dance, and proclaimed a basic reality in life: the triumph of Death. Compared to the Christian imagery surrounding collective death in early Christianity and the Middle Ages, the dance of death exhibited an entirely new sensibility about human mortality. According to historian Philippe Ariès, "the image of universal destruction that the Middle Ages present prior to the fourteenth century is of an altogether different order: it is dust, not decomposition, not worm-ridden corruption."[3] This transition from a predominantly collective awareness of death to a more personal preoccupation with physical, individual death and judgment played itself out in the cultural productions of artists, printers, authors and religious authorities, who found numerous ways to bring rotting corpses and dry bones into the popular imagination.

Ariès describes the danse macabre as "an eternal round in which the dead alternate with the living. The dead lead the dance; indeed, they are the only ones dancing. Each couple consists of a naked mummy, rotting, sexless, and highly animated, and a man or woman, dressed according to his or her social condition and paralyzed by surprise. . . . The moral purpose was to remind the viewer both of the uncertainty of the hour of death and of the equality of all people in the face of death."[4] It also communicates an older monastic commitment to hold in contempt the things of this world, especially the body, and remember the inevitability of death—memento mori, in Latin. Although this macabre vision arose during a period of great distress and high mortality rates, and was primarily used by the church to frighten people with repellant images of bodily corruption in order to save their souls, it should not be tied exclusively to a concern about the life to come. Instead, it can also express, in the historical context of an expanding mercantile, capitalist economy increasingly centered on individual lives, growing attachment to the things of this world, including worldly possessions, close relations, and the pleasures of the body itself.

As Ariès and other historians have noted, however, the danse macabre had various cultural incarnations in Western and Central Europe, ranging from the early depictions of the living and dead literally dancing to the more mundane narratives of Death personified as a towering figure, often carrying a scythe and visiting the home of the rich and poor, to the more repulsive, violent images of Death raping young women. According to historian Jean Delumeau, even as the macabre became a dominant, familiar iconographic system in these cultural settings, its meanings remained ambiguous, a play of "diverging significations" that could easily deviate from a traditional Christian frame of reference.[5] He describes two possible non-Christian meanings associated with the popularity of the macabre before the birth of the modern world:

> In a climate of anguish and morbidity, the allure of the macabre risked leading the people of the time (and it did not fail to do so) in two directions, each of which was ultimately opposed to the initial religious message. The first of these blind alleys was a taste for spectacles of suffering and violence. This syndrome started with the crucifixions

and flagellations of *The Golden Legend* and other saints' lives, eventually culminating in willfully pernicious scenes of tortures, executions, and
slaughters. Departing from the moral and religious lesson, there was a
gradual sliding into sadistic pleasure. The macabre eventually became
exalted for its own sake.

The second detour away from the path approved by the church
consisted of the turning of the memento mori into a memento vivere.
Since life is so short, let us hasten to enjoy it. Since the dead body will
be so repulsive, let us hurry to gain all possible pleasure from it while it
is still in good health. Here it is important to recall what took place
during outbreaks of the plague. Some people rushed off to churches
while others greedily indulged in the worst debaucheries.[6]

The meaning of the Grim Reaper in American popular culture today
is perhaps more complex than before the modern era, primarily for two
reasons. First, it is so completely removed from the evangelism of fear
propagated by Christians who understood the corruptible body as an
unmistakable sign of the need for salvation. Cut loose from its traditional symbolic anchors, the image of the Grim Reaper no longer
conveys any specific moral messages or inspires any particular fear.
Second, the demographic picture in the United States at the turn of the
twentieth-century is the diametric opposite to the dismal picture in
the late Middle Ages. Americans do not have to live with the widespread presence of corpses in their midst. Indeed, most rarely encounter
the dead throughout their life journey—in most cases, of course, this
encounter takes place at the funeral home after ritual specialists have
prepared it for a final appearance in public.

The Grim Reaper has been recast for the current generation, dancing
his way into American hearts and minds—often morbidly amusing rather
than disgustingly macabre—and assuming a variety of representational
forms suited to modern sensibilities, desires, and outlooks. In a hilarious
2001 episode of the animated prime-time series, *The Family Guy*, the
cartoon father dies and must find a suitable date for Death in order to
get out of his unfortunate predicament (he dies on his anniversary) and
live again. Given the preoccupations evident from the time of the earliest
desecrations of Native American graves by colonists hungry for collect-
ible artifacts to keep for themselves or sell on the market, it is not
surprising that American culture remains possessed by an engrossing
attraction to the dead, and has found numerous creative ways to enliven

the worn-out stereotype of the "King of Terrors."[7] Death haunts and inspires Americans, who live with a cultural system that unabashedly brings the dead to life for public consumption, sometimes in the recognizable, singular skeletal and robed form, sometimes as grave artifacts on display, sometimes as the recently deceased, and sometimes as a ghost present in, but unencumbered by, the physical world of the living.

This proclivity both to let go of and hold on to the dead simultaneously has animated cultural life from the Puritans to the present. Americans often conjure the dead and reflect on death without resort to the well-known Grim Reaper. The dead come to life in dreams, visions, civic commemorations, personal and shared memories, bestsellers, songs, public space, photographs—in other words, dancing across a spectrum of cultural productions, social rituals, and private fantasies. Illustrations abound. Take, Madonna's 1998 CD release, *Ray of Light*. The final cut on this platinum-selling album, "Mer Girl," describes the singer's voyage of self-discovery that leads smack into the cemetery and, ultimately, to the corpse of her dead mother. It does not hide behind sentimental images of innocence lost or domestic salvation—it is, a "material girl" keeping it, well, material. After running from home, her man, the memories of her mother, and her daughter, the heroine races through the forest to the cemetery and experiences being buried alive: "I saw the crumbling tombstones / The forgotten names . . . /I tasted my tears/I cursed the angels/I tasted my fears/And the ground gave way beneath my feet / And the earth took me in her arms/Leaves covered my face / Ants marched across my back."[8] Still running in search of herself after this episode, Madonna sings of smelling her mother's burning flesh and rotting bones. At the end of a musically and lyrically compelling disc, one of America's most popular stars leaves her audience in the graveyard with yet another troubling corpse. In a memorable music video for Tom Petty's 1990s hit "Mary Jane's Last Dance," Kim Basinger plays a corpse recently deposited at the local morgue. Petty plays the attendant on the night watch who cannot resist sneaking the beautiful body home for more than a last dance.

In another popular example from the end of the twentieth century, M. Night Shyamalan's 1999 film, *The Sixth Sense*, focuses on a young boy who claims he can "see dead people." This cinema sensation—like *Ghost*, a 1980s film that gave audiences entertaining insights into life after death and became one of the top grossing films of all time—displayed a winning combination of script, direction, and star power. It also offered an innovative treatment of one of America's favorite movie pleasures from the earliest years of cinema: seeing the dead live again. Lured into the theater by a suspenseful trailer anchored by the now famous line "I see dead people," the audience arrived anticipating the vicarious thrill of seeing the dead through the eyes of a child. The story follows the life of a psychiatrist after one of his former patients breaks into the doctor's home and shoots him in the stomach. Several months later the troubled doctor finally decides to take on a new patient, the young boy with a "sixth sense." The film provides viewers with some frightening images of the walking, talking dead, but the shock of the story, revealed at its conclusion, is that the doctor is not alive at all, but one of the wandering dead himself. No doubt the thrilling and chilling opportunity for this kind of intimacy with the dead accounted for some its success.

And to return to the genre with which we began, the advertisement, in February 2001, the *New York Times* carried an observant article on a current trend in "shock advertising." After describing a Toshiba copier ad that featured a man having a heart attack on a hospital bed and receiving shock treatment, the author explains: "In today's world, where 'shock advertising' featuring sex is hardly a novelty and where the public, bombarded by suggestive imagery, has grown increasingly jaded, Toshiba's spot, called 'Flatline,' represents a new trend in marketing. Like many other recent pitches seeking attention, [the new Toshiba commercial] eschews prurient themes, instead embracing subjects that are even more shocking and taboo—death and dying."[9] The article mentions a number of recent television commercials that embody this new spirit of transgression for Madison Avenue, including a Federal Express ad with Steve Irwin, of Crocodile Hunter fame, getting bitten by a snake and dying while waiting for the antidote to be delivered by a different delivery company. Death and dying may have remained "taboo" in advertising until the last decades of the century, but by the start of the twenty-first century, they have become quite difficult to avoid in most areas of American social and cultural life.

Another barometer of American interest in death, of course, is the reappearance of the undertaker in public culture. Since Mitford's time, his image has expanded in some unusual, and other rather typical, directions. On the one hand, the mortician has become something of a dreadful figure in the cultural production of horror, and the funeral home a common site of fictional murder and mayhem. Popular in 1950s comic books, the monster mortician has become a stock-in-trade for Hollywood horror films. In the 1979 fright fest, *Phantasm*, for example, two inquisitive brothers encounter the "Tall Man," a gangly, emaciated mortician with extraordinary powers, an army of menacing dwarves, and a special flying, spinning ball that extracts human brains from helpless victims. This cult favorite, which spawned a series of successful sequels, extends the dominant stereotype of the corrupt, sinister undertaker into the realm of the supernatural, where the diabolic Lord of Death enters everyday reality in search of fresh cadavers to ensure his dominion over the world.

On the other hand, a few more humane, sympathetic portrayals of funeral directors have appeared in film as well. In *My Girl*, the 1991 release directed by Howard Zieff, Dan Aykroyd plays a widowed mortician raising his only child, a girl of eleven. Set in the summer of 1972, the film presents a complicated portrait of the mortician, who is struggling with real-life issues like parenting, grieving, and dating. He falls for a freelance makeup artist, played by Jamie Lee Curtis, who eventually starts working for him as a cosmetician in his funeral home. This coming-of-age story touches on a range of familiar cultural themes, including first love, non-traditional families, cultures in conflict, and the dream of starting over. The fact that the main character is a funeral director brings a certain fresh perspective to these themes, as well as an unconventional spotlight on life in the funeral business.

Beyond cinema, funeral directors have surfaced in a variety of unexpected arenas, including the wrestling ring. The Undertaker, sometimes simply referred to as "Taker," is a character in World Wrestling Federation lore with a tremendous cult following. Surrounding himself with such personalities as The Embalmer and Paul Bearer, this wrestling phenomenon has even been turned into a popular comic-book figure by Chaos! Comics. At the other end of the cultural spectrum, funeral director and poet Thomas Lynch, one of the interview subjects for this study, achieved remarkable literary success with the publication of his book, *The Undertaking: Studies in Life's Dismal Trade* (1997). This volume, as well as numerous essays he has written for the *Harper's*, the *New York Times*, and other magazines and newspapers, has given the public image of the funeral industry something of a face-lift. In his writings, Lynch offers a portrait of his world, the world of the dead—and of the living with the dead—that complicates the stereotypical representations of undertakers historically so dominant in the popular imagination.

The HBO series, *Six Feet Under*, offers Americans a peek into the lives of the Fishers, a funeral family trying to survive the opening-episode tragic death of the patriarch, hit by a bus on his way to pick up a body. Before long, it is clear that the family plot is driven by sexual appetites as well as funereal black humor. The show was created by Alan Ball, writer of *American Beauty*, another popular and critically acclaimed film that relies on death and the presence of the dead to bring the story to life. Like other popular HBO shows, such as *The Sopranos* and *Sex and the City*, *Six Feet Under* taps into enduring interests that animate America's search for good entertainment—in other words, it stimulates America's mythic sensibilities. Instead of crime and the mafia, or the power and bounty of feminine sexuality, Ball's show offers viewers death and the ritual specialists who live with the dead in their own homes. It also resurrects the dead, with departed souls like the father returning as familiar-looking apparitions who come back into the lives of friends and family members.

Six Feet Under is a ratings hit, and presents an unusual portrait of people involved in the funeral industry. Compared with most popular representations in the past, the characters running this funeral home are complex individuals. They have fears, phobias, lusts, secrets, good humor and other traits that arouse sympathy and identification instead of disgust or ridicule. They are clearly ambivalent about their lot in life, and temporarily escape from their lives with typically American diversions, including sex, drugs, and fantasy. Ball understands the world of the funeral home, making reference to such historical tidbits as the fact that hearses once served as ambulances. He also plays off of a range of procedures and products associated with embalming, and injects dead-on dialogue that employs commonplace industry rhetoric. Finally, he addresses a pressing development that is currently having a tremendous impact on the formalities of human disposition in the United States and, indeed, around the world: the entrance of multinational corporations into the funeral business. The fictional show draws from the real-life drama caused by huge death-care conglomerates that emerged on the funereal scene in the 1980s and 1990s. Along with trying to deal with their own grief, as well as confronting the anger and confusion of their clientele, the Fishers must contend with financial giants who want to buy out the family business.

Booming Business for the Grim Reaper: From Family Homes
to Corporate Facilities

An early and highly successful tactic deployed by mortuary men with corporate mentalities was simply to buy out small, independently-owned funeral home owners like the Fishers, raise prices, keep the name of the familiar family business—sometimes even putting the former owner on the payroll as a consultant—and consolidate clusters of mortuary facilities in various regions of the country, creating economies of scale that yielded monster profits. At the end of the last century, the typical news story about American funerals was in many ways the same as it always has been, the economics of death, though now the victims include local funeral home owners as well as innocent, vulnerable consumers in grief. Publicly traded corporations, including the "big three,"—Service Corporation International (SCI), the Loewen Group, and Stewart Enterprises—are the new dance partners at the funereal ball, more than happy to lead the bereaved through the ritual motions attending bodily disposition. Family-owned and operated funeral homes have been experiencing the same kinds of economic threats from large corporations hungry for higher prof-its as small-town drug stores and other independently-owned businesses.

Why the recent corporate interest in what was once awkwardly called the "dismal trade" and is now gently referred to as "death care"? Early in the twentieth century, most never imagined a time when the financial records of funeral homes and existing market conditions would entice large investors. At the forty-seventh convention of Kentucky's state funer-al association in 1929, Professor Clifford G. Askin from Indiana spoke to the audience about the future of the death business. In a *Southern Funeral Director* report, the professor is quoted as predicting that "chain organiza-tions will not invade the funeral direction profession [because] the return on capital invested in the profession is not sufficient to attract large bank-ing interests." Citing statistics that show funeral directors realizing a prof-it on only seventy-five percent of the deaths they handle, Askin explains that the numbers simply do not add up to anything substantial enough to "attract large financial houses."[10] For much of the century, industry ana-lysts tended to paint a bleak economic picture for the nation's funeral homes, an image drastically at odds with prevailing popular assumptions about the riches made from exploiting grief.

By the 1970s, a new awareness about the profitability of death led to strategic and innovative ways of rethinking the business of death. In an award-winning essay for the National Foundation of Funeral Service, Kansas City, Missouri, funeral director Eugene Kennon addresses "The Future of Funeral Service." Along with advocating more open dialogue with local community members, especially ministers, and encouraging more educational opportunities in the area of "mental hygiene," Kennon impresses on the reader the urgency of facing major structural shifts in the funeral industry that will follow in the wake of greater migration to urban areas: "Because of the constant move of rural to city, the large funeral home will continue its expansion, edging out the small owner, because he can't compete in service, price or facility. As expansion and mergers occur, increased economies will be made by greater utilization of personnel with constant scrutiny of operating expense."[11] Kennon, as well as many others, began to see the writing on the wall, and knew it would only be a matter of time before the business of death became very big business.

The growth of funeral home chains in urban areas, a clear sign of entrepreneurial unrest and a corporate mortuary mentality, began to transform the economic landscape in the second half of the twentieth century. But even more essential to the rise of funeral home dynasties monopolizing human disposal in the United States from the 1970s on is a belief in a simple demographic fact: Whether they are rich or poor, celebrated or anonymous, millions of baby boomers will soon have their own round with Death. Numerous features on the funeral industry appeared in the 1990s, each highlighting how big business is banking on this seemingly obvious certainty. A reporter for *TIME* magazine wrote, for example, that "The death-care companies seek to ready themselves for what stock market analyst Steve Saltzman of the Chicago Corp. calls the 'golden era' of death, the fast-approaching epoch when baby boomers begin dropping like flies."[12]

Aging and soon-to-be dying baby boomers, who comprise a vast generation of people born between 1946 and 1964, may not exactly "drop like flies," but they will start to "drop" and need ritual specialists to prepare their bodies. Like many other sectors of the consumer economy, funerals have become a passage that conforms to a fundamental value in American society: Only buy what suits your individual personality. In an article on consumer-conscious funeral shoppers, a *Los Angeles Times* writer explains that the aging of the baby boom generation "represents the crest of a wave poised to engulf the funeral industry with demands for reasonably priced, often individually tailored celebrations of passage."[13] The consumer desires of this generation will no doubt make a tremendous impact on the goods and services provided by funeral homes; less bound by modern American traditions, baby boomers are more likely to improvise and innovate when planning rituals to accompany the dead to their final, this-worldly destinations. Dead baby boomers, most believe, will bring many happy returns to stockholders who, unlike their source of capital, have only one foot in the grave rather than both.

During the so-called baby boom, over 70 million babies were born, with close to 45 million from the years 1955 to 1964. By the end of the century, the products of this demographic explosion entered their middle age and now see the final frontier closing in on them, and their parents. In the introduction to a 1999 collection called *America's Demographic Tapestry: Baseline for the New Millennium*, the editors write:

> A maturing of America is the demographic transformation of the late twentieth and early twenty-first centuries. . . . Throughout each phase of its life cycle since the 1950s, the baby boom has dominated America and, since the 1960s, has shaped the nation's political life. It was originally the Hula-Hoop generation of the 1950s, overwhelming the nation's educational infrastructure. It then became the Woodstock generation in the 1960s, inundating our colleges and universities. It eventually swamped our labor and housing markets in the 1970s and then formed the yuppie brigades of the 1980s. Mature professionals supplanted yuppies, and the generation as a whole began reproducing itself in earnest, spawning the baby boom echo. Thus, the fabled youth society—in terms of demographic reality and vision—succumbed to its inevitable evolution into middle age. . . . As America moves into the second decade of the twenty-first century, the baby boom will finally transition into retirement.[14]

The authors do not mention the transition following retirement: death. The tremendous impact of this generation on a range of social, political, and cultural values has yet to be fully realized, but their encounter with death—first with parents, and soon their own—is beginning to move closer on the horizon.

In the early 1980s, in the midst of a demographic explosion in the number of people seventy-five years and older, the prospects in the field of death care seemed promising indeed. Even though consumer rebellion against the industry still dominated the press, customer satisfaction with goods and services continued fueling an industry generating billions and billions of dollars. Beginning in the 1970s, savvy businessmen inside and outside the industry started to take notice of revenues and the encouraging demographic future, and capitalized on a market many believed to be replete with financial opportunities.

At the start of the Federal Trade Commission investigations in the middle 1970s, at least two major, publicly-owned companies had entered the market by purchasing funeral homes that, in most cases, had been family-owned for generations. According to a 1976 New York Times article, the Houston-based SCI, with more than 150 funeral homes and several cemeteries throughout the country, earned over five million dollars on revenues totaling eighty million dollars. The Des Moines–based International Funeral Services, Inc., operated on a smaller scale, with just over a hundred funeral homes and sixteen cemeteries. Together, the two companies had a hand in close to 4 percent of the funerals undertaken in the U.S. in 1975. The article also reports on the FTC's special investigation of SCI for a number of ethical and legal transgressions. After some study, the agency filed complaints against the corporation that ranged from making a profit on so-called "cash advance items," such as obituary notices and flowers, to overcharging on cremations and providing kickbacks to other professionals able to pass along information on the recent dead, like medical examiners, morgue attendants, hospital staff, and police. In summer, 1976, the report explains, the company entered into a "tentative consent agreement" with the FTC which did not mention the kickback charges, but included the others. If approved by the commission, SCI would have to refund anyone over charged in the previous five years.[15]

In spite of these and other setbacks, the next two decades brought explosive financial growth to companies that anticipated immediate as well as long-term prosperity for investors in a market that will never disappear or be at the mercy of passing consumer fads. The Atlanta Journal Constitution reported that, in 1995, SCI owned over 1,500 funeral homes and close to 250 cemeteries. SCI and a few other major corporations now had control of almost 20 percent of the American funeral market, and were continuing to voraciously eat up smaller funeral establishments. For most of these publicly-traded, international corporations, the formula for success embodied typical capitalist virtues, especially entrepreneurial ingenuity and an ultimate commitment to the bottom line. Robert Waltrip, a funeral director since 1952 and current chief executive officer at SCI, exemplified these virtues when he began buying other funeral homes early in his career. He realized the need to look for more efficient ways to run his homes and created such business innovations as hearse pools and regional embalming centers so that the company could more tightly control and centralize corpse traffic. By the 1980s, SCI began to acquire other relevant companies, including those related to casket manufacturing, insurance policies, and even cremation, like the ash-scattering Neptune Society, earning it the reputation as the biggest death-care giant in the business. Its 1995 revenues: 1.652 billion dollars, a 48 percent increase from the previous year.[16]

The corporatization of death has not only restructured basic ingredients in the modern traditions invented in the early part of the twentieth century, it also greatly accelerated a trend with deep roots in the history of American funerals: preneed sales. Former NFDA executive director Raether wrote in 1990, "The history of funeral service will probably define preneed as the phenomenon of the 1980s."[17] Originally associated with burial certificates, burial organizations, and burial insurance for the poor, the idea of prepaying for funeral services was opposed by many funeral directors in the early decades of the twentieth century. After cemetery owners got into the business of selling prearranged and prefunded funerals in the early 1950s, members of the NFDA still hesitated following in their footsteps, fearful this practice would have the appearance of promoting "rank commercialism of the marketplace." By 1982, a special committee created by the NFDA to study preneed possibilities came up with the following conclusions: "Preneed exists as a business reality for funeral directors now and increasingly for the future. It cannot be ignored or denied. Preneed is something the consumer wants. Preneed is a means to provide the resource to pay for a consumer's desired funeral or in some cases to place limits on the amount that should be spent on the consumer's desired funeral." At the following convention, an official resolution was passed stating NFDA's approval of a list of positions on the issue, including an endorsement of prearranging and preplanning the funeral, disposition of human remains, or any form of ceremonial memorialization.[18]

During a time of heightened consumer empowerment when entering the funeral market, and in the midst of a death awareness movement in popular culture, prepurchasing funeral plans made sense to a sizable number of consumers who wanted to take ultimate matters about their body into their own hands. In this more receptive atmosphere, preplanning can

arouse a great deal of public attention, especially if the preplanner is a
major public figure. In January 2001, the popular *Star* tabloid carried the
front-page headline, "Oprah Plans Her Own Funeral," with a picture of
the megastar superimposed against an image of a cemetery. Inside, the
story, entitled "Oprah's Bizarre Death Wish," explains that although she
is only 47, Winfrey has carefully planned every element of her funeral,
including the desired casket, music to be played (Motown favorites like
the Temptations and Marvin Gaye) and a video eulogy she reportedly has
already prepared.[19] While not exactly a font of wisdom and truth, this
tabloid tapped into a widespread consumer interest in shaping funerals to
embody and celebrate the life lived rather than conform to conventional
traditions that suppress or limit expressive ceremonies.

With the rise of the corporate mortuary mentality came more aggressive
selling tactics in the area of preneed sales, primarily because this service to
the customer promised to bring a windfall of immediate revenues to stockholders, company leaders, and employees managing funeral houses. Indeed,
in 1997, SCI had presold over three billion dollars worth of funerals, adding
substantial capital without having touched a single corpse. Now many funeral homes, whether part of a franchise or not, work hard to inform the public
that they have the power to control both the ceremonial trappings and the
bottom line before they die. In other words, as long as they desire capable,
well-trained handlers of the dead, let consumers determine their own fate
while alive. After all, as in the case for democratizing embalming, if Egyptian
kings could preplan their not-so-final disposition in the pyramids, why not
all Americans?

Unfortunately for the death care giants, however, modern capitalist
America is not ancient Egypt. While many Americans may want royal
treatment, providing what customers want in this sector of the economy
proved much more difficult than expected. Preselling funeral plans and
other business strategies to corner the mortuary market has not yet
established the financial domination many stock market analysts predicted for death care. Instead, it has, in some instances, led to consumer
outrage. At the beginning of the twenty-first century—and way before
the anticipated flush of baby boom corpses—these companies have had
dramatic financial setbacks and stock market catastrophes. A variety of
developments have contributed to the difficulties recently experienced
by the big three, including lawsuits, stiff competition (a favorite phrase
in press coverage of the industry) between companies that led to

outrageous bidding wars, and most surprising of all, diminishing rather than increasing death rates.

In 1995, one of the "big three" was ordered by a jury in Jackson, Mississippi, to pay a local funeral home, in the business for generations, a whopping 500 million dollars in compensatory and punitive damages. Funeral owner Jeremiah O'Keefe sued the Canadian-owned Loewen Group, one of the most promising smaller giants in the funeral market whose stocks had risen twenty times the initial offering in 1987, for predatory trade practices. During the course of the civil trial, the jury heard evidence about monopolizing local markets, forcing competitors out of business, and raising prices on caskets and other items to outrageous levels over wholesale costs. They heard testimony from former Loewen employees that their jobs could be in jeopardy if they did not follow company orders and dramatically increase prices. O'Keefe settled the case for 175 million dollars, which saved Loewen from bankruptcy after its stock lost close to half its value when the verdict was announced.[20]

Not long after this financial trauma, SCI made its own predatory moves to improve its financial position and corporate reach in the death care market by attempting a takeover of Loewen. Although the attempt ended in failure, the hostile rivalry spurred competitive bidding wars over various properties that sent prices sky high. Unfortunately for Loewen, this put them two billion dollars in the red and they are still on the brink of bankruptcy. According to an analyst at J. P. Morgan, SCI began to suffer from guilt by association with Loewen and, in mid-1998, their stock began to fall, too. The delayed release of the company's earning report early the next year, providing investors with depressing news of per share stock earnings considerably lower than expected, contributed to the precipitous decline of SCI stock by over 40 percent.[21]

The *Houston Chronicle*, which carefully monitors one of its most famous hometown multinational corporations, reported that SCI's net income dropped from 28 to 12 cents per share in the second quarter of 2000. The cemetery segment of the corporation saw revenues drop from 257.2 million dollars in the second quarter of 1999 to 236.5 million dollars in 2000; gross profits for the funeral segment dipped from 84 million dollars to 67.4 million dollars in the same period. According to the newspaper, one of SCI's strategic plans to climb out of its financial hole is to participate in joint ventures with partners that enhance access to consumers in the global marketplace, such as improving its operations in

Spanish-speaking communities by creating a partnership with a Miami-based company. In the report, Jeff Curtiss, senior vice president and chief financial officer of SCI, discusses the possibility of a joint venture with operations in Cuban communities in Miami, as well as in Latin America and parts of Europe.[22] These multinational corporations, fueled by global capitalism and the potential for worldwide profits, are particularly open to cultural differences as well as consumer satisfaction.

The article also quotes Curtiss's explanation for the company's financial reversals: "People aren't dying at the pace actuaries expect them to die. . . . The rate of death is lower than expected. . . . It's clearly down from the prior year. The entire industry has had issues in terms of the death rate this year and many of the companies, including SCI, have had fewer sources of income that relate to undeveloped cemetery property." Curtiss, of course, is not the only one with "issues" about death rates. As more and more people continue to live longer, and as medical technologies and research continue to make headway in the drive to prolong life, the exact impact, and timing, of dying baby boomers on the death care market remains to be seen. Die they will, but in the meantime, as Curtiss and others witnessed in concrete, economic terms, the number of funeral services actually decreased between 1999 and 2000.[23]

In addition to the financial setbacks plaguing companies, a number of lawsuits have generated bad publicity in daily newspapers around the country. One is a class action lawsuit by SCI shareholders in revolt over top-level management business practices. Other suits have been filed by customers charging a variety of misdeeds, as well as by former employees.[24] A report in the "Law and Order" section of *The Atlanta Journal Constitution*, for example, described a "sex suit" in 2000 that alleged employees at one of SCI's Georgia funeral homes "kissed and groped each other while working and sexually harassed employees who didn't participate."[25] Recent entrepreneurial maneuvering by smaller businesses in the death sector, capitalizing on both the century-long consumer protest against the industry and the more recent cutthroat tactics of the death giants, is beginning to make its mark on the consumer landscape as well. The popular appearance of small, independent casket dealers on American streets and in cyberspace threatens to impinge on one of the most profitable commodities in the industry: the casket. The large corporations, as well as various state and national funeral-related organizations, are vigorously lobbying to dispose of this economic threat. But more and more states are striking down laws giving funeral directors exclusive rights to casket sales.

The news is not all bad for big business death care, however. The funeral is now, and no doubt will continue to be, a money-making enterprise. As the headline in a May 2001, *Houston Chronicle* reports, "Service Corp. Funerals Dip, But Profit Up."[26] Even with a decline in the number of funerals performed by SCI-owned funeral homes in the first quarter of 2001, the company made more money than during the same period the previous year. Several days after the article, the paper published a list of the hundred leading companies in Houston.[27] SCI was number 29. A report on Carriage Services Inc., a start-up, and much smaller, funeral service company with headquarters in Houston, indicated that the misfortunes of the big players may not sound the death knell for the corporate presence in the market. Indeed, Mark Duffy, CEO of Carriage, explains that they will follow an entirely different strategy from the aggressive, free-for-all tactics of the now-crippled big three: "We look for large funeral home businesses with first-class management. . . . They must pass extensive due diligence. When you make sure the businesses you acquire have good fundamentals, there is less operating risk. Our performance is a good indicator that we don't have a problem with integration of our acquisitions."[28] The funeral business has come a long way from the early days of embalming in the home of the deceased. Even though acquisitions and mergers, consolidations, and economies of scale are on the minds of mortuary entrepreneurs, they want the same thing as their early counterparts: control of the dead from last breath to final disposition.

The rise of death care conglomerates, along with significant changes in the landscape of the death market—thanks to such developments as independent casket stores and customized funeral celebrations—have led to a new round of governmental investigations of the industry and calls to revisit and revise the FTC trade rule. One example of these efforts is the 2000 Senate Special Committee on Aging. Iowa Senator Charles Grassley, the committee chairman, claimed in a CBS news report that the industry needs more consistent regulation. Numerous horror stories were told in the hearings, including a description by a woman who charged that her grandmother's remains had "spilled out of a faulty coffin into a mausoleum."[29] A press release from NFDA headquarters in Milwaukee the same day as the CBS report said the hearings were clearly distorted, complaining that only one person was invited to testify on behalf of funeral directors, the president-elect of the Iowa Funeral Directors Association, Jay Jacobson. The release expressed Jacobson's outrage at being the only funeral service professional invited to testify, and his insistence that the majority of America's funeral homes are privately owned. He wanted to make sure that the committee distinguished between the majority of independently-owned and operated funeral homes and the minority of chains in thrall to global corporations.[30]

As the corporatization of American funerals generated increasingly bad press, representatives from state and national organizations, and the majority of independent funeral directors around the country, realized that the economic upheavals of the present and recent past had produced a new and potentially valuable foil in the ongoing, century-long effort to carve out a legitimate professional identity in the consumer marketplace. Like communists in the 1950s, and longhairs in the 1960s, the corporate acquisitions and merger mentality represents a contemporary foreign threat to indigenous myths and rituals undergirding American traditions passed on from funeral forefathers in the early part of the twentieth century. By defining themselves against the now-familiar image of multinational, publicly-traded corporations voraciously gobbling up the death trade, funeral directors who have not sold out stake their claims of professional integrity, moral purity, and ritual competence on a combination of core middle-class American values and personal religious convictions.

In death care, as in most sectors of the savage consumer economy, one company's bad press is another company's public relations golden opportunity. Journalist Miriam Horn published a story in *U.S. News & World Report* titled, "The Deathcare Business." The cover of the issue featured a close-up of a young, even sexy, veiled widow and the legend, "DON'T DIE BEFORE YOU READ THIS, How the funeral business makes money off your grief." In a subsequent issue, the magazine published a letter from the president and executive director of NFDA. According to the funeral magazine *The Director*, *U.S. News* had omitted a portion of the letter challenging Horn's economic portrait of the industry, including the suggestion that undertakers make six-figure salaries. The letter, published in its entirety by the funeral trade magazine, shifts attention away from the Goliaths in death care generating billions of dollars, and focuses on the remainder—the clear-cut majority—of multigenerational, independently-owned, community-rooted, small funeral homes in the country. In addition to asserting that funeral directors earn a much more modest income than suggested by the article, the letter says that they can take pride in an unexpected social reality: Americans trust them with their dead.

> More than 80 percent of [American funeral homes] are "mom and pop" small businesses that have been owned by the same family for generations. The funeral service professionals and family owners in these firms provide honest, ethical, caring and compassionate service to the people of their community 24 hours a day, seven days a week. . . . The American people rate funeral directors as among the top ten most honest and ethical professions, according to a recent Gallup Poll. The Federal Trade Commission recently reported 85 percent of funeral homes were obeying federal law requiring funeral price disclosure. The Gallup Poll, the FTC report and other studies confirm that an overwhelming majority of funeral directors are providing honest, ethical, and fairly priced services to the communities in which they serve.[31]

Many funeral directors now take special care to differentiate themselves, their business practices, and their work ethic from corporate models in death care, and use these differences to bolster claims of vocational devotion to tending the dead, and consumer satisfaction with their production of ritual order when death occurs. Ironically, warnings from independent undertakers about insensitive, greedy corporate predators on the prowl for vulnerable, grieving consumers echo the warnings voiced by consumer advocates of funeral reform earlier in the last century. When asked about the changes he has seen in the past several decades and whether consumer tastes have transformed the industry, Trevino Morales responds, "I think the changes have come in the last few years as the corporations are buying family-owned funeral homes. Consumers didn't change [the funeral], corporations did." He elaborates further on the impact of conglomerates: "There's a big difference between corporations and family-owned funeral homes. You get personal service at the family-owned funeral homes. Corporations are an assembly line. 'When you've got them in your office sell them everything you can.' The interest of the sole proprietor is providing good service, helping a family through trying times. They do get paid but it is not as demanding as corporate-owned funeral homes because you've got to answer to your stockholders. [A] sole proprietor only answers to himself and his conscience."[32]

Bill Monday also identifies corporate interest in funerals as the most significant change in the industry in the recent past. He explains how this affects the family in grief, and the body once tenderly cared for in the traditional family home. "Our business is a twenty-four hours a day, seven days a week business. I had a friend who worked for a firm. If he started embalming a body and four o'clock came around, which was his [stopping] time, he stopped because the next embalmer would come in and finish it. If you made arrangements with a family, you followed that family through. [An employee working for a major corporation] might make arrangements with a family and you're off Friday, Saturday, and Sunday. You might not ever see that family again. I guess this is the way business and our society are going."[33] Across the country, funeral directors understand the presence of the multinational corporations as a mortal threat to an American way of life.

Surprisingly, the rise of the death-care giants has not only provided local funeral directors with rhetorical ammunition to mark out their professional territory, it has also produced a subtle and quite remarkable change in the tenor and tone of press reports profiling local funeral homes. A great deal of negative media attention on SCI and other multibillion dollar companies has accompanied their ride to the top of the death market, focusing on a slew of offensive corporate-minded strategies like retaining recognizable names of family funeral homes after buying the owner out, or buying into the African-American market, where cost-efficient measures like cremation have not yet made an economic impact.[34] At the same time the press has condemned these corporate tactics, and after the corporate buying frenzy of the past two decades lost some steam, a strange nostalgia began to emerge at the turn of the millennium about funerals in the long-lost days of early twentieth-century America—the time before the corporate monsters came and altered the relations between modern ritual specialists and the living.

In one of numerous examples from the late 1990s, the *Philadelphia Inquirer* reported in the "Neighbors" section on the Donohues, a family of undertakers with their own small chain of homes in Newtown Square, West Chester, Downingtown, and Upper Darby. "Where Funerals are Truly a Family Affair," tells the entire, one-hundred-year history of the family business, beginning with Nicholas Donahue, who set up shop in South Philadelphia after his parents immigrated from Kerry County, Ireland.[35] After Nicholas died from tuberculosis during the Spanish-

American War, his brother John P. took over and now his descendants, all the way to his great grandsons, are keeping the business thriving.

Most of the story covers life in the old days, as reported by the living family members. John A., the oldest brother in the family, speculated about how his grandfather got into the business: "I think the Irish always laid claim to this business because of their sense of humor. That may sound macabre, but the Irish accept death as an inevitability. You know, 'She's in a better place.'" The article describes funerals in the old days, when the undertaker would enter the home of the deceased, prepare the body, and often put it on ice "because there was no way of preserving bodies." It describes the disposal challenge the family faced during the deadly flu epidemic in 1918, when people stole caskets piled up in the street because so many were dying so quickly, and the public relations expertise of grandfather Donahue, who belonged to over 33 organizations in the city and won the people's confidence as "a friend, someone they felt they could trust, to do the burying."[36]

A rather complimentary picture is painted of the Donahues and their small family business in an uncomfortable, but inevitable, venture in the American economy. By the end of the piece, the reader learns that the Donahues perform "about 700" funerals a year from their four homes, catering to a wide-ranging clientele that includes Korean Catholics, Buddhists, and Reform Jews, as well as the increasingly choosy consumer who wants customized treatment like, "laser engraving on the outside of the casket to commemorate the deceased's special interests; a drawing of a fisherman and another of a golf club, for example." A final point made in the piece is that the Donahue's generate significant business by preplanning funerals with consumers who want to pay ahead of time, and that Raymond, another grandson, has his planned out already.[37]

Compared with the heartless giants in death care, the smaller, family owned business—even with multiple home locations—is often depicted as run by traditional, humane, authentic, even humorous Americans who have a unique, often charming perspective on local history. In a recent *Los Angeles Times* story on the city in the section "Then and Now," the Pierce Brothers were profiled as mortuary mavericks who made a fortune taking care of the dead, and had intimate contact with the Hollywood dead. "A Lively Business in Funerals" begins with the brothers' early years as livery stable owners and rapid rise to the top of the funeral market. The piece covers the excitement of opening the "first full-service funeral home in the city," in 1924, the impact of such innovations as using trolley cars in funeral processions, and the "marketing schemes" of the brothers, such as providing tours of mortuaries and embalming rooms to local church groups.[38]

Their role as funeral directors to the stars is also explored, as in the 1935 death of actress and comedian Thelma Todd, known as "Vamping Venus," and the "thousands of mourners" who descended on the Washington Boulevard Pierce Brother Mortuary after she died. The article also gives Ralph Head, who worked with the brothers for 50 years, the final word on the infamous story of Errol Flynn stealing the dead body of John Barrymore from the mortuary and bringing it to a Beverly Hills hotel, so Barrymore could participate in his own wake: "It never happened. It just made a colorful story for Flynn's autobiography."[39] At the end of the harmless, entertaining history of the Pierce brothers, the reader learns that the family sold their mortuary interests—funeral home, cemeteries, crematoria, insurance—in 1959, and that today, Pierce Bros. is owned by SCI.

Although fears of death-care giants monopolizing the funeral business do not currently get as much press as in the early 1990s, their undeniable impact in American society, and the kind of coverage they receive in the media, contributes to a cultural nostalgia for the traditional values now associated with the family-owned funeral home. The values—trustworthiness, candor, humor, familiarity—could only emerge in the wake of the discovery of new media scapegoats responsible for the victimization of grieving innocents. The long-term consequences of death-care conglomerates for the vitality of privately-owned, family-run funeral homes are difficult to predict, but significant changes in the kinds of students entering mortuary colleges raise a number of relevant issues in this time of transition in the death market.

As part of its series on the funeral business, the *Pittsburgh Post-Gazette* ran an article entitled "Quiet! Morticians in Training Here." The writer investigates student life at the Pittsburgh Institute of Mortuary Science, one of a handful of similar free-standing educational institutions in the United States in the business of preparing future funeral men and women. Provided is evidence of a dramatically changing student population enrolled in this and other mortuary programs around the country. For example, only 20 percent of the students in the program come from families already in the business, a marked drop in recent years. Also, the number of women morticians in training has increased substantially in the last few decades, with roughly 40 percent in the program when the piece was published in 1999. Overall, the article reports, enrollment in mortuary training programs has increased throughout the country. Why are more people, especially those with no connection to the funeral business, looking to live a professional life as an undertaker? The article offers the perspective of Gordon Bigelow, executive director of the American Board of Funeral Service Education, who says "There are about 3,200 mortuary students nationally, with enrollment growing during the 1980s and 1990s, perhaps from a sense that death care is largely a recession-proof industry for future employment."[40]

In November 2000, a *New York Times* article on "Funeral Business's New Look," journalist Edward Wong reports on the increasingly diversifying work force in the industry, and the changing composition of the student body at mortuary schools. Mentioning the recent financial turmoil confronting big death-care corporations, Wong also reinforces the growing perception that funerals are going to be big business in the future, no matter what may be occurring at the moment. The setbacks for major companies like SCI are understood to be a boon for individually-owned funeral homes, with students anticipating the luxury of being their own boss, garnering a respectable income, and participating in a fulfilling career. The inevitable surge in baby boomer deaths, the report intimates, as well as an expectation that there simply will not be enough funeral directors to handle their corpses, is contributing to the growing interest among new enrollees, many of whom are female, non-white, and novices with no family ties to the business.[41]

No matter what the future of death care looks like in the coming century, the Grim Reaper will remain a fixture of the popular imagination, dancing in and out of American lives. Whether in television commercials, music videos, film, or other popular media, the Grim Reaper reminds everyone, especially aging baby boomers, of their ultimate fate in the coming century. But, as we have seen, his appearance can signal a light-hearted approach rather than an ominous intrusion. In a humorous *New York Times* opinion piece from June 2001, Jenny Lyn Bader writes about recent changes in public and popular culture that have altered the image and respectability of America's funeral directors. Thanks to numerous high school and college death education courses that write the funeral industry into the curriculum, as well as powerful new shows like *Six Feet Under*, depicting sympathetic, complex, and realistic characters, undertakers are currently enjoying a "new lease on life." At the end of her piece, Bader considers other occupations that might benefit from special treatment on television, including accountants, senators, and H.M.O managers. Her final suggestion? Make the gravest occupation of all TV-friendly: "The Grim Reaper himself is in serious trouble. In 'Death Gets a Makeover,' he could be given better clothes and a less daunting scythe—perhaps a gadget from the *Sharper Image* catalog."[42]

Regardless of contemporary perceptions of the Grim Reaper, or the humor often wrung from his wretched presence as the personification of Death, Americans continue to be focused on mortality, both as a challenge to the imagination as well as a condition that demands ritual action. Many place a great deal of stock in the power of science—to slow the aging process, freeze bodies for future animation, or put an end to death completely—but it is highly unlikely that mortality will cease to be a fundamental, constitutive element of human life any time soon. Although it is dangerous to put too much stock in demographics, according to the National Center for Health Statistics, the death rate will rise from 8.6 people per 1,000 in 1999 to 10.24 in 2020. No doubt, the dead will continue to pose a peculiar dilemma that must be solved by both ritual specialists as well as by consumers themselves. Perhaps the most important question the funeral industry will face in the twenty-first century gets to the heart and soul of its very existence: Whither the body?

Not Yet a "Cremation Nation"

In July 1996, Jessica Mitford died at the age of 78 in Oakland, California. Although she jokingly stated her desire for a traditional funeral, with plumed horses, public ceremonies, and a plush casket with her embalmed body, Mitford actually preplanned her final disposition according to a dramatically different logic from that found behind modern American traditions. She chose to have her body cremated and her ashes dispersed in the Pacific Ocean. Her family requested that well-wishers who wanted to express their regrets at her passing make donations to her son's "Send a Piana to Havana Fund."[43] At her memorial service a week later, with over 600 people gathered, Mitford received a hero's tribute from a number of well-known literary figures, including Maya Angelou, and from journalists and Bay Area activists. In addition to the touching and funny reminiscences of her close friends and family at the service inside, there were two funeral hearses outside, one set up in the plaza with photos and mementos from her life, the other on the street, being pulled by six black plumed horses and followed by a twelve-piece brass band.[44] While she preferred that people forget her dead body, memories of her embodied life drew close relations and admirers to gather together in ritual celebration.

No doubt, some in the funeral industry would like to forget Mitford ever lived. However, many have accepted her presence in their lives, and will live with her for as long as she is championed by funeral reform-ers intent on undermining the ritual authority of America's funeral directors. While her body has disappeared from view, the public author-ity of her critique survives in the popular media, thanks to such consumer advocates as Lisa Carlson, who started the nonprofit Funeral and Memorial Societies Association and has written on caring for one's own dead, and Karen Leonard, former research assistant to Mitford, who contributed to the 1998 revised edition of *The American Way of Death*. The rerelease of this book after Mitford's death began a new round of media frenzy over the outrages of the funeral industry—though nothing like the sensation created by the first edition in 1963. The new edition included updates in some chapters, entirely new sections on corporati-zation, an account of her guest appearance at a 1995 Funeral Service Seminar in Tiburon, California, and an amusing introduction, with Mitford's reflections on the birth of the book and her response to its incredible, worldwide popularity.

Mitford's final wish, to be cremated and scattered, was characterized in the title of one local newspaper article on her passing as a "last snub" aimed at the funeral industry, and the numerous funeral directors from around the country who called to offer their services when news broke of her death.[45] Although many understand incineration of the body as a rebuke of modern American funeral traditions, it is clear that the recent surge in cremation rates signals both institutional approval of the practice within the industry and a seismic cultural shift in consumer sensibilities about the value and purposes of the body. Between the death of President Kennedy one month after the publication of Mitford's book and the recent scattering of his son's ashes at sea, cremation rates have skyrocketed from under 5 percent to close to 25 percent. Rates may be especially high in California and parts of the Southwest, but burning bodies is clearly becoming a nationwide phenomenon. The future looks bright, however, for the funeral home, an American institution that will continue to thrive by living simultaneously with tradition and invention, changing with the times but remaining fundamentally the same.

Cremation has a much longer history in American society than the past few decades, when it became the second, and really the only, alternative to burial. As historian of religions Stephen Prothero expertly demonstrates in his 2000 book, *Purified By Fire: A History of Cremation in America*, the practice achieved a fairly limited degree of acceptability in some communities by the early 1900s, roughly 25 years after the body of Charles De Palm, member of the Theosophical Society and an Austrian immigrant who had been in the country just one year before his death, burned in the nation's first cremation. Between the turn of the twentieth century and the 1963 publication of Mitford's book, the "bricks and mortar stage" in Prothero's schematization, the cremation movement moderately expanded both geographically and demographically—from a small group of cultural elites in the late-nineteenth century to a broader swath of American society in most regions of the country other than the South, including early-twentieth-century Sikh, Hindu, and Buddhist immigrants.[46] More importantly for its future, however, was the dedication of resourceful men who worked together to address a series of challenges—what Prothero describes as "the everyday challenges of improving crematory technologies, constructing crematories and columbaria, and administering a burgeoning infrastructure."[47] Although limited in clientele, and still shunned by the conservative funeral industry, cremation achieved only a small degree of institutional viability before the 1960s.

Cremation catches fire, so to speak, after Mitford's book in 1963, which opened the crematory door for consumers disenchanted with the mythology emanating from the funeral industry, and gripped by a combination of practical and deeply religious concerns. With only a small number of cremations taking place in the first half of the twentieth century, the incredible increase in its popularity in the second half led many in the funeral industry to rethink their initial skepticism, if not downright condemnation, of the practice and reinvent American funeral traditions once again. Many funeral directors in the early and middle decades simply ignored the rather marginal and, in America at least, still highly unusual practice. However, after Mitford's book, cremation could no longer be ignored, and with the Federal Trade Commission's insistence that funeral homes provide disposal alternatives, including cremation and direct, immediate disposition, funeral directors once again saw the wisdom in taking a more progressive posture and warmly embracing consumer tastes.

It took some time for many in the industry to come around on cremation, but most morticians eventually ceased their public attacks on the emergent practice, which had equated incineration and bodiless ceremonies with indecency, insensitivity, and secularism, and found a way to live with and profit from burning bodies, either by contracting with freestanding crematoria, or building their own furnaces. One of the more respected commentators on American funerals, the Reverend Paul Irion, published a book in support of cremation as a psychologically and theologically legitimate means to dispose of the body. Writing in 1968, Irion notes the structural shifts within the industry already taking place because of cremation, and the prevalent distrust and competition between funeral directors and crematorium operators. "Discussions with both funeral directors and crematorium managers reveal mutual suspicion of conflicting interests. The crematorium manager feels that funeral directors, through laws which require a licensed funeral director to secure certification of death and permission to bury or cremate, have made themselves indispensable adjuncts to the cremation process."[48] In the end, Irion encourages not just an acceptance of cremation, but pastoral involvement in all phases of postmortem activity, including, if appropriate, the final scattering. He even provides a thought exercise, "How Do You Feel About Cremation?" as an appendix to assist readers in clarifying their own opinions on the matter.

How did cremation become a viable, and increasingly popular, consumer choice in the second half of the century? It is not simply a matter of economics, with vultures preying on the poor—most surveys demonstrate that the majority of people who opt for cremation are from the upper classes.[49] In addition to the popular impact of Mitford's book, and the political ramifications of the FTC investigations, a number of institutional, cultural, legal, demographic, and religious changes in the 1960s and 1970s contributed to the growing social acceptance of this disposal choice. During the Second Vatican Council, in the summer of 1963, before the release of Mitford's book and Kennedy's assassination and funeral, the Roman Catholic Church stepped away from its nearly one-hundred-year ban on cremations. The church continued to advocate traditional practices that preserved a ceremonial role for the body before burial, practices Catholic and Protestant undertakers could easily manage. But by lifting the prohibition against cremation, Pope Paul VI ensured that members of one of America's largest religious communities could at least consider this option, and not be troubled by the question of bodily destruction before the resurrection. Catholic consumers, like their fellow American shoppers, now had an additional choice at the time of death.

Another reason for the ascent and cultural legitimation of cremation in the United States is the critical change in immigration policy that occurred in 1965, when Congress rewrote immigration law and allowed more South and East Asians to enter the country. As the religious and cultural landscapes of metropolitan areas became more diverse, funeral homes found themselves catering to communities with funeral traditions entirely different from those invented by pioneering American ritual specialists. While early cremationists in this country drew on eastern religious traditions to make their case about the values associated with burning corpses, funeral directors in post-1965 America encountered recently arrived Hindus, Buddhists, and others who understood cremation as a traditional religious duty rather than a consumer statement about funeral reform. For these communities, cremation had particular religious meanings that were mythologically locked in to significant cultural practices.

Perhaps no other community in the United States did more to help funeral directors see the religious and ritual virtues of cremation than Americans affected by AIDS. As we have seen, many in the industry initially responded to the arrival of AIDS corpses with fear, disrespect and, in some cases, downright malignity. Most family members wanted to dispose of the disease-ravaged body as quickly as possible, whether out of shame stemming from the terrible social stigma attached to AIDS, or out of love that overcomes socially-constructed stereotypes and seeks new forms of ritual appropriate to the life and death of the deceased. Now funeral directors often speak about the human face of AIDS, their initial promotion of cremation and direct disposition, a short-lived trend to charge more for embalming, and their own mixed feelings when they were called upon to perform their work.

Wayne Baxter speaks frankly about the early fears associated with AIDS and what some funeral directors had to face when dealing with the families. "Little by little we found out what we had to do. It was . . . stressful to see families torn apart with that. The shame of that disease causing people to have direct cremations that they never would have had if their son or daughter had died of pneumonia, cancer, or something else.

Often the victims were people in the gay community. So they felt this rejection. I think one of the most painful things was to see parents reject their son or daughter who died of AIDS and have direct cremation."[50] Thomas Lynch explains that "there was this sense that victims of AIDS should be cremated immediately so you don't expose yourself. . . . This was terribly hurtful to those families. Many families came in with the social stigma of this disease. In my experience it was never a gay disease, it was a human disease. In funeral service there was a great fear about it. People would charge extra for embalming because of the possible exposure. There was a great deal of misinformation."[51] The bodies of these victims were a source of pollution and humiliation for many funeral directors and family members who did not desire a rehabilitated, visible, purified living presence to look at and remember. On the other hand, a last glimpse of the too-fragile, long-suffering AIDS body was not necessary for many close relations who found other means to create and hold on to memories of the life lost.

The choice of cremation, arising from a wide range of emotions, motivations, and rationalizations, became a common, familiar scene in AIDS-related literature, particularly in the many memoirs and biographies that have appeared in the last two decades. Mark Doty's elegant memoir of life with his partner Wally, and Wally's death from AIDS, is one of numerous examples. After Wally finally succumbed to the disease, employees from the local funeral home came out of the cold winter air to retrieve the corpse and take it away. The body as Doty knew and experienced it never played a role in any final ceremonies for Wally. The cremated remains, however, were present during the memorial service. In the book, Doty explores his own uncertainty about the ashes, knowing that Wally had wished them to be scattered in a favorite natural spot that had special meaning for the two of them, but also strangely attached to them and relieved when Wally's mother asks him to wait before performing the final ritual act of dispersal. He writes, "I didn't know until that moment that I'd be relieved, too. I wasn't ready to relinquish the evidence of his body." Doty recognizes this attachment when he realizes that, although still retaining some of Wally's personal belongings that are "full of the psychic scent of a man," the physical presence of his partner will disappear forever when the ashes are scattered.[52]

Struggling with his mixed feelings about the ashes, Doty discloses his comfort with the body, as ashes, remaining in his home, and his greater appreciation for traditional rituals:

What I'd soon feel, about that little cannister of ash, was that it was fine to have with me. . . . It's a comfortable presence. It represents, perhaps, the way that a part of Wally's with me always, but it's not like I thought—I thought I'd need to hold on to this symbol, this proof of his having been.

I understand, differently, the longing of Antigone to bury her brother properly. Something shifts, with the body where it belongs; Wally's body belongs in the huge sun-burnished field of the salt marsh beside our tiny airport.[53]

By the time he finally decides to scatter the ashes in the marsh, Doty is at peace with letting them go, knowing full well this would please his partner. He even writes of being surprised at his own happiness when the ashes, the last physical trace of Wally, blew back onto his own body and he rubbed his cheeks with the "grit of him" left on his hands.[54]

A broad range of Americans could identify with and appreciate the religious ingredients captured in this scene—the attachment to the body, the necessity of ritual to make sense of life at the time of death, and the recognition that there is more to a life than its material trace. Over time, moving, humane scenes like this became increasingly familiar to the American public, and funeral directors gradually determined that they could continue to play their traditional role in planning religious ceremonies for all Americans who make this choice, instead of simply and distantly arranging the body's final consumption by fire. Major corporate interest in all facets of death care, and unabashed enthusiasm for cornering the market even if it means arranging cremations and subsequent memorializations, also contributed to broader industry acceptance of the practice. Because of these social developments and cultural encounters, many funeral directors, who claim to have the utmost concern for the future well-being of their customers, are finally convinced of its genuine religious meaning for many, and its potential to reap profits for those who change with the times.

The most important factor in the growing popularity of cremation, of course, is the consumers themselves, who desire burning bodies and disposing of ashes over traditional ceremonies that keep the body intact. It is difficult to compose an exact profile of cremation consumers, but many surveys attempt to identify certain characteristics, finding that these individuals generally come from the wealthier classes, are well-educated, favor a progressive political agenda, support doctor-assisted suicide, have deep concerns about the environment, and represent a variety of religious communities, including Unitarian, Christian Science, Episcopalian, Reform Jewish, Catholic, Buddhist, Hindu, and New Age communities.[55] At the turn of the twenty-first century, even this broad range of identity markers is in flux and, as mentioned earlier, regions of the country that have been resistant to this practice, like the South, are beginning to show increasing cremation rates in the larger metropolitan centers.

Despite its complex history, and its association with funeral reform, cremation is here to stay. Indeed, according to the oft-quoted executive director of the Cremation Association of North America, Jack Springer, cremation will be the norm in the next few decades.[56] Although many see cremation as a way to avoid dealing with local funeral directors, it is certain to become an easily routinized method of disposal in the repertoire of services offered by funeral homes throughout the country, homes responding to consumer desires to annihilate the corpse as quickly as possible, but remember the life through rituals and symbols uniquely crafted for the lost loved one. This desire is as much about "style," to use Prothero's key analytical frame,[57] as it is about "substance." The body matters to Americans, even if the body is reduced to ashes, and rituals must be employed when disposing of bodily matter. The kinds of issues raised in Doty's moving account of his relationship to the ashes of his partner, issues that surface in both ritual practice and popular representations across many different communities, indicate a crucial fact about cremation: the sacred remains present, still lingering around the substance produced after the body is put to the fire.

America's ritual specialists who are charged with handling the dead body and molding fitting and meaningful ritual activity to get rid of it finally understand that this choice does not necessarily signal a coming scourge of atheism, communism, or God forbid, a society without funerals. Instead, it is still a matter of the deeply problematic, yet uncannily sacred, quality of the dead body, whether it is embalmed and viewed first in the funeral home, then cremated, and transferred as ashes to the family, or immediately put to the fire at an independent crematory with the remains unceremoniously handed over to the family who perform their own private memorial service. Funeral directors prefer the former to the latter option, of course, and many will try to persuade consumers that this choice has greater overall benefits for the living. Their future financial success will depend on how effective they are in steering Americans who want cremation in this direction.

The funeral industry, now heavily invested in the cremation business, has already produced a number of publications geared toward assisting undertakers in this endeavor. Michael Kubasak, a funeral home owner in Burbank, California, who went on to become a vice president at SCI, wrote *Cremation and the Funeral Director* in 1990. This book, highly regarded in the industry, echoed the themes of many progressives in the 1970s and 1980s, who encouraged their brethren to change with the times, alter traditional attitudes, and see consumer desires as potential business opportunities. Most important of all, according to Kubasak, is not to run from the cremation option for fear it represents an economic threat, but to assist clients in shaping the details of the final disposition by pointing out the value of having a ceremonial, communal last look at the casketed, embalmed body before it goes up in flames.[58]

Many newspaper reports on cremation delight in publicizing the once-exotic, now rather familiar range of rituals surrounding this alternative to burial. The litany of celebrities consigned to immediate consumption in a furnace is quite impressive, though the coverage often features the outrageous as well as the pious elements of the fate of the celebrated celebrity cinders. In 1997, *TIME* magazine published a brief, informative follow-up to the murder of the famous designer, Versace, and his subsequent memorial service. Entitled "Cremation Nation," it begins: "Designer Gianni Versace joined Janis Joplin, Albert Einstein and John Lennon by being cremated upon death. Forty years ago fewer than 4% of Americans chose cremation, but in 1995 21% did. That figure is expected to rise to 40% by 2010."[59] Many other well-known figures have joined the cremation nation as well, including Kurt Cobain, whose ashes reportedly produced an image of Jesus after they were left at a psychic's house by his widow, Courtney Love,[60] and Jerry Garcia, who had his ashes scattered in the sacred Hindu river, the Ganges.[61] Perhaps the most famous anecdote is the launching of cremated remains into space, an honor shared by two Americans who inhabited the frontiers of the popular imagination, Gene Roddenberry and Timothy Leary.

Many media reports about cremation also highlight the way funeral directors are trying to remain indispensable when planning for this mode of final disposition. In a 1996 article from *Forbes*, "The New (and More Convenient) American Way of Death," the author identifies one way undertakers, acutely aware of the fashion for cremation, stay afloat: sales of receptacles for the cremated remains. "Of course, the $10 billion funeral industry is wise to the trend, and will be happy to oblige you if you choose cremation over burial. There are now close to 100 varieties of urns on the market, costing as little as $20 for a plastic one to as much as $3,500 for a 24k-gold-plated number encrusted with sapphires. Batesville Casket, the country's largest maker of caskets, now markets 'keepsake' urns—5 inches high or so—to encourage people to divide ashes among family members."[62] A more recent article in USA *Today Magazine* reports, "With a trend toward cremation, the funeral industry has tried to find ways to make it more profitable. While crematories require only that the body be delivered in a combustible container, it is not uncommon to find funeral homes listing alternative containers for as much as $200 or more."[63] As these and other reports make clear, funeral directors who want to stay in business remain susceptible to the still culturally charged accusation of putting personal profit before social propriety—in other words, these reports still ask a question that echoed throughout the twentieth century: How can anyone profit off of death?

In addition to providing receptacles to the consumer, many funeral directors who are committed to a bright future either contract with separate crematoria facilities to take care of their local clients, or have purchased their own facilities to ensure they maintain their intimate, privileged connections with dead bodies. Signs of this commitment are increasingly present in cyberspace. For example, surfers can click on cremation at the Bluefield, West Virginia, home page of Mercer Funeral Home, "a family owned, independent business serving Southern West Virginia and Southwest Virginia for over 77 years." Here they read that this funeral home has its own crematory to serve local families who would like to pursue this option, and learn some general facts about this increasingly common choice. While it "dates back to ancient times," readers are told that today cremation is a method of choice for a variety of environmental, religious, philosophical, and practical reasons. No matter what motivates the choice, the site informs the reader, cremation does not have to be without ritual—or "options," to use language from the text:

> Many people believe that choosing cremation means limiting your options. Actually, there are a variety of options available with cremation. Most families hold services of some kind which help the

bereaved cope with the loss of a loved one. It may be a funeral or memorial or a simple prayer at graveside or other place of remembrance. Services or ceremonies may precede or follow that actual cremation. Prior to cremation, there may be a period of visitation, either public or private with an open or closed casket.[64]

Another example can be found at the home page of McHenry Funeral Home, located in Corvallis, Oregon. Five generations of McHenrys have been involved with burying the local community and, "unlike other chain-owned corporations that operate for the sole purpose of showing the bottom line profits for its out-of-town owners, McHenry's provides full-service burial and cremation arrangements at lower prices, discounts for hardships, special payment arrangements and has never turned down a family due to their inability to pay." Some of the cremation packages advertised here include "Traditional Service Followed by Cremation," "Celebration of Life/Memorial Service in McHenry's Chapel," "Celebration of Life/Memorial Service Outside Facility," and "Direct Cremation with Limited Viewing (ID Viewing)."[65] The latter option consists of "basic services of funeral director and staff," such as keeping the body refrigerated for one day, engaging in minimal cleaning and handling of the unembalmed body, offering facilities for limited visitations from the family, removing body from the place of death and transportation to the crematory, and providing family members with grief recovery materials.[66]

Cremation specialists at the Meyers Funeral Home, in Delmar, New York, another independently-owned business, also offer information online that indicates how standardized this practice has become in recent years. The website notes that cremation is now the second most popular disposal choice in the United States, and that many people do not realize that this can include "a funeral with all the traditional aspects [visitation or viewing, for example] of the ceremony."[67] Warning against making the cremation choice as a way to avoid meaningful grieving, the specialists encourage visitors to make an informed decision about how to organize and ritualize the final disposition for themselves or loved ones. Whether the choice is made for financial reasons ("A traditional burial can cost about twice as much as a cremation with similar ceremonies"), environmental reasons ("Cremation saves land for the living and offers an immediate return to nature"), religious reasons ("Cremation is accepted among almost all Christian denominations. Reform Judaism accepts cremation, but Orthodox and Conservative Judaism are opposed."), or personal reasons ("Some people are very uncomfortable with the full service funeral and body burial. Others are equally uncomfortable with the idea of cremation without any accompanying services."), the specialists at Meyers assure you they can assist at every stage of planning and execution.[68]

Sometimes funeral directors are called upon in unusual circumstances, when loved ones try to perform their own invented religious rites of scattering ashes in public, crowded settings. When questions arise about human disposal, the obvious expert with hands-on experience can be found at the local funeral home. Ned Phillips describes one peculiar case from his experience in the funeral business in Las Vegas. He received a call from the manager of a nearby hotel who informed Phillips that a section of the casino had been cordoned off and they needed his help.

> I went and it turned out that this woman from out of state had brought in her husband's remains and spread them around the twenty-one table. . . . Well, this state doesn't have any particular scattering laws other than the fact that you can't scatter on private property unless you have permission of the property holder. . . . So it took me probably a half hour or more to persuade the individual that she couldn't leave her husband there, even though that was his wish. . . . And that we needed to retrieve the cremains. I remembered that I had seen . . . a wooden urn that had a poker hand on it. And I said, 'You know, I know your husband just loved to play twenty-one [but] I don't have anything with a twenty-one hand on it but I do have another urn in our main office with a poker hand on it and I would be more than happy to help put your husband in that urn.'[69]

She did eventually buy the urn with the poker hand and, according to Phillips, left the home a satisfied customer.

Public perceptions about cremation are also shaped by news reports, which often bring to light profoundly disturbing American stories that reinforce the deep-rooted suspicions about every element of the business of death. Like the media stories of corruption, exploitation, and irresponsible behavior that shadowed the rise of the American funeral home, recent news reports of cremation catastrophes continue to reinforce century-old stereotypes associated with the industry. Accusations about overcharging for cremation, mixing animal ashes with human remains, misidentifying burned bodies, cremating corpses at the wrong time, as well as inflicting other ritual indignities on the dead and living will no doubt attract local and national attention to the changing cultural values at stake in twenty-first century modes of disposition. In one example of this kind, a Georgia funeral home is facing litigation over the cremation of a member of the Buddhist community. According to the lawyer representing the family, the home cremated the body prematurely, before a seven-day period of ritual action around the visible body had been completed, and thereby greatly affected the postmortem destiny of his consciousness. Ironically, the funeral home cheated the mourners of what they needed so desperately, and what the funeral industry has been so desperate to provide to mourners: a visible body.[70]

What people ultimately do with bodily remains varies widely in America today. In most media stories, as well as scholarly studies on the topic, rising cremation rates are explicitly tied to baby boomers who, now facing the final frontier of death, base their wishes on a combination of consumer entitlement to choice, and religious freedom. Whether cremated remains are incorporated into a fireworks display ignited in a commemorative celebration, mixed into concrete and molded into "reef balls" used to rehabilitate damaged coral reefs around the globe, scattered to the wind or over the ocean to be united with the natural world, or simply placed in an urn that either stays in the home or is put in a columbarium at a local cemetery, the last ritual acts signify religious and social sensibilities that speak to American commitments to find an appropriate mode of disposal. Funeral directors, especially those who are themselves baby boomers, understand these commitments and are betting that their future prosperity will be assured if they can convince Americans that, even with cremation, they have the knowledge, sympathies, and tolerance to ensure a meaningful funeral service and the successful transcendence of grief.

Heaven Can Wait: The Dead Here, Now

In the end, the dead come back to life in American society. Indeed, American society comes to life thanks to the luminous presence of the dead in the imaginative and physical landscapes of its citizens. The American way of death is motivated not by fears or disavowals, but by attachments and fixations; it is more like a cult of the dead than a symptom of a culture in denial. The national ritual calendar of holidays and commemorations is dominated by civic obligations to remember American dead; pilgrimage spots marked by death and memories of the dead draw American tourists from across the country; widely dispersed but tightly focused communities devoted to dead military, entertainment, and political heroes provide a source of meaningful, though often hidden, identity to members; popular culture thrives on the inspirational and compelling appearance of the dead in a wide range of media; and the individual ceremonies to let go of the dead often depend on their temporary close proximity to the mourners, who desire to see the body, touch the casket, or walk away with the cremated remains.

In ancient Egypt, the physical remains of pharaohs were preserved because they would serve a future purpose: reanimation at the return of an immortal soul that stays close by the body. Although they were embalmed, these bodies were also mummified, wrapped up according to elaborate ritual formulas, and hidden from the view of the living. In American history, the future utility of the dead body as a vehicle for reanimation has grown less and less important. What matters is the immediate value of a visual encounter with the corpse and the expectation that it will stay in place when disposed of by the family. Bodies of the recently dead have been brought back to family and friends because of a strong desire to see the corpse of the once-living individual, to consider in person the face that embodied the spirit, personality, and essence of the deceased. In most cases, the dead return in the American imagination and stay there as spirits whose postmortem identities are intimately tied to their appearance when alive. Individual eternal identities are not based on an inner nature, or an ethereal substance inhabiting a useless body, but instead they are given life in the minds of the living only because the body itself, the material form fated to age and ultimately disintegrate, is the sacred source for envisioning personal identity in the afterlife. In other words, returning spirits often have all the physical attributes they did before life was extinguished, even though freed from the flesh. Americans prefer to recognize their dead when they return rather than contemplate postmortem existence, and the ongoing intimate presence of the dead, without familiar physical features.

In an acclaimed children's history book, published in 1998, the spirit of George Washington steps out from his portrait in the White House to lead young Sara, visiting with fellow classmates from George Washington Elementary School, on a private tour of the national home, which is, like the funeral home, a complex space that is simultaneously a private residence, a place of business, and a sacred center of profound religious meaning in American culture. *Ghosts of the White House*, by Cheryl Harness, brings American history to life for students in comic book form by illustrating a crucial source of the landmark's religious meaning: It is a haunted house. When Sara gives America's first president her hand, "POOF," she is no longer constrained by time and space and is taken on a journey through the residence, where she is introduced to other dead presidents who offer the young girl informative historical and architectural tidbits.[71] Rather than fear and trembling, Sara is filled with awe and wonder by her brief contact with these impressive ghosts. In her last individual encounter with a dead president she meets John F. Kennedy, looking young, serious, and presidential. He interacts with Sara but also repeats the immortal words countlessly replayed in American society: "Ask not what your country can do for you, but what you can do for your country." After this exchange, all the ghosts head for the White House backyard to send Sara back to the land of the living with a hearty, fond farewell. Even not-yet-dead former Presidents Bush and Clinton like the book, according to quotations on Harness's home page, which also advertises her forthcoming book in the series, *Ghosts of the Civil War*. In this history lesson, the spirit of Willie Lincoln, the child whose death during the war between the states broke the heart of his father, President Abraham Lincoln, transports a boy back in time to learn important facts about America's past.

When George Washington died in 1799, Americans throughout the nation held funeral ceremonies that often included an empty casket with a virtual body inside. Communities with no access to the real body in Mount Vernon found popular ways to conjure the tangible presence of the dead American hero in order to to make those ceremonies more meaningful and fulfilling expressions of personal loss and collective sorrow.[72] The spirit of Washington continues to live two hundred years later because of his preeminent place in the pantheon of American leaders. He is a familiar ghost whose unpleasant decomposing body was immediately replaced by an attractive ideal vision of a triumphant spiritual body that wears the same clothes and looks exactly like Washington at a moment in his fifties. From the very beginning of national life, Americans have looked to the eternally returning dead as gods, heroes, guardians, temporary visitors, and even as monsters. Their form and identity, however, often depends on living memories of the physical appearance of the deceased when alive.

Funeral directors are very clear about the value and popularity of a last look at the deceased and that this intimate moment will have future consequences for the living destined to interact with the returning dead. The past and future successes of the funeral industry depend on convincing Americans of this essential social, psychological, and religious fact, and that funeral directors have the expertise to preside over the crucial, short-lived window of opportunity for the living to be with their dead. For America's family funeral homes, this challenge has grown even more difficult because of developments on two fronts. First, multinational corporations have not only posed a very real threat to economic survival for many funeral homes around the country, they have also provided new fodder for the general bad press surrounding the business of disposal. Second, the base of their support, the local community, is in many places much more diversified and fluid than in the past. Increasing social mobility, fragmenting families, declining religious attendance—these social forces can have a damaging impact on the number of funerals with a body present. These recent developments represent a dangerous mix to many in the funeral industry today, corrosive to both the local communal body and the larger national body.

But America's funeral directors will continue to fight for the value of protecting, presenting, and preserving the dead, reaching out to communities in whatever ways they can, and earning the trust of consumers who want the dead off their hands, but not out of view quite so fast. One obvious strategy funeral directors will explore is to get on-line with their fellow boomers and utilize the Web as a place to showcase their services and place their name before a global community. The Web is being used as a medium to introduce innovative cyber-rituals that can facilitate healing actions as well as soothing memories to those in grief. Cyberspace offers consumers another arena to purchase services, as well as enact rituals, that with a click of a button allows the living to interact with the dead but also put them in their place, immediately and in perpetuity. A brief E-commerce update in March 2001, "Net Brings Life to Funeral Industry," projects that, in stark opposition to the bleak news associated with dot-com failures, death care has a bright future indeed: "While some firms are dying at the hands of the Internet, the medium is breathing new life into others. And ironically, some of these are part of the multibillion dollar U.S. death industry, according to a Reuters report."[73] How will funeral homes participate in this invisible and timeless universe? Will undertakers be able to maintain their

status as ritual specialists who are especially equipped to prepare the dead
for their journey beyond the grave, after the fire, or into cyberspace? If the
past is any indication, funeral homes will find their place in the brave new
world of cyberspace and embrace change in order to preserve tradition.

Even without involvement from the funeral industry, the Web has
become a popular way for Americans to manage their relations with the
dead and keep them around. A proliferation of death-related Web
sites—perhaps only rivaled by the popularity of cyberporn—has emerged
in the past decade, ranging from independent casket sellers attempting
to enter the lucrative market of disposal containers, to memorial pages
where visitors can e-mail messages to the dead, to graphic, often violent
scenes of death and bodily destruction, to on-line support groups for
grieving relations. The proliferation speaks to the uncannily appropriate
fit between modern fixations on death and the fecund ritual possibilities
in cyberspace; whether one is acquiring information about low-cost
funerals or participating in deeply moving E-testimonials about the
dearly departed, Americans have found yet another medium to express
their profound longings to remain intimate with the dead and the details
of death.

Some pioneers in the funeral industry—though not too many at the
moment—see the Web as yet another frontier to open and establish their
own special forms of on-line intimacy with the dead, as well as the living.
A Scripps Howard News Service report recently claimed that "increasingly, funeral homes use the Web to offer everything from memorial pages to
flower delivery to real-time funeral videos. Industry leaders are encouraging a very traditional business to respond to increasingly Internet-expec-
tant customers"[74]—which means, of course, aging baby boomers. In
October 2000, the *New York Times* reported on the slow-growing trend of
some funeral homes to provide Web-casting for funerals, and in some
cases, a "cremation cam" that assures grieving relations that no mistakes
are made when the body of the deceased enters the fiery furnace. On this
admittedly rare option, the article reports that "the family can witness the
body (in a combustible box) being sent down a conveyor belt into the
retort, where, once the doors are closed, the corpse will be turned into
ashes. The wall-mounted Cremation-Cam was installed because many
potential customers had heard horror stories about crematoriums where
the wrong corpse would be cremated or where people would be cremated
along with animals."[75]

Wherever Americans take leave of the body—over the Web, in a marsh by an airport, next to an open casket with an embalmed body—undertakers will make themselves available, twenty-four hours a day, seven days a week, to prepare it before the final exit. The funeral home, whether part of a corporate chain, or run independently by a single family for generations, will no doubt remain the primary site for this preparation, an intermediary stop for the body between home, hospice, or hospital, and its last resting place on earth, or in the stars, for some very basic reasons: public trust that funeral directors know what to do with it, consumer satisfaction with its treatment, and a deep-seated desire to be near the deceased but avoid disturbing signs of its inevitable physical disintegration. Whether the choice is immediate translation into ashes, or preservation of physical appearance through embalming, Americans cannot, and will not, countenance the naked truth of bodily corruption when saying their final farewell to friends and relatives.

Even with the increased popularity of alternative forms of disposal and growing experimentation on the Web, most Americans will pay funeral men and women to bring out their dead one last time. To be sure, the dead will return to the living whether they are tenderly prepared to be seen in the warm light of the funeral home or abruptly disposed of under cover and without the gaze of the living. The dead will not be denied. Funeral directors know this reality and see it at work in the lives of people who walk through their doors asking them for help. Thomas Lynch speaks to this truth in American society: "The body is technologically, psychologically neutral. The dead don't care. Only the living do. The idea is the living need to take leave of their dead. They don't farm that part out. Of course, you can get on your cell phone and get out your gold card and have the dead disappeared. You might not have to deal with the dead, but you will have to deal with their death. In the end it is not about what we spend or what we save. It is about what we do."[76] Most Americans do not want the dead body to disappear too quickly. But on the other hand, they do not want it lingering around for too long. A brief, intimate moment with the dead—looking at the face, touching the casket, being in the presence of the corpse for a short time—is an ingrained ritual gesture that brings meaningful, and material, order out of the chaos of death.

⊕ EPILOGUE: 9/11 ⊕

I FINISHED WRITING THE MAIN BODY OF THIS TEXT AT THE END OF AUGUST 2001, relieved that the four-year journey was finally over. Nearly finished with another book about death, I knew I would make the same vow I had made at the end of the first book: No more death! I was looking forward to a research future without death and a wonderful array of possible topics to occupy my mind in the coming years. For the last ten years of my life, I have been thinking, reading, and writing about death. I thought it was time for a change.

Then on September 11, 2001, terrorists made their fateful and fatal attack on the United States, using commercial airplanes as bombs to destroy New York City's Twin Towers, the Pentagon in Washington, D.C., and perhaps the White House if one of the planes had not crashed in Pennsylvania. The days and weeks after these events were surreal at times, filled with anguish, disbelief, astonishment, sadness, outrage, and anxiety. Like many, I found it very difficult to stay focused and be productive in the immediate aftermath of the brutal attacks. I even forgot about the book in the confusing, confounding period between 9/11 and Thanksgiving. In time, however, I could not get away from the book or shake the feeling that this tragic day would have the last word in it.

This book asks the following question: How do Americans live with their dead? The terrorist act against the nation was an awesome spectacle of death and destruction—an extraordinary, impressive morning of horror and fascination that had annihilated thousands of lives in vital national centers by lunchtime. The success of the attack, the chilling impact it had on the life of the nation in the months after, and the declaration of war on terrorism by President George W. Bush will forever change the course of American history. The loss of these innocents, the incineration of their bodies, and their irretrievable condition in the ruins will leave scars in American life that both transcend history and propel it forward. The dead will remain eternally present in our memories and be models of virtue and heroism—they are the first martyrs of the twenty-first century, and their blood and ash, mixed with concrete and steel, will become valuable relics in the national effort to memorialize the atrocities of 9/11.

As many commentators have repeatedly asserted, what took place on that day was unprecedented. The only remotely comparable events are the terrorist attack in Oklahoma City, which led to the execution of Timothy McVeigh, and the Japanese attack on Pearl Harbor, which led to the dropping of the atomic bomb on two cities in Japan and America's full involvement in the Second World War. In the nineteenth century, the Civil War offered Americans a firsthand account of human carnage never before witnessed on our national soil. But try as we might, we do not have an adequate frame of reference within which the events of September 11 can be comprehended. Certain individual deaths have made a dramatic impact on the national psyche, including those of Abraham Lincoln, John F. Kennedy, Martin Luther King Jr., and Christa McAuliffe on the space shuttle Challenger. After these individuals died, Americans found new and innovative ways to memorialize and celebrate them; public displays of communal mourning, sometimes officially organized, sometimes more spontaneous expressions of collective loss, often brought large groups of people together across class, gender, religious, and racial lines. In all cases, these can be considered public forms of civil religious community united in grief. By that very unity, communities were able to transcend the sad, terrible circumstances of their individual deaths.

The cold, brute facts of September's acts of terror, and the vast bloodbath in their wake, will not be easy to overcome for those most directly affected or for the rest of us, psychically marked by the images, news accounts, and nightmares of hijacked planes and exploding buildings. Institutional religion provides the most gratifying answers to the questions associated with larger metaphysical issues related to evil and suffering, and punishment and forgiveness. But when it comes down to the physical, most religious traditions take the body seriously at death and require its presence—seen or hidden, close or distant—to address essential questions about the ultimate meaning of life, the unavoidable truth about identity, and the crucial value of social relations among the living and between the living and the dead.

Media coverage emphasized the profound importance of having a body in the ritual ceremonies to say a proper farewell in a number of different religious communities affected by 9/11. Within three weeks, the *New York Times* ran the story, "Rites of Grief, Without a Body to Cry Over." In it, the article explains that hundreds of families from a variety of religious communities had been "robbed . . . of intimacy" and "cheated out of . . . rituals" because of missing bodies. "Having the deceased dressed in her favorite clothes for a Catholic wake, scattering ashes in a river for a Hindu ceremony, reading prayers at the Jewish cemetery, cocooning the body in a white shroud for a Muslim burial. . . . none of them are possible." The article goes on to offer heartbreaking examples of families needing to improvise, to rely on photographs or other memorabilia that do not seem enough or quite right for the occasion.[1] One *San Francisco Chronicle* article mentions Muslims, Buddhists, and Jews, all ritually enfeebled without access to whole bodies of the dead. It also reports former Mayor Giuliani's desperate and disturbing gesture of providing survivors with something material from the Twin Towers: An urn with ash and other materials from the site of the destruction.[2]

Making sense of the dead and putting them in their place without bodies is a very troubling matter, and churches, synagogues, and other houses of worship cannot always control how the living relate to them. Another *New York Times* report at the end of September noted a "sad and inevitable change" that recently took place at ground zero. More and more family members who lost a loved one began to visit the site—so many that a new ferry between Midtown and the World Financial Center had to be set up—to leave mementos, flowers, personal notes, photographs, and other intimate objects that connected them with their dead. "Hundreds of people . . . have quietly toured what they now reluctantly regard as a final resting place—perhaps the only semblance of a graveyard the 5,000 or so lost will ever know." For many affected by this nightmare, a pilgrimage to the site brought them physically closer to their missing relations, now and forever intermingled with rubble and ash.[3]

Without identifiable bodies to ground our responses, and absent funeral rituals that can provide an orderly manner to dispose of them individually, close family members and all Americans were left with literally nothing to focus their hearts and minds on. Instead, the wrenching sight of homemade flyers with pictures of the missing and the common memorial street scenes, displaying personal expressions of grief, inhabit our imaginations. The photographs, so many pictures of life, of individuals in the midst of life, provide visual evidence for specific, individual identities lost in the debris and speak to the deep yearning to have something more than an image to commemorate the death of a close relation or friend. In ordinary circumstances, the dead body cries out for ritual, and whether it is ultimately cremated and dispersed to the wind, embalmed and put on display, or cared for by community members and placed in the ground, Americans rely on its temporary presence to properly and meaningfully say good-bye.

Some media outlets covered the reaction of local funeral directors in the days after the horrible events, the very people normally charged with managing the body's temporary presence after death and before it vanishes. On September 22, *Newsweek* carried the story, "Final Respects: New York's Funeral Industry Prepares for an Onslaught." In it, the reader learns of companies shifting casket inventories closer to New York City, state agencies surveying open cemetery space in the surrounding areas, and medical authorities providing sobering details about the small number of bodies recovered and the disturbingly large number of unidentifiable body parts. The article then reports on the impact of the carnage on different New York City funeral homes, including the well-known Manhattan institution, Frank E. Campbell's Funeral Home, which, the author notes, is continuing its policy of giving free funerals to public servants killed in the line of duty. The piece explains that even though bodies were missing, Americans who lost close relations were turning to America's death specialists to assist in planning the appropriate ceremonies. It also mentions that recent historical changes in the funeral industry should prepare them for the wide variety of celebrations and ceremonies desired by devastated family and friends: "Still, it helps that in recent years, funeral etiquette has loosened up, and funeral directors are more accustomed to hosting nontraditional memorial services. 'We used to think of funerals as just tending to the dead,' says Vincent O'Conner of the Dennis O'Conner Funeral Home in Rockaway, N.Y. 'Now we see them as an opportunity to celebrate the person's life.'"[4]

While family members and friends will find their own way to ritually say good-bye to loved ones without the body present, the nation will draw regenerative strength from permanent memorials likely to be erected at or near the sites of destruction. These sacred sites dedicated to remembering the dead, so prominent at the mall in Washington D.C., but also found at Civil War battlefields and other numerous locations throughout the country, transform the physical landscape, and become pilgrimage centers that reinforce the ties that bind the national community. After all, Americans throughout the twentieth century have shown a marked ability to find ways to commune with their dead, who often stick around rather than finding peace in the grave. The dead from these attacks will no doubt return to us as subjects in a variety of popular culture offerings as well, including films about the events of September, television specials focused on specific acts of heroism and tragedy, and even websites devoted to memorializing those who died. In most cases, rather than trivializing the horror, or exploiting those most affected by it, popular culture will serve as a significant arena to remember the dead and grapple with the psychic, imaginative, and symbolic aftereffects of all this carnage. Disconnected from normal rituals of disposal, and from individual gravesites, these dead will not go away. They will stay with us, and will be part of the American cultural landscape for many, many years to come.

⊕NOTES⊕

Prologue

1. Sherwin B. Nuland, *How We Die: Reflections on Life's Final Chapter* (New York: Alfred A. Knopf, 1998), 122.
2. James L. Watson, "Funeral Specialists in Cantonese Society: Pollution, Performance, and Social Hierarchy," in *Death Ritual in Late Imperial and Modern China*, ed. James L. Watson and Evelyn S. Rawski (Berkeley: University of California Press, 1988), 133.
3. Jonathan P. Parry, *Death in Banaras* (New York: Cambridge University Press, 1994), 4.
4. Pascal Boyer, *Religion Explained: The Evolutionary Origins of Religious Thoughts* (New York: Basic Books, 2001), 214.
5. "History of Embalming," *Wyoming Funeral Directors Association* [Online] Available: *http://www.wyfda.org/basics_3.html* [January 27, 2002].

Introduction

1. Jessica Mitford, *The American Way of Death* (New York: Simon and Schuster, 1963), 15.
2. Mitford reminisces about this anxiety and anticipation within the industry in the revised version of her book, *The American Way of Death Revisited* (New York: Alfred A. Knopf), 1998), xvi.
3. "'The Undertaker's Racket' by Jessica Mitford," *The Director*, 33, 6 (June 1963): 13.
4. "The Only Answer—A Profession," *The Director*, 33, 6 (June 1963): 9.
5. Mitford remarks about reviewers getting the joke in the recent edition of the book, *The American Way of Death Revisited*, xvi.
6. David Cort, "Ambush on the Styx," *Saturday Review* (August 31, 1963): 21.
7. Cort, "Ambush," 22.
8. Advertisement from the *New York Times*, September 9, 1963. Butler Library, Columbia University, Manuscripts Collection, Leroy Bowman Collection, Box 63.
9. Sydney H. Schanberg, "Funeral Pricing Studied by State," the *New York Times* (November 20, 1963): 1.
10. Schanberg, "Funeral Pricing," 44.
11. Mitchell Gordon, "The Funeral Furor: Top-Selling Book Spurs Expansion of Societies Promoting Simple Rites," *Wall Street Journal* (September 30, 1963): 1, 18.
12. Gordon, "The Funeral Furor," 1.
13. Ben Gross, "The High Cost of Dying Discussed on CBS Hour," New York *Daily News* (October 25, 1963): 74. Rutgers University Library, Special Collections and Archives, Consumer Research Inc. Records, Box 865.
14. "'CBS Reports' On Funerals Set for TV On October 16 or 30," *The Southern Funeral Director* (October, 1963): 4.
15. "The Furor over Funerals: Why the Cry of Scandal?" *Changing Times: The Kiplinger Magazine* (November 1963): 7.
16. "Furor over Funerals," 7.
17. "Furor over Funerals," 8.
18. "Furor over Funerals," 12. Italics in original.
19. "Letters to the Editor," *TIME* (October 4, 1963): 21.
20. "Letters to the Editor," *National Review* (November 19, 1963): 455. Italics in original.
21. William M. Lamers, *A Centurama of Conventions: A Review of all the Conventions of NFDA Focusing on the Words and Deeds of Funeral Service Practitioners* (Milwaukee, Wisc.: NFDA, 1981), 60.

22. Lamers, *A Centurama of Conventions*, 61.

23. Lamers, *A Centurama of Conventions*, 61.

24. For a study of Abraham Lincoln's death and funeral journey, see Gary Laderman, *The Sacred Remains: American Attitudes Toward Death, 1799–1883* (New Haven, Conn.: Yale University Press, 1996), 157–163.

25. Arthur M. Schlesinger Jr., *Robert Kennedy and His Times* (Boston: Houghton Mifflin, 1978), 610.

26. Mitford, *The American Way of Death Revisited*, 134–137.

27. William Manchester, *The Death of a President: November 20–November 25, 1963* (New York: Harper & Row, 1967), 292.

28. Manchester, *The Death of a President*, 293–294.

29. Manchester, *The Death of a President*, 294.

30. A detailed account of this episode can be found in Manchester, *The Death of a President*, 297–307; also see Gerald Posner, *Case Closed: Lee Harvey Oswald and the Assassination of JFK* (New York: Random House, 1993), 294–295.

31. Manchester, *The Death of a President*, 300.

32. Manchester, *The Death of a President*, 305–306.

33. Manchester, *The Death of a President*, 309, and Mitford, *The American Way of Death Revisited*, 135.

34. Manchester, *The Death of a President*, 381–382.

35. Manchester, *The Death of a President*, 383.

36. Manchester, *The Death of a President*, 430–431.

37. Manchester, *The Death of a President*, 432.; also see Mitford's own description of these decisions, *The American Way of Death Revisited*, 135–136.

38. Jim Bishop, *The Day Kennedy Was Shot* (New York: Funk & Wagnalls, 1968), 644.

39. Quoted in Manchester, *The Death of a President*, 433.

40. Quoted in Manchester, *The Death of a President*, 433.

41. Bishop, *The Day Kennedy Was Shot*, 662.

42. Manchester, *The Death of a President*, 435.

43. Manchester, *The Death of a President*, 437.

44. Schlesinger, *Robert Kennedy and His Times*, 610.

45. Manchester, *The Death of a President*, 442.

46. Manchester, *The Death of a President*, 443.

47. Quoted in Manchester, *The Death of a President*, 443. Italics in original.

48. "The Family in Mourning," *TIME* (December 6, 1963): 28.

49. Manchester, *The Death of a President*, 443.

50. "Mrs. Kennedy's Opposition to Open Coffin Explained," the *New York Times* (November 27, 1963): 18.

51. Jack Raymond, "Kennedy Lies in State in East Room," the *New York Times* (November 24, 1963): 1.

52. Manchester, *The Death of a President*, 510.

53. Manchester, *The Death of a President*, 517. Italics in original.

54. For descriptions of these events, see Marjorie Hunter, "Mrs. Kennedy Leads Public Mourning," the *New York Times* (November 25, 1963): 2; and "Four Days: The Historical Record of the Death of President Kennedy," compiled by United Press International and American Heritage Magazine (New York: American Heritage Publishing, Company, 1964), 68–84.

55. "Thousands Pass Bier at Night Despite the Cold and Long Wait," the *New York Times* (November 25, 1963): 2.

56. "Thousands Pass Bier," 2.

57. Manchester, *The Death of a President*, 490–492.

58. "Oswald is Buried," *San Francisco Chronicle* (November 26, 1963): 1.

59. "The President's Funeral," the *New York Times* (November 26, 1963): 36.

60. Robert L. Fulton and Howard C. Raether, "The World Stood Still," *The Director*, 33, 12 (December 1963): 4–5.

61. Fulton and Raether, "The World Stood Still," 5.

62. Albert R. Kates, "Editorial," *The American Funeral Director* (December 1963): 21.

63. Kates, "Editorial," 22.

64. Ralph W. Loew, "Mrs. Kennedy's Fortitude Fine Example to U.S.," *Buffalo Courier Express* (December 2, 1963): 14.

Chapter 1

1. One of the best discussions of changing mortality rates in the twentieth century can be found in Michel Vovelle's history of death in the West, "La victoire et L'angoisse." *La mort et L'Occident de 1300 à nos jours* (Paris: Gallimard, 1983), 673–686.

2. Peter Uhlenberg and James B. Kirby, "Longevity," *The Encyclopedia of Human Biology*, 2nd ed., ed. Renato Dulbecco (San Diego: Academic Press, 1997): 231.

3. For discussions of these changes in mortality rates, and debates over the reasons for these changes, see Judith Walzer Leavitt and Ronald L. Numbers, "Sickness and Health in America: An Overview," in *Sickness and Health in America: Readings in the History of Medicine and Public Health*, ed. Judith Walzer Leavitt and Ronald L. Numbers (Madison, Wisc.: University of Wisconsin Press, 1985), 1–10; Gretchen A. Condran, Henry Williams, and Rose A. Cheney, "The Decline in Mortality in Philadelphia from 1870 to 1930: The Role of Municipal Services," in *Sickness and Health*, 422–423; Stephen Kunitz, "Mortality Change in America, 1620–1920," in *Human Biology*, 56 (1984): 569–577; *Mortality and Morbidity in the United States*, ed. Carl L. Erhardt and Joyce E. Berlin (Cambridge: Harvard University Press, 1974); Robert V. Wells, *Uncle Sam's Family: Issues in and Perspectives on American Demographic History* (Albany: State University of New York Press, 1985), 57–94; and Paul E. Zopf Jr., *Mortality Patterns and Trends in the United States* (Westport, Conn.: Greenwood, 1992).

4. Condran, Williams, and Cheney, "The Decline in Mortality," 421; for a more general discussion, see Thomas McKeown, *The Role of Medicine: Dream, Mirage or Nemesis* (Princeton: Princeton University Press, 1979), 29–44.

5. This revolution took place in rural, as well as urban, areas. According to demographer Robert Higgs, the rural crude death rate dropped about a third between 1870 and 1920. He concludes, "in a half century after 1870 nothing less than a 'vital revolution' occurred in the American countryside." Robert Higgs, "Mortality in Rural America, 1870–1920: Estimates and Conjectures," *Explorations in Economic History*, 10, 2 (Winter 1973): 176–195 (quotation from 182).

6. Peter Uhlenberg, "Death and the Family," *Journal of Family History*, 5, 3 (Fall 1980): 313.

7. Uhlenberg, "Death and the Family," 319–320; also see his more recent analysis, "Mortality Decline in the Twentieth Century and Supply of Kin Over the Life Course," *The Gerontologist*, 36, 5 (1996): 681–685.

8. See graph in Leavitt and Numbers, *Sickness and Health*, 7. Their source for this information is the U.S. Bureau of the Census, *Historical Statistics of the United States: Colonial Times to 1970* (Washington, D.C.: Government Printing Office, 1975). Part 1. 57. A more intricate, detailed discussion of these rates in terms of race, ethnicity, region, and other variables can be found in Zopf Jr., *Mortality Patterns*, 73–122.

9. Mortimer Spiegleman and Carl L. Erhardt, "Mortality and Longevity in the United States," *Mortality and Morbidity in the United States*, 4.

10. Zopf Jr., *Mortality Patterns*, 230.

11. Zopf Jr., *Mortality Patterns*, 2.

12. Zopf Jr., *Mortality Patterns*, 252.

13. The complexity behind these numbers, relating to social differences across class, gender, race, and region, provides a critical dimension to any social history of American life. See, for example, Zopf Jr., *Mortality Patterns*, 163–203.

14. See, for example, Ronald L. Numbers, "The Fall and Rise of the American Medical Profession" in *Sickness and Health*, 185–196; also see Charles Rosenberg's comprehensive history of the hospital in nineteenth-century America, *The Care of Strangers: The Rise of America's Hospital System* (New York: Basic Books, 1987).

15. Thomas J. Schlereth, *Victorian America: Transformations in Everyday Life, 1876–1914* (New York: HarperCollins, 1991), 286.

16. Philippe Ariès, *The Hour of Our Death*, trans. Helen Weaver (New York: Alfred A. Knopf, 1981), 584.

17. For discussions of this process in western culture generally, see Vovelle, *La mort et l'Occident*, 707; Ariès, *The Hour of Our Death*, 583–588; and Ivan Illich, *Medical Nemesis: The Expropriation of Death* (New York: Pantheon, 1976). On the medicalization of death in America, see David Sudnow, *Passing On* (Englewood Cliffs, N.J.: Prentice-Hall, 1967); and David Wendell Moller, *Confronting Death: Values, Institutions, and Human Mortality* (New York: Oxford University Press, 1996), 24–39.

18. Ariès, *The Hour of Our Death*, 586.

19. For an important historical analysis of the emergence of the "clinical gaze," see Michel Foucault, *The Birth of the Clinic: An Archaeology of Medical Perception*, trans. A. M. Sheridan Smith (New York: Pantheon, 1973).

20. On professionalization in this period, see Burton Bledstein, *The Culture of Professionalism* (New York: Alfred A. Knopf, 1977).

21. This change in title was discussed in the very first meeting of the National Funeral Director's Association. See Gary Laderman, *The Sacred Remains: American Attitudes Toward Death, 1799–1883* (New Haven, Conn.: Yale University Press, 1996), 168. Another title proposed early in the century that figured into the funeral industry's quest as a full-fledged profession, and one I will occasionally use, is the less popular "mortician." In an early article that advocated the use of this word, the author writes: "The word most appropriate, most applicable, and that has the ring of professionalism is a new word that is not as yet found in our dictionaries. The word to which I refer is 'Mortician.' It is derived from the word 'mort,' meaning death, consequently a mortician is one who cares for the dead." A. W. Stout, "'Undertaker' or 'Embalmer' Objectionable," *American Funeral Director*, 43, 1 (January 1920): 13.

22. See Schlereth for a brief discussion of this shift, *Victorian America*, 118–124.

23. Laderman, *The Sacred Remains*, 34–35.

24. Robert W. Habenstein and William M. Lamers, *The History of American Funeral Directing*, 4th ed. (Milwaukee, Wisc.: National Funeral Directors Association, 1996), 328–330.

25. Silas E. Ross, *Recollections of Life at Glendale, Nevada, Work at the University of Nevada, and Western Funeral Practice*, Part II, 1971. Oral History Project, University of Nevada, Reno, Library. Special Collections. 404.

26. Advertisement, *Southern Funeral Director*, 21, 1 (July 1929): 5.

27. Jessica Mitford, *The American Way of Death* (New York: Simon and Schuster, 1963), 17–21. A comprehensive discussion of these theories will take place in chapter three.

28. Myth is commonly used by historians of religion as a category of stories that serve as sacred narratives for specific communities, providing members with a sense of meaning, order, and orientation in the cosmos. In this investigation it is not a question of whether myths are true or false, but rather exploring what meanings they have to those communities who cling so tightly to them.

29. Antonia Lant, "The Curse of the Pharaoh, or How Cinema Contracted Egyptomania," in *Visions of the East: Orientalism in Film*, ed. Matthew Bernstein and Gaylyn Studlar (New Brunswick, N.J.: Rutgers University Press), 71–72. André Bazin, one of the most influential French film critics from the 1960s, made another significant connection between preserving bodies and preserving images on-screen. He characterized photography, the building block of cinema, as a medium that "embalms time, rescuing it from its proper condition." *What is Cinema?* (Berkeley: University of California Press, 1967), 14.

30. Lant, "The Curse of the Pharaoh," 83.

31. Thomas E. Kelly and Evan B. Johnson, *The Evolution of the American Funeral Director* (New York: Traverauld Press, 1934).

32. Kelly and Johnson, *The Evolution of the American Funeral Director*, 3.

33. Kelly and Johnson, *The Evolution of the American Funeral Director*, 100–102.

34. Kelly and Johnson, *The Evolution of the American Funeral Director*, 107.

35. Simon Mendelsohn, *Embalming Fluids: Their Historical Development and Formulation, from the Standpoint of the Chemical Aspects of the Scientific Art of Embalming* (New York: Chemical Publishing, 1940), 1.

36. Industry fascination with ancient Egypt is evident in the names of some early embalming chemical companies as well, such as the Egyptian Chemical Company or the Egyptian Embalmer Company, and the names of embalming fluids produced in the first half of the century, such as The Oriental and simply Egyptian. See Habenstein and Lamers, *The History of American Funeral Directing*, 348.

37. *Funeral Customs Through the Ages* (Saint Louis, Miss.: F. C. Riddle & Brothers Casket Company, 1929). Fiftieth anniversary booklet. Archives, National Museum of Funeral Directing, Houston, Texas.

38. *Funeral Customs*.

39. John H. Eckels, *Modern Mortuary Science* (Philadelphia: Westerbrook, 1948), 49.

40. For early discussions of Holmes see Kelly and Johnson, *The Evolution of the American Funeral Director*, 107; Eckels, *Modern Mortuary Science*, 48; or A. O. Spriggs, *Champion Textbook on Embalming and Anatomy for Embalmers* (Springfield, Ohio: Champion Company, 1946), 15.

41. For a detailed discussion of Holmes' role in embalming in the United States, see Habenstein and Lamers, *The History of American Funeral Directing*, rev. ed., 205–219.

42. For early discussions of Holmes, see Mendelsohn, *Embalming Fluids*, 15; Eckels, *Modern Mortuary Science*, 48, and Spriggs, *Champion Textbook on Embalming*, 15.

43. C. F. Callaway, *Text Book of Mortuary Practice: The Pathological Conditions of, and the Embalming Treatments for over 150 Diseases, Arranged Alphabetically for Easy Reference* (Chicago: Undertakers Supply Company, 1943), 10.

44. Habenstein and Lamers, *The History of American Funeral Directing*, 218.

45. Habenstein and Lamers, *The History of American Funeral Directing*, 222–225; also see Spriggs, *Champion Textbook on Embalming*, 15.

46. *Funeral Customs Through the Ages*; also see John C. Gebhart, *Funeral Costs: What They Average; Are They Too High? Can They Be Reduced?* (New York: G. P. Putnam's Sons, 1928), 16.

47. Habenstein and Lamers, *The History of American Funeral Directing*, 225; also see Robert E. Mayer, *Embalming: History, Theory, Practice* (Stamford, Conn.: Appleton and Lang, 1996), 47–55 for a more comprehensive discussion.

48. Habenstein and Lamers, *The History of American Funeral Directing*, rev. ed., 262.

49. For an overview of the institutional history, see Habenstein and Lamers, *The History of American Funeral Directing*, 291–359.

50. *The American Funeral Record: A Ready Day-Book for Undertakers* (St. Louis, Miss.: F. J. Feineman, no date). In Stout Manuscript Collection, Frank Hintzman Funeral Home, Funeral

Records, 1907–1910. Volume 1. State Historical Society of Wisconsin, Archives Division, Milwaukee, Wisconsin.

51. *The American Funeral Record.*

52. Interview with Thomas Kearns, Leo F. Kearns Funeral Home, Richmond Hill, New York. June 23, 1998.

53. Habenstein and Lamers, *The History of American Funeral Directing*, 308.

54. Habenstein and Lamers, *The History of American Funeral Directing*, 260, and Vanderlyn R. Pine, *Caretaker of the Dead: The American Funeral Director* (New York: Irvington Publishers, 1975), 15.

55. *What To Do: A Booklet of Funeral Facts That Everyone Should Know* (National Casket Company, 1935), 21–22. Archives, National Museum of Funeral Directing, Houston, Texas.

56. William M. Lamers, *A Centurama of Conventions: A Review of all the Conventions of NFDA Focusing on the Words and Deeds of Funeral Service Practitioners* (Milwaukee, Wisc.: National Funeral Directors Association, 1981), 31.

57. Charles W. Berg, *The Confessions of an Undertaker* (Wichita, Kans.: McCormick-Armstrong Press, 1920), 30.

58. Berg, *Confessions*, 37–42.

59. Interview with Trevino Morales, Morales Funeral Home, Houston, Texas. July 28, 1998.

60. Reverend G. B. Carpenter, "Funeral Director's Chief Concern Should be to Get the Family Comfortably Through the Service and Burial," *American Funeral Director*, 43, 1 (January 1920): 35.

61. T. B. Bailey, "Funeral Directing Through the Ages," *Southern Funeral Director*, 20, 5 (May 1929): 41.

62. On post-mortem photography, see Jay Ruby, *Secure the Shadow: Death and Photography in America* (Cambridge, Mass.: MIT Press, 1995) and Stanley B. Burns, *Sleeping Beauty: Memorial Photography in America* (New York: Twelvetree Press, 1990).

63. Edward A. Martin, "Psychology of the Funeral Service," *Casket & Sunnyside*, 70, 2 (February 1940): 21–22.

64. *Funeral Customs Through the Ages.*

65. National Funeral Director's Association Pamphlet. "Speaking Frankly: A Plain Talk about Funeral Service," 1940, 9. National Funeral Director's Association Library, Milwaukee, Wisconsin.

66. "The Public Relations of the Funeral Director," *Southern Funeral Director*, 20, 4 (April 1929): 39.

67. Mabel Hamlin, "A Woman's Viewpoint on Children's Funerals; How to Achieve an Effective 'Memory Picture' Which Will Assuage Parents' Grief and Build Good Will and Profit for the Funeral Director," *Casket & Sunnyside*, 70, 6 (June 1940): 26–27.

68. E. T. Eilsom, "The Chapel: Product of New Competition," *Southern Funeral Director*, 20, 1 (January 1929):53.

69. Advertisement in *Southern Funeral Director*, 21, 1 (July 1929): 20.

70. "Crowds Throng Hartford Opening," *Southern Funeral Director*, 20, 5 (May 1929): 39.

71. Silas Ross, "Educational Evening, May 13, 1932." University of Nevada, Reno, Library, Special Collections, Silas Earl Ross Papers, NC820, box 1.

72. Charles M. Anderson, "The Funeral Director Was 'Explained' to the Rotary Club of Springfield, Ohio," *Casket & Sunnyside*, 58, 8 (April 1928): 4.

73. Christine Quigley, *The Corpse: A History* (Jefferson, North Carolina: McFarland, 1996), 272.

74. Jimmy Fletcher Interview, Pasley-Fletcher Funeral Home, Thomaston, Georgia. October 30, 1998.

75. "Texas Morticians Uphold Tradition of Profession," *American Funeral Director*, 60, 4 (April 1937): 31.

76. Berg, *Confession*, 112–113.

77. Gebhart, *Funeral Costs*, viii.

78. Gebhart, *Funeral Costs*, xii.

79. Gebhart, *Funeral Costs*, 22.

80. Gebhart, *Funeral Costs*, 22.

81. Maxwell Lehman, "Can You Afford To Die?" *The Woman* (December 1938): 28–32, quote from 30. Consumer Research, Inc. Records, 1910–1983. Special Collections and University Archives, Rutgers University Library. Box n. 865, folder 26.

82. Federal Trade Commission, Washington. Press release in afternoon newspapers, Thursday, April 6, 1939. Consumer Research, Inc. Records. Special Collections and Archives, Rutgers University Library. Box n. 865, folder 26.

83. Federal Trade Commission. April 6, 1939.

84. Irving Shulman, *Valentino* (New York: Trident, 1967), ix.

85. Shulman, *Valentino*, 1.

86. Shulman, *Valentino*, 4.

87. Shulman, *Valentino*, 13.

88. Shulman, *Valentino*, 14–15.

89. Shulman, *Valentino*, 17.

90. Shulman, *Valentino*, 18.

91. Shulman, *Valentino*, 21.

92. Thornton Wilder, *Our Town: A Play in Three Acts* (New York: Harper & Row, 1957 [1938]), 79.

93. Wilder, *Our Town*, 8.

94. Wilder, *Our Town*, 10.

95. Wilder, *Our Town*, 81. Italics in original.

96. Wilder, *Our Town*, 81.

97. Wilder, *Our Town*, 82. The crucial anthropological work on this topic is Robert Hertz, "Contributions to the Study of the Collective Representations of Death." In *Death and the Right Hand*, trans. Rodney and Claudia Needham (Glencoe, Ill.: Free Press, 1960 [1907]).

98. Wilder, *Our Town*, 82.

99. Wilder, *Our Town*, 83.

100. Wilder, *Our Town*, 83.

101. See, for example, Donald Haberman, *Our Town: An American Play* (Boston: Twayne Publishers, 1989).

102. When the play was turned into a film in 1940, Emily does not die, but has a strange deathlike dream that allows her and the audience to learn about the meaning of life, and death. See Haberman, *Our Town*, 72.

103. For a recent discussion of Walt Disney in America, see Steven Watts, *The Magic Kingdom: Walt Disney and the American Way of Life* (Boston: Houghton Mifflin, 1997).

104. Gary Laderman, "The Disney Way of Death," *Journal of American Academy of Religion*, 68, 1 (March 2000): 205–255.

105. Maria Tatar, *The Hard Facts of the Grimms' Tales* (Princeton: Princeton University Press, 1987), and Marian S. Pyles, *Death and Dying in Children's and Young People's Literature: A Survey and Bibliography* (Jefferson, N.C.: McFarland, 1988).

106. Bob Thomas, *Walt Disney: An American Original* (New York: Simon and Schuster, 1976), 99.

107. Leonard Mosley, *Disney's World: A Biography* (New York: Random House, 1985), 123. Italics in original.

108. Mosley, *Disney's World*, 124.

109. Thomas, *Walt Disney*, 100.

110. Richard Schickel, *The Disney Vision: The Life, Times, Art and Commerce of Walt Disney*, rev. ed. (New York: Simon and Schuster, 1985), 146.

111. Thomas, *Walt Disney*, 135–136.

Chapter 2

1. Eugene W. Baxter to Alex G. Baxter, November 25, 1946. Schenectady, New York. Baxter Family Papers, Special Collections, University of Nevada, Reno, Library. Reno, Nevada.

2. Quote and discussion in G. Kurt Piehler, "The War Dead and the Gold Star: American Commemoration of the First World War," in *Commemorations: The Politics of National Identity*, ed. John R. Gillis (Princeton: Princeton University Press, 1994), 172–173.

3. Mark Meigs, *Optimism at Armageddon: Voices of American Participants in the First World War* (London: Macmillan, 1997), 143–187; Erna Risch, *Quartermaster Support of the U.S. Army: A History of the Corps, 1775–1939* (Washington, D.C.: Office of the Quartermaster General, 1962); Edward Steere, *The Graves Registration Service in World War II* (Washington, D.C.: Office of the Quartermaster General, 1951), 12-14.

4. Meigs, *Optimism at Armageddon*, 177.

5. Ralph Hayes, "A Report to the Secretary of War on American Military Dead Overseas," in *The Care of the Fallen* (Washington, D.C.: Government Printing Office, 1920), 12.

6. Hayes, "A Report to the Secretary of War," 12; also see Piehler, "The War Dead and the Gold Star," 172.

7. Hayes, "A Report to the Secretary of War," 13–14.

8. Hayes, "A Report to the Secretary of War," 14.

9. Hayes, "A Report to the Secretary of War," 24. Also see Piehler, "The War Dead and the Gold Star," 172–173; and Ron Robin, *Enclaves of America: The Rhetoric of American Political Architecture Abroad, 1900–1965* (Princeton: Princeton University Press, 1992), 36–39.

10. Hayes, "A Report to the Secretary of War," 24.

11. Meigs, *Optimism at Armageddon*, 178–179.

12. Hayes, "A Report to the Secretary of War," 15.

13. Hayes, "A Report to the Secretary of War," 14.

14. Meigs, *Optimism at Armageddon*, 180.

15. "*The Casket* Causes a Sensation in Congress During Debate on Bringing Home the Soldier Dead," *The Casket*, 45, 1 (January 1, 1920): 1.

16. "*The Casket* Causes a Sensation," 35.

17. "Concerning the 'Field of Honor,'" *The Casket*, 45, 1 (January 1, 1920): 47.

18. "Concerning the 'Field of Honor,'" 47.

19. "Who is Behind the Legislation For the Return of the Soldier Dead?" *The Casket*, 45, 3 (March 1, 1920): 30.

20. "Who is Behind the Legislation," 30.

21. Much has been written on the topic, including Meigs, *Optimism at Armageddon*, 143–149; and Piehler, "The War Dead and the Gold Star," 174–175.

22. Quincy L. Dowd, *Funeral Management and Costs: A World-Survey of Burial and Cremation* (Chicago: University of Chicago Press, 1921), vii.

23. Dowd, *Funeral Management*, 47, 1. See Dowd's position on cremation in chapter 10, 225–246. Also see Stephen Prothero's historical investigation of cremation in the United States, *Purified By Fire: A History of Cremation in America* (Berkeley: University of California Press, 2001). My discussion of cremation will take place in the final chapter.

24. Dowd, *Funeral Management*, 43.

25. Dowd, *Funeral Management*, 43–45.

26. Dowd, *Funeral Management*, 47.

27. Dowd, *Funeral Management*, 57.

28. Dowd, *Funeral Management*, 49.

29. Dowd, *Funeral Management*, 269.

30. John C. Gebhart, *Funeral Costs: What They Average: Are They too High? Can They Be Reduced* (New York: G. P. Putnam's Sons, 1928), 221.

31. Gebhart, *Funeral Costs*, 235.

32. Gebhart, *Funeral Costs*, xxiii. The panel also included clergymen, lawyers, and charity workers.

33. Gebhart, *Funeral Costs*, 23–24.

34. Gebhart, *Funeral Costs*, 68.

35. Gebhart, *Funeral Costs*, 20.

36. Gebhart, *Funeral Costs*, 80–95.

37. Gebhart, *Funeral Costs*, 80.

38. Gebhart, *Funeral Costs*, 148.

39. Gebhart, *Funeral Costs*, 222.

40. Gebhart, *Funeral Costs*, 270–271.

41. F. A. Manaugh, *Thirty Thousand Adventurers: An Informal Disclosure of Observations and Experiences in Research in the Funeral Industry* (Los Angeles: Times-Mirror Press, 1934), 9.

42. H. H. Hathaway, "Undertaker Calls His Business 'Highly Specialized Racket,'" *Washington Times Herald* (March 8, 1945): 1.

43. William M. Kephart, "Status After Death," *American Sociological Review*, 15 (October 1950): 635–643.

44. "The Better Way," *Good Housekeeping* (June 1959): 131.

45. Hugh Stevenson Tigner, "A Foray Into Funeral Customs," *The Christian Century*, 54, 41 (October 13, 1937): 1263.

46. Tigner, "A Foray into Funeral Customs," 1263.

47. Tigner, "A Foray Into Funeral Customs," 1263.

48. Tigner, "A Foray Into Funeral Customs," 1263.

49. Tigner, "A Foray Into Funeral Customs," 1264.

50. Tigner, "A Foray Into Funeral Customs," 1264.

51. Tigner, "A Foray Into Funeral Customs," 1265.

52. Tigner, "A Foray Into Funeral Customs," 1265.

53. For an overview of some of these calls to action, see Leroy Bowman, *The American Funeral: A Study in Guilt, Extravagance, and Sublimity* (Westport, Conn.: Greenwood Press, 1959), 68–69. Also see Ruth Harmer, *The High Cost of Dying* (New York: Crowell-Collier Press, 1963), 149–150.

Also see articles in religious publications, like Thorp McClusky's "Death on Parade," *Christian Herald* (February 1949): 22–24, 90–92. The lead-in to this article reads, "Not only costly but pagan are many of the practices associated with the modern funeral. Here's why, and here's what we can do about it"; "Funerals Should Be Christianized," *The Christian Century*, 77, 32 (August 10, 1960): 918; and "Pastors Call for Simpler Funerals," *The Lutheran Witness*, 79, 13 (June 28, 1960): 341.

54. Wilfrid Sheed and Shirley Feltmann, "The Funeral Business," *Jubilee: Magazine of the Church and Her People* (November 1960): 30.

55. Sheed and Feltmann, "The Funeral Business," 31.

56. Sheed and Feltmann, "The Funeral Business," 35.

57. "High Cost of Dying," *Newsweek* (November 20, 1944): 84, and "Death & Burial," TIME (January 18, 1954): 93–94.

58. Arthur H. DeLong, *Pastor's Ideal Funeral Book: Scripture Selections, Topics, Texts and Outlines, Suggestive Themes and Prayers, Quotations and Illustrations, Forms of Services, Etc., Etc.* (New York: Abingdon Press, 1910), 196. Italics in original.

59. E. G. Haley, *How to Conduct a Funeral* (Cincinnati, Ohio: Standard Publishing, 1918).

60. Andrew Watterson Blackwood, *The Funeral: A Source Book for Minister* (Philadelphia: Westminster Press, 1942), 59.

61. J. Douglas Parker, "How Pagan Are Our Funerals?" *Michigan Christian Advocate* (August 31, 1950): 8.

62. Parker, "How Pagan Are Our Funerals?," 8–9.

63. Anne Hamilton Franz, *Funeral Direction and Management* (Jacksonville, Fla.: State Board of Funeral Directors and Embalmers for Florida, 1947), iv.

64. Franz, *Funeral Direction*, 62.

65. Franz, *Funeral Direction*, 60.

66. Interview with Bill Monday, Runyon Funeral Home, Dunellen, New Jersey. August 16, 1998.

67. Interview with Wayne Baxter, Fox Funeral Home, Forest Hills, New York. June 17, 1998.

68. Letter from Rex C. Kelly to Hubert Eaton. September 27, 1934. Private collection, Forest Lawn Memorial Park. Los Angeles, California.

69. Percival E. Jackson, *The Law of Cadavers and of Burial and Burial Places* (New York: Prentice-Hall, 1950), xxix–lxxxiii.

70. Jackson, *The Law of Cadavers*, 440–441.

71. Interview with Howard Raether, Milwaukee, Wisconsin. August 30, 1998.

72. William M. Lamers, *A Centurama of Conventions: A Review of All the Conventions of NFDA Focusing on the Words and Deeds of Funeral Service Practitioners* (Milwaukee, Wis. National Funeral Director's Association, 1981), 49.

73. Letter from George L. Wittkopp to Louis H. Prange, March 8, 1955. Louis H. Grange, Papers 1952–1957. State Historical Society, Wisconsin, Archives Division. Madison, Wisconsin.

74. Letter from Ray M. Gerend, Gerend's Funeral Home, Sheboygan, Wisconsin, March 7, 1955. Louis H. Grange, Papers 1952–1957. State Historical Society, Wisconsin, Archives Division. Madison, Wisconsin.

75. Reply from Prange to Wittkopp, March 11, 1955. Louis H. Grange, Papers 1952–1957. State Historical Society, Wisconsin, Archives Division. Madison, Wisconsin.

76. Dabney Otis Collins, "The Aim of Advertising," *Casket and Sunnyside*, 80, 12 (December 1950): 21.

77. *Speaking Frankly: A Plain Talk About Funeral Service* (Milwaukee, Wis.: National Funeral Directors Association, 1940), 1.

78. *Speaking Frankly*, 2–11.

79. *Speaking Frankly*, 5.

80. *Speaking Frankly*, 8.

81. *Speaking Frankly*, 9.

82. *Speaking Frankly*, 14.

83. Wilber M Krieger, *Successful Funeral Service and Management* (Englewood Cliffs, N.J.: Prentice-Hall, 1951), 25.

84. Krieger, *Successful Funeral Service*, 133.

85. Krieger, *Successful Funeral Service*, 182–193, quote from 182.

86. Krieger, *Successful Funeral Service*, 183.

87. "Transcripts from the Dan Lundberg Television Show," *Mortuary Management*, 43, 6 (June 1956): 12.

88. "Transcripts," 12.

89. "The Soldier Dead," *Newsweek* (May 29, 1944): 37.

90. Interview with Ralph Turner, Turner & Sons Funeral Home, Atlanta, Georgia. August 12, 1999.

91. J. A. Shaidnagle Jr., and Howard C. Raether, "To Each His Own: The True Story of Repatriation," *The Director*, 18, 2 (February 1948): 4.

92. W. N. Tumlin, Jr., "The American Way," *Casket and Sunnyside*, 70, 7 (July 1940): 25.

93. Interview with Thomas Lynch, Lynch & Sons Funeral Home, Milford, Michigan. October 13, 1999.

94. Galion Metallic Vault Company Advertisement. *The Southern Funeral Director*, 50, 3 (March 1944): 35.

95. "Editorial Outbursts," *Southern Funeral Director*, 59, 5 (November 1948): 10.

96. "Truth vs. Fiction," *American Funeral Director*, 74, 7 (July 1951): 33.

97. "Truth vs. Fiction," 35.

98. In the revised issue of her book, Mitford includes the following point after referencing Gladstone's quotation: "Sometime after publication, I met Francis Gladstone, a direct descendant of the erstwhile *Prime Minister*. When I asked him about his illustrious forebear's comment, he became interested and wrote to scholars of his acquaintance at Oxford. Lengthy correspondence ensued, but no one was able to identify William Gladstone's alleged statement." Jessica Mitford, *The American Way of Death Revisited* (New York: Alfred A. Knopf, 1998), 153.

99. "Show me the manner in which a nation cares for its dead," *The American Funeral Director*, 84, 2 (February 1961 [reprint of 1960 editorial]): 45.

Chapter 3

1. Jessica Mitford, *The American Way of Death* (New York: Simon & Schuster, 1963), 18.

2. Mitford, *The American Way of Death*, 225.

3. Mitford, *The American Way of Death*, 9.

4. Mitford, *The American Way of Death*, 15.

5. Mark Twain, *Life on the Mississippi* (New York: Oxford University Press, 1996), 432–436. Italics in original.

6. Twain, *Life on the Mississippi*, 438.

7. Twain, *Life on the Mississippi*, 440–441. Italics in original.

8. Darlene H. Unrue, "The Gothic Matrix of *Look Homeward, Angel*," in *Critical Essays on Thomas Wolfe*, ed. John S. Phillipson (Boston, Mass.: G. K. Hall, 1985), 48.

9. See, for example, John Hagen, "Structure, Theme, and Metaphor in Thomas Wolfe's *Look Homeward, Angel*," in Phillipson, *Critical Essays*, 32–47; and Richard Steele, *Thomas Wolfe: A Study in Psychoanalytic Literary Criticism* (Philadelphia: Dorrance, 1976), 24–37.

10. Thomas Wolfe, *Look Homeward, Angel: A Story of the Buried Life* (New York: Charles Scribner's Sons, 1929), 471–472.

11. Hagan, "Structure, Theme, and Metaphor," 44.

12. "Introduction," *Critical Essays*, 1.

13. Wolfe, *Look Homeward, Angel*, 474.

14. Wolfe, *Look Homeward, Angel*, 474–476.

15. Wolfe, *Look Homeward, Angel*, 477.

16. Hagan, "Structure, Theme, and Metaphor," 43–44.

17. Hagan, "Structure, Theme, and Metaphor," 46.

18. Wolfe, *Look Homeward, Angel*, 480.

19. There are exceptions, of course. One example is the forgettable play from the 1940s, *Meet A Body*, a murder mystery that takes place inside of a New York funeral home. Francis L. DeVallant discusses this and other literary representations of the funeral director in his article, "Meet a Body . . . " *Casket and Sunnyside*, 74, 11 (November 1974): 26–27.

20. Selina Hastings, *Evelyn Waugh: A Biography* (Boston: Houghton Mifflin, 1994), 520.

21. *The Life of Riley*, "Riley's Tonsillectomy," October 4, 1949. Museum of Television and Radio. Los Angeles, California.

22. *Dr. Kildare*, "The Exploiters," September 1963. Museum of Television and Radio. Los Angeles, California.

23. From *American Masters: Nichols & May: Take Two*. Museum of Television and Radio. Los Angeles, California.

24. Interview with Jimmy Fletcher, Pasley-Fletcher Funeral Home, Thomaston, Georgia. October 30, 1998.

25. Interview with Thomas Kearns, Leo F. Kearns Funeral Home, Richmond Hill, New York. June 23, 1998.

26. "Morticians Propose Code On Prices," *San Francisco Chronicle* (August 13, 1965): 3.

27. Interview with Wayne Baxter, Fox Funeral Home, Forest Hills, New York. June 17, 1998.

28. Interview with Bill Monday, Runyon Funeral Home, Dunallen, New Jersey. August 17, 1998.

29. Donna Pelzel, "Does the Funeral Director do the Devil's Work?' " *Casket & Sunnyside*, 101, 7 (July 1971): 12.

30. Robert Fulton, "The Sacred and the Secular: Attitudes of the American Public Toward Death, Funerals, and Funeral Directors," in *Death and Identity*, ed. Robert Fulton (New York: John Wiley & Sons, 1965), 95.

31. Fulton, "The Sacred and the Secular," 105.

32. Mitford, *The American Way of Death*, 91.

33. Elmer Davis, "The Mortician," *The American Mercury Reader* (New York: The American Mercury, 1943), 59. Originally published in May, 1927.

34. Mitford, *The American Way of Death*, 95.

35. Peter N. Stearns, *American Cool: Constructing a Twentieth-Century Emotional Style* (New York: New York University Press, 1994), 148–154.

36. Stearns, *American Cool*, 154.

37. Stearns, *American Cool*, 156.

38. Eric Lindemann, "Symptomatology and Management of Acute Grief," *American Journal of Psychiatry*, 101 (1944): 141–148.

39. See, for example, John Archer, *The Nature of Grief: The Evolution and Psychology of Reactions to Loss* (London: Routledge, 1999), 12–26.

40. Stearns, *American Cool*, 156–161.

41. Stearns, *American Cool*, 152.

42. A. O. Spriggs, *The Champion Textbook on Embalming and Anatomy for Embalmers* (Springfield, Ohio: Champion Company, 1946), 18.

43. C. F. Callaway, "Rebuilding Features—A Work of Art for the Embalmer," *American Funeral Director*, 51, 8 (August 1928): 60.

44. Thomas Hirst, "Embalming as Practiced Today," *The Casket*, 46, 7 (July 1921): 21.

45. Advertisement, *Casket & Sunnyside*, 58, 8 (April 15, 1928): 13.

46. "The Man of the Hour," *Champion Expanding Encyclopedia of Mortuary Practices*, 2, 78 (December 1936/January 1937): 309. Other titles in the series include, "Massage the Trunk!", "The Trocar," and "Important Considerations for Summer."

47. "The Man of the Hour," 309–311.

48. Edward A. Martin *Psychology of Funeral Service* (No publisher, 1947), v.

49. Edward Martin, "Functions of the Modern Mortician," *American Funeral Director*, 55, 12 (December 1932): 26. Also a favorite quote of many critics, including Mitford, *The American Way of Death*, 225, and Leroy Bowman, *The American Funeral in Guilt, Extravagance, and Sublimity* (Westport, Conn.: Greenwood, 1959), 32.

50. Martin, *The Psychology of Funeral Service*, v.

51. Martin, *The Psychology of the Funeral Service*, 121.

52. Anne Hamilton Franz, *Funeral Direction and Management* (Jacksonville, Fla.: State Board of Funeral Directors and Embalmers for Florida, 1947), 12–15.

53. Franz, *Funeral Direction*, 13.

54. Franz, *Funeral Direction*, 16–17.

55. Mitford, *The American Way of Death*, 17–18.

56. Mitford, *The American Way of Death*, 95.

57. Mitford, *The American Way of Death*, 18.

58. Charles McCabe, "Grief Therapists," *San Francisco Chronicle* (December 8, 1965): 2B.

59. Dr. Joyce Brothers, "Whey They Behave That Way: Even Bizarre Funeral Serves Good Function," *The Milwaukee Journal* (November 2, 1963): C3.

60. Brothers, "Why They Behave That Way," C3.

61. Elisabeth Kubler-Ross, *On Death and Dying* (New York: Macmillan, 1969), 6–7.

62. Theodore W. Landphair, "The Key is 'Managed Grief': How Funeral Directors—and Students—View Their Career," *National Observer* (June 8, 1970): 3.

63. Charles W. Wahl, "Human Mortality and Its Role in Human Affairs," *The Director*, 39, 8 (August 1969): 7.

64. Some examples of their work include Paul E. Irion, *The Funeral and the Mourners: Pastoral Care of the Bereaved* (Nashville, Tenn.: Abingdon-Press, 1954) and *The Funeral: Vestige or Value* (Nashville, Tenn.: Abingdon Press, 1966). Edgar N. Jackson, *Understanding Grief* (Nashville, Tenn.: Abingdon Press, 1957) and *The Christian Funeral: Its Meaning, Its Purpose, and Its Practice* (New York: Channel Press, 1966).

65. William M. Lamers, *A Centurama of Conventions: A Review of all the Conventions of NFDA Focusing on the Words and Deeds of Funeral Service Practitioners* (Milwaukee, Wis.: National Funeral Directors Association, 1981), 61.

66. Edgar N. Jackson, *For the Living* (Des Moines, Iowa: Channel Press, 1963), 9–11.

67. Jackson, *For the Living*, 53.

68. Irion, *The Funeral*, 100–103.

69. Irion, *The Funeral*, 106.

70. Irion, *The Funeral*, 107.

71. Irion, *The Funeral*, 166.

72. Rev. James L. Kidd, "An Ecumenical Funeral Service for the 'New' Church," *The Director*, 39, 3 (March 1969): 3.

73. Kidd, "An Ecumenical Funeral Service," 3.

74. Rev. R. Earl Allen, "A Pastor's View of Funerals," *Baptist Standard* (April 21, 1971). Reprinted in *The Director*, 41, 7 (July 1971): 10.

75. Jack P. Lowndes, "How Can the Minister and the Mortician Work Together for the Benefit of the Bereaved?" *Casket & Sunnyside*, 101, 8 (August 1971): 16.

76. Lowndes, "How Can the Minister and Mortician Work Together," 48.

77. "Should the Body be Present at the Funeral?" Brochure, National Funeral Directors Association.

Chapter 4

1. Jonathan Lake Crane, *Terror and Everyday Life: Singular Moments in the History of the Horror Film* (Thousand Oaks, Calif.: Sage, 1994), 11.

2. For some discussion of the historical significance of Romero's film, see Crane, Terror and Everyday Life, 10–15; Gregory A. Waller, "Introduction," *American Horrors: Essays on the Modern American Horror Film*, ed. Gregory A. Waller (Urbana, Ill.: University of Illinois Press, 1987), 1–13; and Gregory A. Waller, *The Living and the Undead: From Stoker's Dracula to Romero's Dawn of the Dead* (Urbana, Ill.: University of Illinois Press, 1986), 272–327.

3. Shaila K. Dewan, "Do Horror Films Filter the Horrors of History?" the *New York Times* (October 14, 2000): 17, 19. This article also discusses an important documentary on the horror film, *The American Nightmare*, directed by Adam Simon.

4. Crane, *Terror and Everyday Life*, 31–32.

5. Albert R. Kates, "Conduct of Mortuary College Students Reflects Their Professional Attitude," *American Funeral Director*, 91, 8 (August 1968): 24.

6. William T. Grafe, "My Three Years in the Army's Mortuary Affairs Program," *Mortuary Management*, 26, 5 (May 1969): 14–15.

7. Grafe, "My Three Years," 16, 87.

8. Grafe, "My Three Years," 87–88.

9. William T. Grafe, "1968 Tet Offensive—A Tough Job," *Mortuary Management*, 26, 9 (September 1969): 13.

10. Grafe, "1968 Tet Offensive," 13.

11. Grafe, "1968 Tet Offensive," 18.

12. For brief overviews of the death awareness movement see, for example, *The Last Dance: Encountering Death and Dying*, ed. Lynne Ann DeSpelder and Albert Lee Strickland (Mountain View, Calif.: Mayfield, 1999), 31–39, or *Dying: Facing the Facts*, ed. Hannelore Wass and Robert A. Neimeyer (Washington, D.C.: Taylor & Francis, 1995), 126–127.

13. Rev. M. Dudley Rose, "DEATH—Denying It Or Defying It," *Mortuary Management*, 56, 11 (November 1969): 14.

14. Ralph A. Head, "The Reality of Death: What Happens When it is Ignored?" *Casket & Sunnyside*, 101, 6 (September 1971): 24.

15. Head, "The Reality of Death," 36.

16. Alan Trachtenburg, *The Corporatization of America* (New York: Hill and Wang, 1982).

17. Federal Trade Commission Press Release. "For Release in AFTERNOON NEWSPAPERS of Thursday, April 6, 1939." From Consumer's Research, Inc., Archives. Special Collections and University Archives, Rutgers University Library. Box n. 865, folder 26.

18. Federal Trade Commission Report, *Funeral Industry Practices: Final Staff Report to the Federal Trade Commission and Proposed Trade Regulation Rule* (Washington, D.C.: Bureau of Consumer Protection, June 1978), footnote 43, page 17.

19. Letter from F. J. Schlink to Albert F. Murray, October 9, 1952. Consumer's Research, Inc., Archives, Special Collections and University Archive, Rutgers University Library. Box no. 865, folder 25.

20. Response letter from Erma A. Hinek, July 29, 1963. Consumer's Research, Inc., Archives, Special Collections and University Archive, Rutgers University Library. Box no. 865, folder 24. After 1963, the files in this collections related to complaints about the industry get much, much thicker.

21. FTC Report, *Funeral Industry Practices*, 1978, 16, footnote 38.

22. FTC Report, *Funeral Industry Practices*, 16–18.

23. "FTC Report on Funeral Homes." Consumer News Bulletin. Department of Health, Education & Welfare, 3, 24 (March 15, 1974).

24. William M. Lamers, *A Centurama of Conventions: A Review of All the Conventions of NFDA Focusing on the Words and Deeds of Funeral Service Practitioners* (Milwaukee, Wis.: National Funeral Directors Assocation, 1981), 70–71.

25. Lamers, *A Centurama of Conventions*, 71.

26. "FTC Proposes Funeral Practice Rule." *Federal Trade Commission News* (August 28, 1975): 1–2. Consumer Research, Inc., Archives, Box 865, folder 24. Rutgers University Library, Special Collections. Rutgers, New Jersey.

27. "Giving Undertakers Something To Cry About," *Business Week* (October 6, 1975): 93–94. Pine has published numerous studies of the positive sociological value of the funeral, including, *Caretakers of the Dead: The American Funeral Director* (New York: Irvington Publishers, 1975).

28. "The Distrusted Undertaking," *San Francisco Chronicle* (October 26, 1975): 17.

29. Lamers, *A Centurama of Conventions*, 71.

30. Lamers, *A Centurama of Conventions*, 72.

31. Richard Severo, "Funeral Industry Is Striving to Improve Its Image in Face of Charges of Deception and Abuses of the Public," the *New York Times* (April 25, 1978): 20.

32. Severo, "Funeral Industry is Trying to Improve," 20.

33. Severo, "Funeral Industry is Trying to Improve," 21.

34. Federal Trade Commission, *Compliance Guidelines: Trade Regulation Rule on Funeral Industry Practices* (Washington, D.C., 1984).

35. For various discussions of the FTC rule, see *Dying: Facing the Facts*, 180–182; Lynne Ann DeSpelder and Albert Lee Strickland, *The Last Dance: Encountering Death and Dying*, 276–290; Robert W. Habenstein and William M. Lamers, *The History of American Funeral Directing* (Milwaukee, Wis.: National Funeral Directors Association, 1996), 364–365; and, in one of the additional new chapters in Jessica Mitford's *The American Way of Death Revisited* (New York: Alfred A. Knopf, 1998), 176–187.

36. Federal Trade Commission. *Report of the Presiding Officer on a Trade Regulation Rule Proceeding: Review of the Funeral Industry Practices Trade Regulation Rule* (Washington, D.C., July 1990), 164.

37. Mitford, *The American Way of Death Revisited*, 182.

38. DeSpelder and Strickland, *The Last Dance*, 278.

39. Interview with Trevino Morales, Morales Funeral Home, Houston, Texas. July 28, 1998.

40. Interview with Thomas Lynch, Lynch & Sons Funeral Home, Milford, Michigan. October 13, 1999.

41. Interview with Wayne Baxter, Fox Funeral Home, Forest Hills, New York. June 17, 1998.

42. "Funerals: A Consumer Guide." [Online] June 2000. Available: *http://www.ftc.gov/bcp/con-line/pubs/services/funeral.htm*. [December 12, 2001].

43. Interview with Ralph Turner, Turner & Sons Funeral Home, Atlanta, Georgia. August 12, 1999.

44. Interview with Bill Monday, Runyon's Funeral Home, Dunellen, New Jersey. August 17, 1998.

45. Robert Mayer, *Embalming: History, Theory, Method* (Stamford, Conn.: Appleton and Lange, 1996), 4–13.

46. Mayer, *Embalming*, 13.

47. Interview with Baxter.

48. Consuelo M. Beck-Sague, et al., "Universal Precautions and Mortuary Practitioners: Influence on Practices and Risk of Occupationally Acquired Infection," *Journal of Occupational Medicine*, 33, 8 (August 1991): 874–878, 876.

49. "Refusal to Embalm AIDS Victims OK'd," *The San Diego Union-Tribune* (November 16, 1985): 13.

50. Interview with George Cabot, Cabot & Sons Funeral Home, Pasadena, California. July 12, 1999.

51. Interview with Howard Raether, Milwaukee, Wisconsin. August 30, 1998.

52. Interview with Bill Head, Bill Head Funeral Home, Tucker, Georgia. September 6, 1999.

53. On the dramatic rise in cremation in AIDS cases see, for example, "AIDS and Cremation," the *New York Times* (December 27, 1988): 8. Also see T. A. Jacobs and M. S. Wilkes, "Cremation Patterns for Patients Dying with AIDS in New York City," *New York State Journal of Medicine*, 88 (1988): 628–632.

54. Jack G. Ebner, "Let's Change the Changers," *Casket & Sunnyside*, 57, 6 (June 1970): 16.

55. Charles O. Kates, "Did This Survey Prove Anything?" *Casket & Sunnyside*, 94, 6 (June 1971): 29.

56. "What's Happening to Our Funerals?" *San Francisco Chronicle* (July 27, 1973): 3.

57. "Californians Note More Unconventional Funerals," *American Funeral Director*, 47, 10 (October 1974): 12.

58. William M. Lamers, *A Centurama of Conventions: A Review of all the Conventions of NFDA Focusing on the Words and Deeds of Funeral Service Practitioners* (Milwaukee, Wis.: NFDA, 1981), 68.

59. Lamers, *A Centurama of Conventions*, 69.

60. Lamers, *A Centurama of Conventions*, 75.

61. "What Was The Most Important Contribution That Was Made To Funeral Service in the Past 100 Years?" *Casket & Sunnyside*. Special Centennial Issue, 1971: 10.

62. "What Was the Most Important Contribution?" 11.

63. Jeannett R. Folta, "Attitudes Toward the Contemporary Funeral," *The Director*, 42, 7 (July 1972): 6.

64. Folta, "Attitudes Toward the Contemporary Funeral," 8–10.

65. Bill Bates, "The Adaptive Funeral," *Mortuary Management*, 62, 6 (June 1975): 10.

66. Bates, "The Adaptive Funeral," 10.

67. "Tailor-Made Funeral Service in Hawaii," *Casket & Sunnyside*, 70, 2 (February 1940): 31.

68. "Tailor-Made Funeral Service," 31–32.

69. "Tailor-Made Funeral Service," 32.

70. "Charley Boston's Funeral a Blend of Old and New," *Casket & Sunnyside*, 60, 3 (February 1930): 4.

71. "Charley Boston's Funeral," 4.

72. "Charley Boston's Funeral," 4–5.

73. For some discussion of traditional Jewish views on the funeral, see the brief synopsis of Israel Klavan, Executive Secretary, Rabbinical Council of America, in Robert W. Habenstein and William L. Lamers's, *Funeral Customs the World Over* (Milwaukee, Wisc.: Bulfin, 1963), 825–826; Arnold M. Goodman, *A Plain Pine Box: A Return to Simple Jewish Funerals and Eternal Traditions* (New York: Ktav Publishing House, 1981); and Maurice Lamm, *The Jewish Way in Death and Mourning* (New York: Jonathan David, 1969).

74. Arthur A. Goren, *The Politics and Public Culture of American Jews* (Bloomington: Indiana University Press, 1999), 48–82.

75. Goren, *Politics and Public Culture*, 73–75.

76. Goren, *Politics and Public Culture*, 58–59.

77. Jenna Weissman Joselit, *The Wonders of America: Reinventing Jewish Culture, 1880–1950* (New York: Hill and Wang, 1994), 286.

78. Joselit, *Wonders of America*, 268.

79. Interview with Donald Snider. Columbus Jewish Historical Society, Oral History Program. [Online] Available: *http://www.gcis.net/cjhs/Interviews/HTML/snider_donald.htm*. [June 13, 2001].

80. Phyllis H. Williams, *South Italian Folkways in Europe and America: A Handbook for Social Workers, Visiting Nurses, School Teachers, and Physicians* (New York: Russell & Russell, 1969 [1938]), 206–207.

81. Williams, *South Italian Folkways*, 209.

82. Elizabeth Mathias, "The Italian-American Funeral: Persistence Through Change," *Western Folklore*, 33 (January 1974): 43–44.

83. Mathias, "The Italian-American Funeral," 45.

84. James E. Douthitt and Kenneth L. Dunn, "The Changing Role of the Funeral," *The Director*, 42, 9 (September 1972): 6.

85. Ronald G. E. Smith, *The Death Care Industries in the United States* (Jefferson, N.C.: McFarland, 1996), 245.

86. Michael A. Plater, *African-American Entrepreneurship in Richmond, 1890–1940* (New York: Garland, 1996), 22.

87. Plater, *African-American Entrepreneurship*, xvii.

88. Plater, *African-American Entrepreneurship*, 23.

89. Plater, *African-American Entrepreneurship*, 162.

90. Peter Metcalf and Richard Huntington, *Celebrations of Death: The Anthropology of Mortuary Ritual* (Cambridge: Cambridge University Press, 1979), 194.

91. Interview with Thomas Kearns, Leo F. Kearns Funeral Home, Richmond Hill, New York. June 13, 1998.

92. Mitra Kalita, "Longevity in Death: Funeral Home Thrives with Rich Diversity of its Clients," *Newsday* (March 23, 2001): 56.

93. Interview with Ned Phillips, Palm Mortuary, Las Vegas, Nevada. September 22, 2000.

94. Charles C. Munzy, *The Vietnamese in Oklahoma City: A Study in Ethnic Change* (New York: AMS Press, 1989), 155–159.

95. Kimberly Winston, "The American Way is Changing, Even in Death," *The Argus* (June 22, 1997): 1.

96. Celia W. Dugger, "Outward Bound From the Mosaic: Where Dead are Mourned, Many Traditions Mingle," the *New York Times* (October 28, 1997): 18.

97. LaVone V. Hazell, "Cross-Cultural Funeral Rites," *The Director*, 69, 10 (October 1997): 53.

98. Hazell, "Cross-Cultural Funeral Rites," 55.

Chapter 5

1. "The Grim Reaper Comes to Philadelphia with 'Don't Smoke' Messages *For Youth, By Youth.*" Available: *http://www.onyx-group.com/Uptown.htm* [July 10, 2001].

2. Philippe Ariès, *The Hour of Our Death* (New York: Vintage, 1981), 110–123; Jean Delumeau, *Sin and Fear: The Emergence of a Western Guilt Culture 13th–18th Centuries* (New York: St. Martin's Press, 1990), 86–114; and Johan Huizinga, *The Waning of the Middle Ages* (Garden City, N.Y.: Doubleday, 1954).

3. Ariès, *The Hour of Our Death*, 111.

4. Ariès, *The Hour of Our Death*, 116.

5. Delumeau, *Sin and Fear*, 109.

6. Delumeau, *Sin and Fear*, 113.

7. See the title of historian Robert V. Wells's recent analysis of death in Schenectady, New York, *Facing the "King of Terrors": Death and Society in an American Community, 1750–1990* (Cambridge: Cambridge University Press, 2000).

8. Madonna, "Mer Girl," *Ray of Light*, Warner Brothers, 1998.

9. Bernard Stamler, "Advertising: Shock Advertisers Make Use of Death and Dying," the *New York Times* (February 2, 2001): 2.

10. "Kentucky's 47th Convention," *The Southern Funeral Director*, 21, 1 (July 1929): 62.

11. Gene Kennon, "The Future of Funeral Service," *Mortuary Management*, 57, 3 (March 1970): 32.

12. Erik Larson, "Fight to the Death," TIME (December 9, 1996): 63.

13. Steve Emmons, "Funeral Firms Feel Pressure of New Shoppers," *Los Angeles Times* (December 7, 1998): 1.

14. James W. Hughes and Joseph J. Seneca, "Introduction: The Demographic Trajectory and Public Policy," in *America's Demographic Tapestry: Baseline for the New Millennium*, ed. James W. Hughes and Joseph J. Seneca (New Brunswick, N.J.: Rutgers University Press, 1999), 3.

15. Ron Chernow, "FTC Studies the Cost of Dying," the *New York Times* (September 26, 1976): 3.

16. Allen R. Myerson, "Hardball on Hallowed Grounds," the *New York Times* (September 27, 1996): 3.

17. Howard C. Raether, *Funeral Service: A Historical Perspective* (Milwaukee, Wis.: National Directors Association, 1990), 67.

18. Raether, *Funeral Service*, 69–70.

19. Paul Bannister and Jeff Samuels, "Oprah's Bizarre Death Wish," *Star* (January 30, 2001): 6.

20. For one detailed discussion of the case, see Jonathan Harr, "The Burial," *The New Yorker* (November 1, 1999): 70–96.

21. Risa E. Kaplan, "Sickly Funeral Industry on Death's Door," *Money Central*. [On-line] September 19, 1999. Available: *http://www.moneycentral.com/articles/invest/sectors/4683.asp* [August 3, 2001].

22. Mary Sit-DuVall, "As Death Rates Decline, So Do Earnings," *Houston Chronicle* (August 9, 2000): 2.

23. Sit-DuVall, "Sickly Funeral Industry," 2.

24. See for example Robert Bryce, "The Dying Giant," *Salon*. [On-line] September 29, 1999. Available: *http://www.salon.com/news/features/1999/09/29/sci* [August 6, 2001].

25. "Funeral Homes Hit with Sex Suit," *Atlanta Journal Constitution* (March 4, 2000): 8.

26. Greg Hassell, "Service Corp. Funerals Dip, But Profit Up," *Houston Chronicle* (May 10, 2001): 2.

27. "Chronicle 100 Leading Companies of Houston," *Houston Chronicle* (May 20, 2001): 8.

28. Monica Perin, "Smaller Funeral Industry Players Thrive after Near-Death Experience," *Houston Business Journal* (May 7, 1999): 429. "Death On the Installment Plan," National CBS News report. [Online]. April 10, 2000. Available: *http://www.cbsnews.com/now/story/0,1597,182419–412,00.html*. [July 15, 2001].

30. "Funeral Directors Suggest Senate Hearings are Unfair," Press Release, National Funeral Directors Associations. [On-line] April 20, 2000. Available: *http://www.nfda.org/aging/apr10.html*. [July 18, 2001].

31. "The Deathcare Business Responds," *The Director* (May 1988): 54.

32. Interview with Trevino Morales, Morales Funeral Home, Houston, Texas. July 28, 1998.

33. Interview with Bill Monday, Runyon Funeral Home, Dunellen, New Jersey. August 18, 1998.

34. Gary Rotstein, "Owners Change, But Names Remain," *Pittsburgh Post-Gazette* [On-line] May 23, 1999. *http://www.post-gazette.com/regionstate/19990522finalregs9.asp*. [August14, 2001]. Dianna Marder, "The Conflict of Conglomerates," *The Philadelphia Inquirer* (May 3, 1999): 1.

35. Kay Raftery, "Where Funerals are Truly a Family Affair," *Philadelphia Inquirer* (January 6, 1998): 1.

36. Raftery, "Where Funerals Are Truly a Family Affair," 4.

37. Raftery, "Where Funerals Are Truly a Family Affair," 4.

38. Cecilia Rasmussen, "A Lively Business in Funerals," *Los Angeles Times* (July 18, 1999): 6.

39. Rasmussen, "A Lively Business," E6.

40. Gary Rothstein, "Quiet! Morticians in Training Here," *Pittsburgh Post-Gazette*. [On-line] May 23, 1999. *http://www.post-gazette.com/regionstate/19990522finalschool9.asp* [August 17, 2001].

41. Edward Wong, "Funeral Business's New Look," the *New York Times* (November 10, 2000): 1.

42. Jenny Lyn Bader, "Death Be Not Bad For Ratings," the *New York Times* (June 10, 2001). 2.

43. Henry K. Lee, "Mitford Cremation—Last Snub to Funeral Industry," *San Francisco Chronicle* (July 25, 1996): 21.

44. Charles Burress, "Laughter Eclipses Tears at Mitford Tribute," *San Francisco Chronicle* (July 30, 1996): 11.

45. Lee, "Mitford Cremation," 21.

46. Stephen Prothero, *Purified By Fire: A History of Cremation in America* (Berkeley: University of California Press, 2001), 103–160.

47. Prothero, *Purified By Fire*, 111.

48. Paul E. Irion, *Cremation* (Philadelphia: Fortress Press, 1968), 44.

49. See for example, Michael J. Weiss, "Dead But Not Necessarily Buried," *American Demographics*, 23, 4 (April 2001): 40.

50. Interview with Wayne Baxter, Fox Funeral Home, Forest Hills, New York. June 17, 1998.

51. Interview with Thomas Lynch, Lynch & Sons Funeral Home, Milford, Michigan. October 13, 1999.

52. Mark Doty, *Heaven's Coast: A Memoir* (New York: HarperCollins, 1996), 279–280.

53. Doty, *Heaven's Coast*, 283.

54. Doty, *Heaven's Coast*, 283–284.

55. Prothero, *Purified By Fire*, 189, and Weiss, "Dead But Not Necessarily Buried," 40.

56. Weiss, "Dead But Not Necessarily Buried," 42.

57. Prothero, *Purified By Fire*, 211.

58. Michael W. Kubasak, *Cremation and the Funeral Director: Successfully Meeting the Challenge* (Malibu, Calif.: Avalon, 1990).

59. Nadya Labi and Lina Lofaro, "Cremation Nation," TIME (August 4, 1997): 18.

60. Jeannette Walls, "Smells Like Holy Spirit," *Esquire* (April 1997): 30.

61. Prothero, *Purified By Fire*, 188.

62. Alexander Alger and William G. Flanagan, "The New (and More Convenient) American Way of Death," *Forbes* (October 21, 1996): 324.

63. Gene B. Fulton, "Taking the Mystery Out of Funeral Costs," *USA Today Magazine* (July 2001): 22.

64. Mercer Funeral Home. [On-line] Available: *http://www.mercerfuneral.com* [August 23, 2001].

65. McHenry Funeral Home. [On-line]. Available: http://www.mchenryfuneralhome.com/info.html. [August 23, 2001].

66. McHenry Funeral Home. [Online]. Available: *http://www.mchenryfuneralhome.com/cremation4.html*. [August 27, 2001].

67. Meyers Funeral Home. [On-line]. Available: http://www.cremation.com/csc/Meyers/. [August 23, 2001].

68. Meyers Funeral Home. [Online]. Available: *http://www.cremation.com/csc/edu/concerns.html* [August 23, 2001].

69. Interview with Ned Phillips, Palm Mortuary, Las Vegas, Nevada. September 22, 2000.

70. Richmond Eustis, "Cremation Error Angers Buddhists," *Decatur Daily Report* (August 14, 2000): 10.

71. Cheryl Harness, *Ghosts of the White House* (New York: Simon & Schuster, 1998).

72. Gary Laderman, *The Sacred Remains: American Attitudes Toward Death, 1799–1883* (New Haven, Conn.: Yale University Press, 1996), 15–18.

73. Kathleen Haney, "Net Brings Life to Funeral Industry," *Digitrends.net*. [On-line]. Available: http://*www.digitrends.net/ebna/index_14954.html*. [July 26, 2001].

74. Larisa Brass, "Funeral Industry Makes Move to Web," *Nando Times*. [On-line] March 29, 2001. Available: *http://archive.nandotimes.com/noframes/* . . . *1-500717040-503984394-0,00.html?printer*. [July 26, 2001].

75. Edward Wong, "Coffins, Urns and Webcast Funerals," the *New York Times* (October 5, 2000): 10.

76. Interview with Lynch.

Epilogue
1. Somini Sengupta, "Rites of Grief, Without a Body to Cry Over," the *New York Times* (September 27, 2001): E1.
2. Margaret Woodbury, "With Bodies Lost in the Rubble, Mourners Forgo Traditional Rites," *San Francisco Chronicle* (October 14, 2001): 1.
3. Dean E. Murphy, "Slowly, Families Accept the Ruins as Burial Ground," the *New York Times* (September 29, 2001): 1.
4. Jane Spencer and Jennifer Tanaka, "Final Respects: New York's Funeral Industry Prepares for an Onslaught," *Newsweek*, September 22, 2001. [On-line]. Available: http://www.msnbc.com.news/632663.asp [September 25, 2001].

⊕ INDEX ⊕

6/18
$T = 2\ ^2/18$
$\ell = 8$
4/23
$T = 2\ ^2/18$
$L = 4$

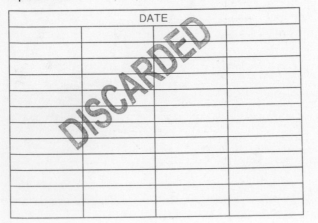